Pederasty and Pedagogy
in Archaic Greece

Pederasty and Pedagogy in Archaic Greece

William Armstrong Percy III

University of Illinois Press
Urbana and Chicago

© 1996 by the Board of Trustees of the University of Illinois
Manufactured in the United States of America
C 5 4 3 2 1

Library of Congress Cataloging-in-Publication Data
Percy, William A.
    Pederasty and pedagogy in archaic Greece /
William Armstrong Percy III.
        p.   cm.
    Includes bibliographical references and index.
    ISBN 0-252-02209-2 (cloth : acid-free paper)
    1. Homosexuality, Male—Greece—History. 2. Anal
intercourse—Greece—History. 3. Homosexuality, Male—
Law and legislation—Greece—History. 4. Greece—History—
To 146 B.C. 5. Greece—Civilization—To 146 B.C.
6. Homosexuality and literature—Greece—History. I. Title.
HQ76.3.G8P47 1996
306.76'62'0938—dc20   95-12864
                                                            CIP

For Theodor Mommsen, Jr.

Contents

Illustrations follow page 98

Acknowledgments

I wish to thank the following:

Three individuals who have been virtual co-authors—my best student, Pedro J. Suarez, for unrivaled chronological knowledge and for insisting that Cretans first institutionalized pederasty; the late polymath Warren Johansson, for unparalleled erudition and translations from the many languages that he commanded; Donald Stone, for his patient, insightful, rigorous editing;

Wayne R. Dynes, for bibliographical help; Eugene F. Rice, for sage counsel; Charley Shively, an inspiring example, for perceptive insights; George Koniaris, for factual corrections; Clive Foss, for technical advice; Mason Hammond, for criticizing a rough draft; the Australian poet and savant Paul Knobel, for clues about vase paintings; Lester Segal, for help on Jewish matters; Beert Verstraete, for information on Rome; Louis Crompton, an inspiration and excellent reader, for correcting the manuscript and putting my findings into perspective; John Onofrey, for help with illustrations; Bennett Hill, Norman Cantor, David Greenberg, Paul Hardman, Loie Hayes, Dorr Legg, Jim Kepner, and Mildred Dickeman; Michael Vickers, who through his inspired articles taught me to reinterpret Greek art; Gregory Nagy, from whose seminar at Harvard's Center for Literary Studies I comprehended the orality and recomposition of early Greek poems. Of course, no one can treat Greek pederasty without an abiding debt to the pathbreaking works of John Addington Symonds, Hans Licht, and Kenneth Dover.

I have had exceptional teachers in addition to Eugene Rice. Theodor Mommsen Jr. at Princeton and Cornell, along with Max Laistner of Cornell, a German trained at Cambridge, taught me how to analyze and respect sources. Their colleagues Morris Kaplan and Lane Cooper were also gay. At Cornell the tradition of the homosexual founding president Andrew D. White still lived on in my day. Another gay, Mommsen's friend Ernst Kantorowicz, biographer of the Hohenstaufen emperor Frederick II and a member of the Stefan George Kreis, helped me with my dissertation on Sicilian history, inspiring me to look imaginatively behind the sources.

His replacement at the Institute for Advanced Studies, Felix Mendelsohn Gilbert, another refugee from Nazism who enriched American scholarship, was a close friend of Mommsen, whom he so fondly memorialized in his autobiography. At Princeton I also studied under Coleman-Norton, who had been adopted by the famous Charles Eliot Norton of Harvard. Werner Jaeger of Harvard and the Russian Mikhail Rostovsteff of Yale, refugee from another totalitarian regime, contributed ideas essential to the present work. Mario Einaudi, who also fled from tyranny, helped me at Cornell. Two of the younger DeSanctis's students taught me: Mario Levi at Cornell and Silvio Accame at Naples. So did Sir Steven Runciman, when he visited Duke one summer along with R. W. Southern, whose son became my assistant for a year in St. Louis. A great geographer, Edward W. Fox supervised my master's thesis at Cornell, and Joseph R. Strayer, once president of the AHA, my dissertation at Princeton. All of those scholars were liberal; most were also gay and/or Jewish. None of them is, of course, responsible for any errors that I may have committed in preparing a work of this scope.

Introduction

> I delight in the prime of a twelve-year old, but a thirteen-year
> old is far more desirable. He who is fourteen is a still sweeter
> flower of the Loves, and one who is just beginning his fifteenth
> year is even more delightful. The sixteenth year belongs to the
> gods, and as for the seventeenth year not for me is it to seek,
> but for Zeus. But whoever desires still older ones is no longer
> playing, but seeking a lover who says "Now let me do it to you"
> [i.e., a Homeric phrase here connoting a demand for the active
> role as well].
> —Strato, *Greek Anthology*, XII, 4[1]

In the fifth dialogue of his *Philosophy in the Bedroom* the Marquis de Sade speaks at some length about pederasty. The pairing will seem self-evident to many: the master of perversion discourses about a favorite immoral act. Yet, in truth, the marquis chooses to defend pederasty for quite different reasons. It is a practice misunderstood and unfairly denounced. "The law-givers of Greece would they have introduced it into their country if they had thought it was [dangerous]? Quite the contrary, they thought it a necessity for a warrior people. Plutarch speaks with enthusiasm about a band of *lovers* and their *beloveds;* for some time they alone protected the freedom of their homeland. This vice held sway over that band of soldiers; it kept it together; the greatest figures practiced it."

This volume is devoted to a discussion of the correctness of Sade's understanding of institutionalized pederasty, a view which, interestingly enough, Friedrich Nietzsche repeated in the nineteenth century.[2] According to that system, most upper-class Greek males, forbidden or strongly discouraged after 600 B.C. from marrying before their thirtieth year, took adolescent males as their beloveds. In his early twenties the young aristocratic lover (*erastes*) took a teen-aged youth, the *eromenos* or beloved, to bond with and train before going on at about age thirty to matrimony and fatherhood. Then, the youth, now grown and having completed compulsory military training, himself in turn took another adolescent to bond with and train before he, too, married. In this form, pederasty embodied a class ethos and the aristocratic desire for self-perpetuation. Those who most fully incarnated the ideal of *kalos k'agathos* (beautiful and good), those who could most aptly promote the interests of the *poleis,* selected the best of their numbers to continue that ideal.[3]

Regarding this practice, it is noteworthy that no less a mind than Plato included pederasty among those features that distinguished classical Hellenic civilization from despotic "barbarian" cultures: "[T]he barbarians because of the rule of despots call [pederasty] ugly, as well as philosophy and nude sports; I suppose it is profitable to their rulers that the subjects should not be great in spirit or make strong friendships and unions, which things love is wont to implant more than anything else" (*Symposium,* 182b). Although in the *Laws* the elderly Plato condemned carnal excesses of every sort, in earlier dialogues he did not hesitate to associate pederasty with an activity that rendered individuals "great in spirit" and laid the foundation for "strong friendships and unions." Nevertheless, the few moderns who have discussed the custom (rather than condemning it summarily) have rarely seen fit to recognize in Greek pederasty its role as an inspiration for learning as well as courage. Dover's book on Greek homosexuality, for example, was, in its avoidance of homophobia, a welcome and needed addition to classical studies. It established the recognition by Greek society of homosexual desire. In its closing pages it further underscored "a consistent Greek tendency to regard homosexual eros as a compound of an educational with a genital relationship."[4] But it afforded no extended discussion of that educational dimension or of those pederastic Greek heroes who became in ancient times the most sensational product of institutionalized pederasty. As a result, one of the aims of this study will be to explore as fully as the extant sources permit how pederastic pedagogy appears to have affected the "spirit" of its *eromenoi* and to suggest that that training may have affected those accomplishments of Greek civilization often referred to as the Greek Miracle.

In addition, in the pages to come I attempt to show that the Greeks did not institutionalize pederasty until the late seventh century B.C., that is, much later than was previously thought. I also argue that Cretan lawgivers or "musicians" (those devoted to the Muses) created the system to control the upper-class population explosion (as Aristotle maintained) and to train and bond warriors. Thereafter, the system spread rapidly to almost all of the rest of Hellas, becoming less regimented in Ionia and Athens but more concerned with intellectual development than had been the case in Crete and Sparta and enduring for a millennium until the Christians suppressed it.

Paucity of Sources

The overwhelming bulk of pagan Greek literature, including especially its erotic texts, has been lost. The *Anacreontea* and the *Greek Anthology* both survived in only one copy (some of the *Anthology* also coming down in the Planudean collection). Book 2 of Theognis also survived in but one manuscript, as did Catullus and Petronius (two of the most lascivious of Latin authors), and Lucretius, the most prominent Latin Epicurean. Although more Latin erotic poetry survives, no manuscript of any Archaic Greek poets of pederastic love except Theognis and Pindar was preserved. However, about twenty of Bacchylides' poems have been found on papyri—our most substantial recovery of the Archaic lyricists from the desert sands. Even what we possess is not necessarily what was originally composed or first written down. The surviving orations have unclear textual histories and may have been bowdlerized or expanded by interpolations. On the other hand, the late prose writers Plutarch, Lucian, and Athenaeus, who have come down to us in substantial volume, attest repeatedly to the flourishing of institutionalized pederasty through nearly a millennium.

Papyrology has been of considerable use in this study, as have numerous terse inscriptions on stones or bronze tablets and on ceramics. No one has ever systematically studied all the surviving graffiti for information on pederasty, but enough has been done to be of crucial help, as we shall see.

The surviving statues (in Roman copies more often than in Greek originals), and thousands of painted vases as well as some other artifacts supplement our meager written resources. First thoroughly analyzed by Beazley, the erotic vase paintings have been exploited for gay history by Dover (1978), Shapiro (1981), Koch-Harnack (1983), Kilmer (1993), and De Vries (unpublished manuscript).

By contrast, no article, much less a book, devoted to the influence of pederasty on Greek sculpture exists, although the notion subtly pervaded Johann Joachim Winckelmann's masterpiece (1764). Surviving examples of nude male sculpture are more sedate and less explicit than the erotic vases (with the exception of the erect phalluses on Delos and those of the herms neither of which has any necessary connection to pederasty or even to homosexuality); here, too, however, our losses are considerable. In his celebrated *Lives of the Artists* (1568), Vasari observed that "what inflicted incomparably greater damage and loss on the arts than [the sacks of Rome by Alaric and Gaiseric] was the fervent enthusiasm of the new Christian religion."

Most of the Greek philosophical works that survive are ascribed to Plato and Aristotle. No pre-Socratic works and no Hellenistic philosophers have come down to us in their entirety, though Diogenes Laertius left us lives of their authors. Plato is the only major classical author all of whose significant works appear to have survived, but no one can agree on their chronology or interpretation, and the authenticity of some is questioned. It is estimated that more than three-fourths of Aristotle's four hundred works have disappeared. Although all of his dialogues—early works modeled on Plato's— are lost, many of his treatises survive, but awkwardly written. Several, if not most, seem to many authorities to represent only rough drafts or the garbled notes of his students, given that his lost dialogues were admired in antiquity for their polished style. Every one of the Epicurean works in Greek—except for a few letters and maxims—perished. Not one of Zeno's works survives, nor do any of those of his early followers, all of whom, like him, endorsed pederasty. The writings of the later Stoics, who generally disparaged sex, including pederasty, fared better because the Christians found them less unacceptable. Even for most philosophers from imperial times we have only fragments, worse, often only titles, or Latin paraphrases or commentaries. Before the Neo-Platonists, Marcus Aurelius and Maximus of Tyre are the only thinkers from whom a complete work survives among the many they composed.

Even the texts of the dramatists, philosophers, historians, orators, poets, grammarians, critics, and scientists that have come down to us survive in such remarkably divergent versions that modern editors with the best methodology frequently disagree as to the very words of these ancient documents. Variations on papyri often add to the uncertainty and confusion. Before the age of printing, books could not be standardized. Some, whose texts exist in only one or in a few marred copies, have enormous lacunae. What information is available to us about the history of the transmission of the *Iliad* reveals that the work underwent considerable revision over the centuries, including a severe pruning by the Hellenistic scholar Zenodotus.

As pupils and imitators of the Greeks, the Romans preserved much Hellenic and Hellenistic thought and art. Well over 90 percent of what survives of classical or Hellenistic sculptures are Roman copies. A small percentage of original Archaic sculptures, which the Romans seldom imitated, have been excavated or retrieved from underwater. Vitruvius tells us more about

Greek architectural theory than any surviving Greek, and Pliny the Elder wrote authoritatively on Greek sculpture. Lucretius, Cicero, Seneca, and Quintilian are our best sources for Hellenistic philosophy and oratorical theories because no originals survive. From Virgil to Nemesianus Roman poets drew inspiration from, translated, and paraphrased Greek poetry. Latin as well as Greek critics commented upon and judged all Greek literature and thought. As a result of this cultural interaction, modern scholars have sometimes supposed that references to pederasty in Latin literature were merely copied from Greek tradition and not indicative of Roman life. Such an argument has been applied to, for instance, Plautus's comedies. This view has today been largely abandoned, and Virgil now seems no less a pederast than Theocritus and Martial as pederastic as Theognis.

Byzantine compendia, encyclopedias, lexicons (especially the *Suda*, c. 1000), and the works of Stobaeus (fl. c. 400), Hesychius (fifth century), Photius (d. 886), Michael Psellus (1018–78), John Tzetzes (fl. c. 1143), and Eustathius of Thessalonica (d. c. 1194), all of which contain commentaries from Hellenistic scholars, preserve fragments, and explicate arcane terms and institutions, are of the greatest utility. The sources may be few and far between, but, as I show, almost every *polis* had a pederastic legendary hero and, even during the Archaic Age, a pederastic general, politician, author, artist, or scholar and/or some pederastic art, if only an inscription or an imported Athenian vase. Every *polis*, even those created in Hellenistic times on foreign soil, had gymnasia—though long without substantial buildings—and symposia, the breeding grounds of pederasty.

In this work of *haute vulgarisation*, which does not rely on unpublished evidence, I present new interpretations by stressing formerly little used material, both ancient and modern.[5] My hypotheses are based for the most part on the opinions of ancient authorities heretofore neglected or disparaged. I have relied especially upon the fragments of the lyric poets and ancient comments about them, on Ephorus, as quoted in Strabo, and on Athenaeus. Both Ephorus and Athenaeus have often been unfairly deemed less reliable than they are. Like Diodorus Siculus and Aelian, they reported events in the Archaic period from the now lost writings of earlier authorities. Today, as archeology increasingly confirms legends about early events, it seems less unreasonable to cite their accounts than it did to the hypercritical school so dominant before the First World War. Likewise, the various lives of philosophers, orators, rhetoricians, and poets, however inaccurate and unhistorical in general, contain many pederastic episodes, as do the lives of politicians and generals, which are considered to be in the main more reliable. Ancient commentaries and *scholia,* some of which have not yet been exploited systematically for pederasty or for other forms of homosexuality, also yield important results. *Scholia* exist on Homer, Hesiod, Pindar, Aeschylus, Sophocles, Euripides, Aristophanes, Apollonius of Rhodes, Theocritus, and other poets. With the exception of Plato and Demosthenes there are only a few on Greek prose writers.[6]

Much is speculative, conjectures abound, hypotheses are shaky, and inferences are based on very delicate, technical discussions about the validity of deductions from fragmentary literary, artistic, linguistic, and archeological evidence. Almost every detail of early Greek history, especially of Greek sexuality, is open to doubt and indeed is hotly debated. More ink has been spilled by authors debating whether Homer knew or Plato approved of male love than in studying the attitudes and opinions on that subject of any other Greek, maybe of all other Greeks put together.[7] Yet the major portion of the Homeric corpus evolved, I believe, before pederasty was institutionalized, and Plato criticized rather than typified Greek attitudes toward sex and sexual practices. Moreover, neglected writings and works of art which are less ambiguously homoerotic and pro-pederastic do exist, and it is on them that I wish to concentrate in the pages to follow.

What the Greeks Did

The picture that even the most objective commentators have been able to sketch of ancient Greek sexual practices and theories is necessarily provisional and conjectural. While customs varied from place to place, whole ages remain dark, some without any surviving writing at all, and for certain regions we are without information for centuries, even after writing became common. We are best informed about Athens, where various sexual customs, beliefs, and practices existed simultaneously, and about Thebes, where pederasty was most completely accepted. No one can agree now, or ever could, regarding Spartan customs. For a number of other *poleis* we have but fleeting glimpses, with a little more than usual about Alcaeus and Sappho's Mytilene, Theognis's Megara, Hiero's Syracuse, and Ptolemaic Alexandria. The reputation of the Eleans for carnal pederasty equaled that of the Thebans. About northern and central Greece, except for Athens, we learn almost nothing from nonmythological literary sources before the third century save for Epaminondas's Thebes and Philip's Macedonia.

Most categories of Greek literature composed after 600 allude to pederasty, but the works are rarely specific as to what if anything actually went on sexually. One school of ancients that still has adherents held that relations between pederastic partners were "pure," that is, nonsexual (or, according to certain moderns, at least until they were corrupted by Near Eastern, "oriental" influences). From the fourth century B.C. certain pro-Spartan writers declared that Spartan lovers were chaste and had been since the days of Lycurgus. Xenophon, who admits that many Greeks were skeptical on this point, claimed that "in Sparta there is no more physical love between men and boys than there is between parents and children or brother and brother" (*Constitution of the Lacedaemonians*, II, 13–14). A second theory, popular among Athenians, held that like the Thebans and Eleans, the Spartans routinely practiced anal intercourse in their pederastic relations. The well-informed Cicero cattily noted about Spartan chastity: "The Lacedemonians, while they permit all things except outrage in the love of youths, certainly distinguish the forbidden by a thin wall of partition from the sanctioned, for they allow embraces and a common couch to lovers" (*Tusculan Disputations*, IV, 4).

Some upper-class males may indeed have limited their physical contact to wrestling nude with their beloveds in gymnasia and reclining with them on couches in symposia, where perhaps they did not even go beyond gazing into the eyes or kisses and embraces. Some presumably ejaculated between the thighs or buttocks of their boys as certain vase paintings may imply. Yet others, perhaps most, penetrated their *eromenoi* anally.[8] While the poets were usually discreet and ambiguous as to what kind of intimacy, if any, occurred, contemporary graffiti described anal intercourse, and the word *katapygon* (ass-fucked, lit. "broad-assed") appeared very early. Oral-genital sexuality, whether pederastic, androphile, or heterosexual, was apparently rare and is much disapproved of in the few passages that mention it. Greek sources do not speak about mutual masturbation or fisting although they did have a word for inserting a finger into the anus.[9]

Using works designed for public buildings, sculptors idealized the male nude but rarely portrayed sexual activity. Vase painters, on the other hand, who do not show anal intercourse between human males (as opposed to satyrs), depicted intercrural sex, foreplay, and gift-giving to boys. Dover's contention that the Greek pederasts practiced intercrural sex is supported not only by vase paintings but also by the term *diamerizein* ("to do between the thighs") in literary sources.[10] Other terms such as *pygizein* ("to have intercourse through the buttocks"), mentioned by Theocritus (*Idyll* 5, 41) and by Strato in the *Greek Anthology* (XII, 245), and *binein* ("to fuck") and *katapygon*, terms used by Old and Middle Comedians as well as by scratch-

ers of graffiti, indicate that buggery also occurred.[11] Indeed, other evidence
indicates that anal intercourse was not so rare an occurrence as Dover once
implied (1978), only to revise his position later (1988). Inscriptions at Thera
(published only in 1899) and elsewhere, the Attic comedians, as well as
Catullus, Petronius, Lucian, Juvenal, Martial, Apuleius, Athenaeus, and the
poets of the *Greek Anthology,* all have expressions for such activity.

If other forms of homosexuality also flourished, no evidence exists for
the Archaic period. The word *kinaidos,* which came to mean a much disparaged adult male, presumed to be extremely effeminate in manner and
dress, who took the passive role in sexual intercourse, is first attested in
Plato's *Gorgias,* c. 380 B.C.).[12] Male adolescent prostitution, first attested in an
Archaic graffito on Thera (*Inscriptiones Graecae,* xii, 3, 536) or more datably
in Aristophanes' *Plutus* (c. 390 B.C.),[13] became common in classical times in
Athens and other ports such as Marseilles (Aeschines, *Contra Timarchum* 119–
24; Plautus, *Casina,* 957ff.). In addition to the inevitable streetwalkers and
occasional hustlers, adolescent slaves often labored as prostitutes for pimps
or male brothels, but oddly enough no Greek master is reported to have
had sex with his own male slave (common as this was reputed to have become in Rome) before the lone case in Xenophon's *Symposium* (c. 390 B.C.)
of a middle- or lower-class entertainer and his adolescent slave lover. This
said, such relations certainly did not include the training of both the mind
and body of the partner and thus cannot be compared to the more consequential upper-class institutionalized pederasty.

Pederasty versus Androphilia

The Greeks faced directly and candidly a fundamental aspect of human experience with which we are only now beginning to come to terms: men
sometimes love (whether spiritually or sexually) adolescent males. However, in Greek society, surviving art and literature imply that only a very
few upper-class men experienced similar feelings for adult males, and as
far as prepubescent boys are concerned, we have no evidence whatsoever
in Greek sources to suggest that they were the object of the attentions of
Greek men.[14] "Greek love" therefore means men loving pubescent boys.
Because almost all *erastai* preferred adolescents between the ages of twelve
and eighteen, or until body hair sprouted and the beard became heavy, we
would classify them as pederasts rather than pedophiles (those loving the
prepubescent) or ephebophiles (those loving eighteen to twenty-two year
olds). On their side, they would be quick to condemn our prevalent andro-

philia as extremely distasteful and even reprehensible in that it serves no pedagogical purpose. Indeed, in their eyes, such behavior would have diminished the prestige and worth of the passive partner because most Greeks (and Romans) seem to have thought that adult citizens should not assume feminine roles. Further, the ancients generally expected citizens to marry and sire offspring as a civic and familial duty.

Despite this quite firm distinction in attitude among the Greeks, homophile investigators, beginning with Hoessli and Ulrichs, have often conflated Greek pederasty with modern androphilia. Edward Perry Warren, using the pseudonym Arthur Lyon Raile, first among writers in English drew the line of demarcation clearly and accurately between the pederasty of Graeco-Roman civilization and the androphile homosexuality that pervades modern Europe and North America. However, his three-volume *Defense of Uranian Love* (1928–30) apparently proved too shocking for his contemporaries. To this day, not one American public library counts Warren's title among the books in its collection. Two more recent works that insist upon a firm distinction between pederasty and androphilia, J. Z. Eglinton's *Greek Love* (1964) and Edward Brongersma's *Loving Boys* (1986–90), have fared only slightly better.[15] Since the 1970s social constructionists, following Michel Foucault, have gone to the opposite extreme, claiming that the Greeks were not homosexuals at all. This is because, in their eyes, homosexuals did not exist until after 1869, when the word was coined, or, according to another branch of that school, before the early eighteenth century, when androphilia became common in northern Europe.[16]

As Dover recognized when he persisted in using the term "Greek homosexuality," the evidence from ancient Greece does not unequivocally support the viewpoint of such Foucault-inspired social constructionists as David Halperin. The Hippocratic essay *Airs, Waters, and Places*, Plato, Aristotle, Lucian, certain astrological treatises (for example, the *Tetrabiblos* of Ptolemy and the *Mathesis* of Firmicus Maternus), and a number of authors in the *Greek Anthology* describe individuals who were attracted to members of their own sex without distinction of age and who were not necessarily passive or effeminate. De Vries is reputed to be collecting vase paintings depicting Greek androphilia for his long-awaited book. Boswell (1994) also noted examples of it.

As significant as such evidence is for the history of homosexuality, I feel it important to stress at the outset of this discussion of Greek love that the Greeks we most admire almost always practiced pederasty, at least before marriage. I refer to poets like Alcaeus, Ibycus, Theognis, Pindar, and Theocritus; sculptors like Phidias; generals and statesmen such as Themistocles, Aristides, Pausanias, Alcibiades, Epaminondas, and Philip and Alexander of Macedonia; and the philosophers Pythagoras, Socrates, Plato, Aristotle, and Zeno (the founder of Stoicism).

In light of such a list, the suggestion as to possible links between pederasty and pedagogy, between pederasty and the great accomplishments of Greek culture must, I trust, seem neither extravagant nor implausible. Still, we must be prepared to approach Greek pederasty on its own terms, that is, both free from confusion with androphilia and replete with the values that fostered it and that it in turn fostered.[17]

Origins

The first part of this volume is devoted to a discussion of the various theories that scholars have advanced to explain the origins of Greek pederasty. These theories, I should point out, refer in the main to initiatory pederasty, that is, a ritualistic practice which, because of its religious orientation, was deemed not to constitute in its essence a sexual act. As the ensuing pages will show, the effort to empty initiatory pederasty of all effective sexual content is not supported by the evidence at hand.

One group of scholars has traced the practice of initiatory pederasty to the original inhabitants of Siberia; another, to the first Indo-European settlers of Europe, and to a time well before the proto-Greeks arrived in Greece. A third school believes the practice began only among the proto-Greeks, whereas yet a fourth ascribes the custom only to the Dorians, who, as the last of the Greeks to enter the peninsula, retained many "primitive" customs. The chapters to follow scrutinize each of these theories and point out what I believe to be their inescapable weaknesses. Although, in my opinion, there is no conclusive evidence to demonstrate that any of those groups institutionalized pederasty, it would be unreasonable to deny that under certain circumstances pederasty and other forms of homosexuality may have existed among the early Hellenes and/or their ancestors.

More recently Sallares, a demographic expert, proposed that pederasty was institutionalized by the proto-Greeks between 2000 and 1500 to keep down the population. Marrou hypothesized that situational homosexuality, arising when males were isolated from women in their castles during the Dark Age (1200 to 800), led thereafter to institutionalized pederasty. These views are examined in the chapters of Part 1. In Part 2 I offer my own theory of a late origin (c. 650) situated on Crete and occasioned primarily by overpopulation.

I ask nonspecialists to be patient with the technicalitics inseparable from any effort to establish a new synthesis, however tentative. For their convenience I shall try to point out where my speculations differ from the commonly received opinions. Without doubt, I have failed to relegate enough scholarly quibbles to the endnotes. Specialists, who will perceive the originality of my interpretations, will, of course, recognize that my evidence, all of which is published, is available to all seekers of knowledge in this field. Throughout I have tried to avoid the errors or omissions that would most cripple my thesis and to point out the misinterpretations or lack of evidence in others.

Although recognizing that a book on Greek pederasty must perforce discuss relationships between males, I aim to attract readers of both sexes; not just homosexuals but heterosexuals too; not just specialists in ancient history and classical culture or people more or less professionally knowledgeable about the history of homosexuality but any sympathetic reader curious about that general topic. The book should also be suitable for courses in gay and lesbian studies or sexuality as well as for more standard courses in anthropology, sociology, or psychology. I hope that priests, pastors, rabbis, psychiatrists, psychotherapists, counselors, politicians, legislators, and legal reformers will also read it. It may even enliven and update traditional courses in Greek history, literature, and art and help them to regain some of the students they have been losing over the years to more "relevant" courses. Finally, it is my earnest desire that a true understanding of Greek institutionalized pederasty will at long last permit the educated world to confront the accomplishments of that practice honestly, without embarrassment or outrage.

Part One

Greece before the Institutionalization of Pederasty

One

Indo-European Pederasty

I thought of entitling [my book] Indo-European Initiatory
Homosexuality. . . . Without doubt the institution which I have
described at such length is attested amongst the Hellenes, the
Taifales, the Macedonians, the Albanians, and more vaguely, the
Celts, among Indo-European speakers, and that fact inclines one
to think that it was an institution inherited from a common
prehistory, for one is tempted to see in pedagogical pederasty,
practiced by these related but very different peoples, the per-
petuation of a very ancient institution going back to the age
when the various Indo-European languages hardly differed from
one another, and where the speakers of these languages, much
closer to one another than in the historical epochs, had a common culture.

—Bernard Sergent, *L'homosexualité initiatique dans l'Europe
ancienne* (Paris, 1987), 215

Ever since the close of the eighteenth century, when philologists discovered that most languages spoken in the lands between Ireland and India
had common words and structures, scholars have posited that those languages evolved from a common source, which was dubbed Indo-European
or Aryan ("noble" in Sanskrit). Scholars further posited various *Urheimaten*
(original homelands) for the Indo-European, Aryan, or, as they were sometimes called, Caucasian peoples as well as the persistence among them of
elements of a common religion, culture, and even sexual customs. From
the racist theories in vogue during the nineteenth century, scholars inferred
that these were the ancestors of the genetically superior white race and the
conquerors of the indigenes of the lands that they invaded.

Against this background, the Danish physician Thorkil Vanggaard (1973),
using little-explored Scandinavian material, advanced the theory that all
Indo-Europeans practiced initiatory pederasty until after their diaspora.

Following Vanggaard's lead, Jan Bremmer (1980) related the presumably ancient initiatory pederasty of the Indo-Europeans to present-day Melanesian
pederasty, speculating that at one time all Euroasians practiced it, not simply
the Indo-Europeans. Bernard Sergent (1986, 1987a), who reluctantly limited
himself in his writing to Indo-Europeans in Europe, seconded Vanggaard's
bold hypothesis about the existence of a pan-Indo-European primitive initiatory pederasty.

Regarding the work of Vanggaard, Bremmer, and Sergent, which John
Boswell (1994) tentatively endorsed, it must be noted that since the time
when philologists first formulated their ideas about the Indo-Europeans,
research has not stood still. Disagreements as to when various languages
branched off from proto-Indo-European and from one another are complicated by more recent theories emphasizing borrowings of vocabulary and
customs from proximate peoples rather than descent from common ancestors. There is even less agreement about the customs of and the long-lost
languages spoken by substrata of indigenes, if indeed there were substantial
numbers of farmers in Europe before the coming of the Indo-Europeans.
These and other disputes make agreement impossible as to where the *Urheimat* of the Aryans was, as to when, how, and by what routes they emigrated
from it, and what numbers and sorts of people they settled among. There
is even less consensus nowadays about their physical appearance and about
the nature and evolution of their mythology and religion, which certain
nineteenth- and early twentieth-century scholars confidently described.

For example, although more than thirty homelands have been proposed,
from the Iberian Peninsula to the Himalayas, most moderns would place
the *Urheimat* somewhere on an arc running from the middle Danube across
the Ukraine to the Caucasus. The proposals of the Soviet philologists T. V.
Gamkrelidze and V. V. Ivanov (1983, 1984) and of the processual archeologist Colin Renfrew (1987), following A. H. Sayce (1927), that Anatolia was
the original Indo-European homeland are merely the most recent in a long
series of conjectures. However, their failure to explain away the presence
of so many non-Indo-European languages in the region somewhat undermines even this hypothesis, as well as similar ones that prefer Armenia or
Kurdistan to Anatolia.

The dates of the beginning of the dispersion of the Indo-Europeans
are currently being pushed back, even by linguists, from 2500, the earliest
favored by nineteenth-century philologists, to the end of the fourth millennium. Throughout the 1970s a leading linguist at UCLA, Marija Gimbutas
(1970, 1973, 1977, 1979, 1980), has revised her estimate from 3400 to 4000,

using the Ukraine as the homeland. Renfrew, however, has their dispersal begin c. 6000 from an Anatolian *Urheimat*.[1]

Just as the notions and conceits of the old philologists constitute a less-than-reliable foundation on which to build new theories, so the pederastic practices among certain contemporary New Guinean tribes signaled by Bremmer (1980) prove to be a very problematic stepping-stone to the mores of the ancient Indo-Europeans. Bremmer was, in fact, reviving an idea first put forth by Erich Bethe (1907). Bethe already knew of the pederastic initiatory practices of some tribes in New Guinea and claimed that Dorian warriors solemnly and ritually injected youths anally with semen to make them grow strong and brave, much as certain primitives societies still did in his day. Bethe's contemporaries almost unanimously rejected the analogy. Nevertheless, Bremmer saw fit in 1980 to propose that primitive tribes from Melanesia to Europe once practiced an initiatory pederasty and that the ancient Greeks and modern Melanesians are merely isolated ponds left from what was once a great Eurasian sea of pederastic tribes.

However, Bethe and Bremmer insisted on an analogy that even the customs of the people of Melanesia do not sustain. Although Sambian warriors feed boys their semen directly from the penis, as Herdt (1981, 1982, 1984) has documented, other primitive tribes of New Guinea inject semen into the anus of boys or feed them their urine or rub them with feces.[2] Yet other tribes there do not practice pederastic initiation at all. The lack of uniformity, even in that relatively small area, indicates that the practice originated locally and was not a common legacy. Although appealing to Sergent, Bremmer, and a number of others, this analogy between a few New Guinea tribes and the ancient Indo-Europeans remains the least plausible explanation of the origins of Greek pederasty. Far more pertinent to our investigation are the known pederastic behaviors of certain Indo-European peoples.

Sacred Ritual or Casual Sex

Evidence about institutionalized pederasty among Indo-Europeans apart from the Greeks is contradictory or ambiguous as well as scanty. Certain members of all tribes and peoples everywhere have undoubtedly practiced pederasty, but it cannot be proven that any in Europe ritualized it without influence from the Greeks. A few passages do indicate that certain tribes of Celts, Germans, and Scandinavians scorned *argrs* (effeminate men) and all adult passives, as most Greeks seem to have done. Several of them also deemed a youth who slew big game or proved his prowess in battle at once marriageable. Such rites of passage were widespread but quite unlike what became the custom among the Greeks who, once they institutionalized pederasty, normally postponed marriage for warriors until age thirty. Some Teutonic or Celtic tribes apparently made boys who had not yet proven themselves dress more like women and use female hairstyles; however, some others may have punished certain types of homosexual acts or ostracized effeminate males.

Greek and Latin sources proffer more evidence about Celtic pederasty than about that of any other early Indo-Europeans.[3] According to Aristotle, the Celts "openly approve of male loves" (*Politics,* II, 1269b). Diodorus observed: "although their wives are comely . . . [Celts] have very little to do with them, but rage with lust, in outlandish fashion, for the embrace of males. It is their practice to sleep upon the ground on the skins of wild beasts and to tumble with a catamite on each side" (V, 32). Athenaeus merely repeated Diodorus: "And among barbarians the Celts also, though they have very beautiful women, enjoy boys more; so that some of them often have two lovers to sleep with on their beds of animal skins" (XIII, 603a). The type of pederasty thus attributed to the Celts possessed apparently nothing whatsoever in common with that of the Greeks, which had, if not sacred duties, at least important societal purposes, and pedagogical uses.[4]

The evidence for ancient Germanic pederasty is scarcer and more conflicting than for Celtic pederasty. To contrast barbaric morality with Roman decadence, Tacitus asserted that Germans drowned in "miry swamps under a cover of wattled hurdles *ignavos et imbelles et corpore infames,* " i.e., those "slothful and unwarlike and infamous in body" (*Germania,* 12). He probably meant by this phrase either "passive homosexuals," perhaps above a certain age, as most have maintained. However, others interpreted the expression to mean cowards in battle, "misshapen children," traitors, or those who mutilated themselves to avoid serving in the army.[5] Because of the ambiguity of this most famous passage about the attitudes of the early Germans toward homosexuality (cited by the Nazis to justify their persecution of homosexuals), we must examine other sources on the subject.

Some German tribes seem to have imposed strict penalties on those who falsely charged others with infamous conduct. Apparently such conduct often included adult male passivity. On the other hand, two historians of the Late Empire who wrote after the triumph of Christianity expressed disgust that Germanic tribes practiced pederasty. Ammianus Marcellinus (c. 380 A.D.) mentioned the Taifales, among whom a youth continued in a passive relationship until he slew a bear or boar (*Gothic Wars,* 2, 14). Procopius (c. 550) cited the Heruls, amongst whom youths remained *douloi* (slaves), presumably sexually available for an adult warrior, and fought without shields until they proved their courage (*History*, 31, 9, 5). Thus, even if the passage from Tacitus referred to adult passives, other evidence shows that the Germans had no single rule of conduct or viewpoint about homosexual behavior. When the various tribes, having established kingdoms on Roman soil, put their legal customs into writing with the help of Christian clergy, only the Visigoths in Spain penalized homosexual acts. Pagan Roman religion and laws never condemned pederasty or male homosexuality as such.[6] Even Gisela Bleibtreu-Ehrenberg, who has carefully marshaled documentary evidence for prejudice against "homosexuals" from the earliest ages, was unable to find condemnations of consensual pederasty before Christianity influenced the Germans, but of course before that time the tribes produced no written documents to record their opinions or practices. Boswell (1980, 1994) has implausibly maintained that Christians did not routinely condemn homosexual acts before the thirteenth century.

Likewise, before the arrival of Christianity, Scandinavian laws and religion, closely related to those of their Germanic cousins, never condemned pederasty (as distinct from adult passivity or from shamanism as manifested in certain *argrs*). Scandinavian literature, which begins only after 1000, when those people became literate after converting, seems to preserve early Germanic myths and customs better than German literature does. It does not contain stories of love between comrades, of homoerotic fidelity between heroes in battle, or of any form of institutionalized pederasty. Sagas and even later texts, reflecting some selection and editing after the introduction of Christianity, do stigmatize as cowardly and slothful the passive or effeminate adult whom other males humiliated and abused sexually. Anyone insulted as an *argr*, which had a connotation of sorcery (a female trait), as well of as passive effeminacy, had the right to slay his accuser to avenge his honor. Of all the Scandinavian laws, none of which were put into writing before the people were converted to Christianity, only chapter 32 of the Norwegian *Gulathinglog*, promulgated by King Magnus Erlingsson in 1164, criminalized homosexual sodomy, prescribing perpetual outlawry and confiscation of all property. Some, then, if not most or all Scandinavians stigmatized adult males involved with sorcery and those who accepted the passive role, but apparently not boys who did so. There is, on the other hand, no evidence whatsoever of any general approval of, much less the institutionalizing of, pederasty. Thus there are fewer parallels between Greek and Scandinavian customs regarding pederasty than between Greek and certain German ones.[7]

Proto-Greeks: "The Coming of the Greeks"

If it is not possible to sustain the theory of Indo-European initiatory pederasty, should we believe instead that the practice originated with the oldest
Indo-European settlers of the Greek peninsula, the proto-Greeks? Robert
Sallares (1991) advanced just such an idea, even though present-day thinking about the proto-Greeks has produced endless disagreements as to their
identity and origin.

Renfrew argued that the proto-Greeks, like all other Indo-Europeans,
entered an essentially vacant Europe, peopled only by a very few hunters and
gatherers, c. 6000, coming across the Aegean with their wives and children
in small bands. Drews, at the other extreme, replied that they came as a small
elite aristocracy, bringing their horses with them across the Aegean c. 1600
and comprising only about one-tenth of the population in their new land.
Others have the proto-Greeks descending by land from the north or cross-
ing from Anatolia any time in between, whether as pastoralists with their
herds of horses or as agriculturalists on foot. The disagreement is patent.
Yet Sallares (1991), undaunted, proposed that it was precisely the proto-
Greeks who between 2000 and 1500 institutionalized pederasty as a part
of their comprehensive age-class system, which he associated with delayed
marriages and with attempts at population control in Mycenean times.

Sallares concluded that pederasty was an essential part of the age-class
system from its beginning and that the system, originally common among
all Greeks, limited births and kept the population down but was abandoned
by all Greek societies except the conservative states of Crete and Sparta
during the severe population shrinkage of the Greek Dark Age (1200–800).
This, he claimed, explains the latter's relative lack of manpower and the
great demographic explosion of the other Greeks after 800.

Circa 6000, Neolithic immigrants, possibly Indo-Europeans from Anatolia, if Renfrew is correct, introduced weaving, pottery making, and domes-
ticated plants and animals or, perhaps, if he is wrong, the folk already settled
in Greece imported such techniques from their neighbors in the absence of
significant immigration. Living in villages rather than in small migratory
bands, with their new techniques they could support as many as 500 times
more people per square mile on good soil as the old hunters and gatherers could. If they were immigrants, as Renfrew argued, they exterminated
or assimilated the few aborigines or pushed them back to the inhospitable
mountains.

In 1989 Michael Everson argued that Europe's agriculturization between

7000 and 6500, long before Renfrew placed it, multiplied its numbers and transmogrified the lifestyle of its population, establishing the worship of a transcendental mother goddess. Everson further concluded that another cultural transformation began c. 4500 when he believed that patriarchal Indo-Europeans first moved in among the already numerous matriarchal agriculturalists.[8] Some theorize that matriarchists tend to tolerate homosexuality while patriarchists normally condemn it. Whether Renfrew or his critics are right, there is no convincing evidence for systematic pederasty among any early Indo-Europeans, matriarchal or patriarchal, matrilineal or patrilineal. The ambiguities created by the evidence that Renfrew and his opponents put forward undermine any attempt to claim that early Europeans institutionalized pederasty or anything else.

If Bernal is even partly right about Egyptian influences on the Greek language[9] and the considerable Phoenician colonization that he imagined in Greece, it is quite likely that the Levantine merchant colonists introduced temple prostitution, both male and female, to the Aegean.[10] But no modern theorist denies that both the Greek language and religion evolved in Greece. So, I assert, did the much less analyzed institution of pederasty. We can tell by its particular nature that this Greek practice did not derive from any Asiatic or Egyptian source. Male temple prostitutes, the *kedeshim* of the Jewish scriptures, did not evolve into warriors the way that *eromenoi* did. Nor were Asiatics more degenerate, or more lustful, than Europeans, however popular that notion became during the nineteenth century.

Even if they ranged over vast stretches of steppe, losing touch with one another, the Indo-European tribes could not have, as linguists once claimed, evolved the Greek language, much less the classical Greek religion, or the age-class society with institutionalized pederasty before their arrival in Greece. Whatever conjecture they make, no one can prove that nomadic warriors are less likely than settled villagers to have had strong taboos against homosexuality. Evidence about tribes who came into Greece before 1000 is too exiguous to make valid generalizations about their sexual practices.[11]

Indo-European religion also presents insurmountable problems. Without fixed places of worship like the temples of the ancient Near East or specialized priests, the Indo-Europeans who settled in the West had apparently managed to progress beyond animism. Before leaving their homeland, they supposedly worshiped the sky father Zeus, perhaps their first anthropomorphic deity and the only one found in all the Indo-European pantheons. Though the Latins may have branched off late from the Greeks and may have evolved common gods with them before doing so, if Greek gods other than Zeus appeared in other pantheons, it was probably due to borrowing.[12] Because we have only bare lists in Linear B of Mycenean gods which include, incidentally, almost all the major classical deities, we remain quite ignorant about the evolution of Greek religion before Homer.

Minoan Origins

Our inability to speak authoritatively about the behavior of the proto-Greeks is enhanced by the difficulties we face when seeking evidence of institutionalized pederasty among the Minoans on Crete or among their Greek imitators, the Myceneans. Whether Minoans spoke an Indo-European language, as some now conjecture,[13] and whether they worshipped a mother goddess, is at present not answerable because the little that they wrote, which we cannot decipher, like the writings of the Myceneans, whose language we can read, seems mostly to have been about bureaucratic matters such as inventorying the king's wealth, not about sexual customs or laws.

Late Minoan paintings and other art contain no depictions of sexual activity. Moreover, nothing indicates that Minoans or for that matter even Myceneans, who virtually everyone now agrees spoke Greek, institutionalized pederasty. Little from the Minoans and Myceneans that survived the Dark Age after their fall could have influenced the Archaic Greeks (800–480). Minoans did have a sensual art dominated by sexual symbols such as snakes and bulls, by the lithe bodies of wasp-waisted youths usually wearing loincloths, and by bare-breasted females. The terra-cotta piece discovered near Phaistus showing four nude males with peaked caps dancing in a ring and the nude fisherman on a fresco from the Mycenean colony at Thera are exceptional, but not even they are overtly pederastic. The fresco of the boxer from Thera does suggest to some a possible continuity from Minoan and Mycenean to Archaic athletics.[14] Certain later vases and terra-cotta figurines also suggest some influence by sub-Mycenean on geometric art but none of the figural decorations that appeared on Mycenean or Minoan vases or walls during the second millennium depict homoerotic, much less pederastic, scenes. If those peoples institutionalized pederasty, their art does not indicate that fact.

In the palace at Cnossos a winding corridor may have allowed ladies to pass from what some have dubbed the Queen's or Women's Hall to the verandas and garden terrace southeast of what has been dubbed the Men's

Hall.[15] Still, there seems to have been no strict seclusion, although frescoes show females separated from the males on public occasions. Indeed, "the fact that the ladies play an important role in the [Minoan] pictures is characteristic of Minoan life in general. . . . It has even been suggested that Minoan society as a whole had a matriarchal basis, but there is no clear proof that this was so."[16] If Minoan and Mycenean women were actually secluded, the custom seems to have lapsed among the Greeks of Homer's time.

Harald Patzer (1982) believed in an Indo-European origin for "pure" (nonsexual) Greek pederasty but somewhat incongruously interpreted a find of Martin P. Nilsson's as supporting the view that the Minoans, whom he regarded as non-Indo-European, might also have institutionalized pederasty. He repeated Nilsson's argument that an artifact found on Crete, dating from the third century B.C., proved the survival of Minoan bull worship in a remote area of the island. Using the "trifunctionalism" of Dumézil (the notion that Indo-Europeans grouped everything into threes), Patzer related the Minoan bull to the ox that in a later period a Dorian Cretan warrior gave to his boyfriend, along with a helmet and a drinking cup, to sacrifice to Zeus and speculated that there might be a connection between Minoan religion and Dorian pederasty on Crete. However, others have observed that from Crete "there is no archaeological evidence which proves the existence of a bull-cult, and such a cult would be inconsistent with our knowledge of the sacrifice of bulls which is derived from the monuments."[17]

Aristotle reported but did not endorse the idea that the Cretans of his day believed that their laws stemmed from the Minoan King Minos (*Politics*, 1271b). He went on to argue that the Dorians on Crete institutionalized pederasty to curb their population explosion (1272a 12). But, as we shall see, the population explosion he was referring to occurred not in Minoan times but in the seventh century. In spite of all the legends connecting Minos with pederasty, the physician Sextus Empiricus (*Pyrrhonian Sketches,* III, 199–200; fl. c. 200 A.D.) was the only ancient philosopher or historian, that is, non-mythmaker, to declare unequivocally that pederasty began in Minoan (not Dorian) Crete. He further asserted that it was practiced first by the chief Idomeneus, Minos's brother, and his squire Meriones. Athenaeus, too, associated pederasty with myths placed in the Minoan period.[18]

Henri Jeanmaire, who thought that the practice of ritual kidnapping was very old, suggested that the account of Ephorus reported by Strabo, our best description of the pederastic system on Crete, attested to the way in which a caste of warriors was enlisted from the citizens and that it was officially or legally recognized.[19] R. F. Willetts, too, suggested that Strabo's text documented a Minoan initiation rite for elite youths and derived the ritual sacrifice of an ox from Minoan practices. He speculated that because of the kidnapping this ritual resembled the Zeus and Ganymede myth.[20]

Tying the scene on the famous Chieftain Cup excavated on the island to the story in Ephorus that Cretan lovers gave their boys a cup, Robert B. Koehl (1986) kept alive the theory of a Minoan origin. He described the hairstyles and dress that elite Minoan youths adopted at different stages of their lives when classified into distinctive age-groups. Koehl proposed that the long-haired figure on the Chieftain Cup was not receiving but "presenting the military gear, an ox hide and the cup itself to the top-knotted figure B as the gifts which Ephoros states the *philetor* offers his chosen one, the *parastates*, as required by law." Thus the scene purportedly represented the initiation stage after the two months in the wild had ended.[21] He thought that the group of youths with long hair might stand for the Minoan counterparts of the youthful friends who assisted the Dorian *parastates* in the staged abduction.

However, it is a great leap of faith to presume that the ritual kidnapping of the Dorian Cretans described by Ephorus and all the other pederastic institutions associated with later Crete and Sparta went back to the Minoan palace society at Cnossos and had continued uninterrupted through the devastations of the Dark Age and even through the Mycenean occupation that took place over two centuries before the Dark Age. Three or four artifacts, all difficult to interpret, especially in the absence of writing, hardly constitute proof that courtiers at Cnossos kidnapped boys, kept them in herds, or ate in all-male dining rooms. If the Minoans, who were literate, did indeed organize their young males into age-groups, as many preliterate tribes do, they may have also encouraged some form of homosexuality among them, but even so there would not necessarily be any direct relation between their sexual customs and Greek *paiderastia*.

Probably the oldest Greek pederastic art object, according to Dover, is the eighteen-centimeter Archaic bronze plaque from Crete dated by the noted Oxford art historian John Boardman to the second half and perhaps the third quarter of the seventh century. It shows a man with a bow grabbing the forearms of a young hunter who is carrying a wild goat. Both wear short tunics, and that of the younger reveals his well-developed genitals; thus, in a certain sense, the plaque announces the Athenian black-figure pederastic vases.[22] The plaque is merely one of several found at Kato Syme on

Crete representing long-haired youths and long-haired but bearded older men bearing hunting equipment and animals to feast on or to sacrifice. Boardman denied but Koehl, accenting a resemblance between the hairstyle of the youth and that of figure A of the Chieftain Cup, affirmed a Minoan background.[23]

David Greenberg has kindly called my attention to the existence of a pair of late geometric ithyphallic bronze figurines, which are nude, helmeted, and age-asymmetrical. They also hold hands. Citing Lembesis (1976), Greenberg dated the figurines to the eighth century B.C., long after the Dorians occupied the island, and insisted that they seem to contradict Dover's thesis that no evidence for institutionalized pederasty predates 630. Even if this artifact depicts a pederastic relationship (a conclusion that is by no means obvious), it must be remembered that we seek evidence, not for any sign of such a relationship, but for a complex of behaviors that implicates pederastic bonding in an articulated program which includes love and training. As the preceding paragraphs have tried to show, evidence for such a program among the Minoans cannot be produced.

Myceneans

There is even a more unequivocal absence of any indication of pederasty from the purely Greek, more male-dominated (at least as far as its deities are concerned), and warlike civilization of the Myceneans. About 1400, the Myceneans occupied Cnossos. Henceforth, dominating Mediterranean trade, they voyaged far afield to Italy and maybe even to Spain and through the Dardanelles into the Black Sea for furs, metals, and slaves. No evidence exists that they proscribed, or for that matter practiced, any form of homosexuality. In the earliest Helladic monumental sculpture and in the "tall limestone slabs" in the shaft graves and throughout Mycenean art, male nudity predominates, in contrast to Minoan art where, as in Egyptian art, loincloths usually cover male genitals.[24] Later Greek myths of men changing into women (e.g., Tiresias and Kaineus) may indeed descend from pre-Olympian cultic transvestism.[25] But Late Archaic Greeks deemed these practices foreign if not repellent and there is little evidence for them in Homeric or other early Greek epics. No Mycenean art is sexually explicit.

Little survives of Mycenean writing. To date, Linear B tablets, first deciphered to a great extent in 1952 by Michael Ventris, contain only administrative lists of people and wealth and names of divinities. We have recovered several thousand tablets and fragments, mainly from Cnossos, Pylos, and Mycenae, but we may never uncover any true literature or even religious inscriptions of prayers or incantations in that script.[26]

For all these many reasons, we cannot trace Greek pederasty to the Minoans or Myceneans any more than we can trace it to the prehistoric Indo-Europeans or proto-Greeks. We turn next, therefore, to the preliterate Dorians, another society once widely associated by scholars with the origins of institutionalized pederasty.

Two

Dorian Knabenliebe

> What the Dorians brought was boy-love as a publicly recog-
> nized and honorable institution. Homer never mentioned . . . a
> pederastic relationship. . . . Legitimate pederasty was then un-
> known among the Asiatic Aeolians and Ionians. The same was
> true about their kinfolk remaining in the motherland. . . . The
> Dorians strictly regulated the love relationship between man
> and boy and treated it as a very important arrangement very
> publicly with honorable earnestness under the protection of the
> family, society, the state, and religion. . . . In Sparta, Crete, and
> Thebes . . . the education of the ruling class, resting on ped-
> erasty, [was directed toward] arete [honor] and manly virtue,
> which principally manifested itself in war.
>
> —Erich Bethe, "Die dorische Knabenliebe: ihre Ethik und ihre
>   Idee," *Rheinisches Museum für Philologie* 62 (1907): 441, 444

The theory of the Dorian origins of initiatory pederasty, although less
sweeping and much older than the idea of an original Indo-European or
proto-Greek practice, has always had the merit of recognizing the absence
of institutionalized pederasty in Homer and all other early Greek literature.
Proponents of the theory argued cogently that the earliest Greek writers,
all of whom were Aeolic or Ionian, ignored pederasty because their societies had not yet instituted it. (If Linear B had then been deciphered, they
could have added that the Myceneans, the earliest to write Greek, had not
mentioned it either.) They concluded that Dorians had institutionalized
pederasty, without specifying whether they did so in their distant *Urheimat*, during their migrations, or upon settling the lands that they conquered
in Greece and Crete. Before entering into further details of this theory,
however, the reader should understand to what degree scholarship has radically revised our thinking about the Dorians and how different that people

appears today from the nineteenth-century portrait that gave rise to the Dorian theory of pederasty.

Legend and Fact

According to legend, the arrival of the Dorians in the Peloponnesus was synonymous with what the Greeks called the "Return of the Heracleidae." Shortly before the Trojan War, they believed, King Eurystheus of Mycenae expelled Heracles' sons from the Peloponnesus. The Heracleidae then roamed from one place to another, lingering for a while at Doris in central Greece, whence the name "Dorians." After an abortive attempt or two to invade the Peloponnesus via the Isthmus of Corinth, they at last successfully attacked across its gulf and occupied most of the Peloponnesus. While some refugees fled inland to Arcadia from Messenia, Sparta, and Argos, others took refuge in Athens, from which their descendants supposedly colonized what came to be called Ionia. The Peloponnesian areas where Dorian was spoken in the classical age, the core of Mycenean civilization, experienced the most devastation. A branch of the Dorians or cousins of theirs who spoke another variety of Northwestern Greek occupied Thessaly, enserfing the natives there as the Spartans did in Laconia and Boeotia. However, in contrast to the Spartans, the conquerors of Thessaly in time adopted certain cultural elements, including the language, of those they enserfed.

Although linguistics would still seem to lend support to this legend,[1] archeologists and their allies now dispute it. Elements were clearly added to explain existing conditions and claims advanced in the classical age. Ephorus repeated the version of the Heracleidae that his teacher Isocrates had elaborated (*Archidamus*, 120). Plato claimed that the Dorians were disinherited Achaeans (*Laws*, I, 3). Apollodorus offered one of the most succinct and popular accounts: "Dorus received the country over against Peloponnese and called the settlers Dorians after himself" (I, vii, 3). Strabo and Pausanias preserved differing legends and manifold details which may come from the poetic and local accounts of early Sparta that Herodotus had tried to sort out. In short, the sources about the Dorians, though relatively plentiful, are both late and contradictory.

Today almost all scholars insist that nineteenth-century philologists hypothesized far too much not only about Dorian physical, martial, and moral traits but also about common inherited Dorian institutions. It is true that by the classical period, the Greeks themselves recognized and in fact highlighted the differences between Dorian and Ionian customs. The rivalry sharpened after the Persian invasions, when Athens and its Ionian allies began to challenge the Peloponnesian League, made up principally of Dorian *poleis.* Beginning with Cleomenes I (c. 519–490), some Spartan kings claimed that they were not Dorian but Achaean to gain support from their non-Dorian allies and subjects. This propaganda contrasted with the Athenian boast that in ancient times Athens had offered refuge to the Ionians as they were fleeing the Dorian invaders of the Peloponnesus. The articulate, sophisticated, luxury-loving Ionians of the sixth and fifth centuries, who in general favored individuality and freedom of choice, distinguished themselves from the inarticulate, rustic, austere, conformist Dorians. However, Dorians and Ionians underscored their social and intellectual differences without ever using the term "Dorian pederasty," a phrase invented by nineteenth-century classicists.

Pertinent, too, is the fact that there were many different areas settled by Dorians. However, northwestern Greece, Leucos, and Acarnania showed no more evidence of early pederasty than did those regions (other than Sparta) settled by Dorians in the Peloponnesus: the Megarid, Epidaurus, the Argolid, and Corinthia. (For Corinthia, some evidence has been advanced. It will be discussed below and disallowed.) Nor did Elis, even though, as Pausanias testifies, it was to become with Thebes a city tolerant of pederastic sex, or Achaea, or Corcyra (Corfu), or any of the Aegean islands (except the Spartan colony of Thera) from Cythera and Milos across to Anatolia. Nor were the Dorian settlements in southern Anatolia famed for pederasty. If the pederastic institution had antedated the Dorian dispersal, it should have shown up in all Dorian areas and perhaps also in all Northwest-Greek-speaking areas.[2] It does not, and yet proponents of the Dorian theory have not explained its absence. (Some of those arguing for the Indo-European origin have posited priestly prohibition and suppression in those societies where, finding no evidence of pederasty, they claim that it once existed and then disappeared.)

"Pure" or "Sacral" Pederasty

The Göttingen classicist Karl Otfried Müller devoted eight pages of his monumental *Die Dorier* (1824) to arguing that prehistoric warriors of the Dorian "race" in the mountains of central Asia institutionalized a pure (non-sexual) pederasty and that the practice contained rituals that continued into historic times in Sparta and Crete. Believing in the superiority of the Dorians as the purest and most undiluted of Aryans to enter Greece, Müller

imputed the "gross" sexual aspects of pederasty to a later Lydian (Near Eastern) influence on the theretofore "pure" Dorian pederasty. Both he and his
followers remained vague as to when and why that chaste practice degenerated into sodomy. He did recognize the special importance of the Cretans,
but felt that pederasty was a pan-Doric or even, as he vaguely hinted, pan-
Hellenic institution, the result of peculiar racial instincts, emotions, and
attitudes. In Müller's words:

> The old national custom had evolved in a still more characteristic
> fashion in Crete, hence this island was even regarded by many as
> the birthplace of love of youths [citing Athenaeus, *Deipnosophistae* 13,
> 601C, 602F; Heraclides of Pontus, *On Constitutions* 3; Christian Gott-
> lob Heyne, *Ad Apollodori Atheniensis Bibliothecam notae* (1783), 3, 1, 2;
> Kretes erotikotatoi according to Plutarch, *Erotikos* 17, p. 37]. Here too
> [as in Sparta] it was a disgrace for a well-educated boy not to have a
> lover; for just this reason the beloved was called *kleinos,* the honored;
> the lover, simply *philetor.* How intimate was the relationship emerges
> from the fact that in many respects it was an imitation of the marital
> one. Like the brides in Lacedaimon, here the boys were abducted. . . .
> Such fixed institutions as these had, to be sure, evolved nowhere else,
> but the underlying emotional attitude was common to all Dorians.
> The love of the Corinthian Bacchiad and legislator of Thebes, Philo-
> laus, and the Olympic champion Diocles [also a Corinthian, hence a
> Dorian] lasted until death, and even their graves were associated as a
> token of friendship. ([1844] 287)[3]

Of particular note here regarding Müller's theory is his statement that
"the custom was instituted by Lycurgus as a check to population."[4] The
text in Aristotle to which he referred (*Politics,* 1272a 12) actually reads: "The
Cretan lawgiver regarded abstemiousness as beneficial and devoted much
ingenuity to securing it, as also to keeping down the birth-rate by keeping
men and women apart and by instituting sexual relations between males."
Müller thought that Aristotle's Cretan lawgiver was Lycurgus, whom he
believed to come from Crete. However, the passage in Aristotle does not
indicate a general Dorian custom, much less a pan-Hellenic one, but rather
a historic origin, occurring after the Dorian diaspora and after a population
explosion that, as we know today, did not begin before 800.

In 1837, in the first lengthy study of Greek pederasty (an extended
encyclopedia article), Moritz Hermann Eduard Meier repeated Müller's

theory but cited more of the ancient sources about Greek pederasty, several of which indicated a specific Cretan origin rather than a general Dorian one.[5] Yet, the theory of Dorian origins long prevailed thereafter.

Among the primitive practices that the Dorian conquerors presumably preserved and brought with them to their new homes was the custom of having every worthy youth attach himself to an older warrior for military training, practical instruction, and social initiation. These elite pairs of what may have been (at least in Victorian theory) homosexually chaste heroic comrades apparently often fought and died side by side. We have no hard evidence at all of what actually went on between Cretan or Spartan lovers, though many have assumed that the ritual kidnapping on Crete, like that of Spartan brides it resembled, implied sexual relations.[6] On the other hand, the nineteenth-century German view of the Dorians' "pure" pederasty emphasized two of the most prolific and authoritative sources of information on the late seventh or early sixth century: Xenophon, who vehemently denied that any anal intercourse occurred between Spartan lovers, and Plutarch, who claimed that their lawgiver Lycurgus had forbidden it.

These writers notwithstanding, graffiti inscribed on the rocks of a cliff on the island of Thera (modern Santorini) in the vicinity of what became a gymnasium recorded anal penetration of youths. Their publication in 1898 dropped like a bombshell on academia. Most resembled inscriptions on the later Athenian *kalos* vases: "Lakydidas is *agathos* (good)," "Korax(?) is *agathos*, the (sc. son) of]ronos," ". . .]x is *aristos* (best)," "Pykimedes is *aristos* of the family of Skamotas," "Kudros is *aristos*," "Krimon is foremost . . . ," "Ainesis is *thaleros* (sturdy), Meniadas is first," "Eumelos is the best dancer," "Barbax is a good dancer and [. . .]," "Helekrates is a good [dancer (?)]." Some, however, proclaimed unequivocally that pederasts were anally active: "Pheidippidas fucked, Timagoras and Empheres and I fucked"; "By (sc. Apollo) Delphinios, Krimon fucked a boy, Bathykles' brother [or son]"; and "Krimon fucked with Amotion here."[7] "Krimon" is mentioned so often that some regard him as a sort of pederastic Don Juan.[8]

These Theran graffiti are our most explicit, unambiguous evidence for anal intercourse in Archaic times. The small bleak island of Thera was seized and recolonized by Spartans a little before 750 when Sparta first began to become overpopulated.[9] Excavations prove that it was relatively prosperous in the later eighth and seventh centuries.[10] Approximately a generation before 600 a seven-year drought struck (Herodotus, IV, 1551). The island was unable to support such a large population, and around 630 its leaders forced some of its males to emigrate to Cyrene on the forbidding Libyan coast. (However, it is not unreasonable to suppose that institutionalized pederasty could also have been an aspect of Theran population control.)

The discoverer of these graffiti, F. Hiller von Gaertringen, felt that the inscriptions were connected with the Carneia, a feast to Dorian Apollo similar in some ways to the Spartan *gymnopaedia,* where naked boys danced to honor the god.[11] To many moderns, however, the graffiti seem to be mere bragging and boasting about homosexual conquests rather than an expression of deep religious feeling. Like Dover (1978), I cannot assume with Hiller von Gaertringen that the Theran inscriptions were religious dedications or that they began in the eighth century.[12] Both Dover and Buffière point out that the boasting in the graffiti by the active males vis-à-vis their conquests, which may even amount to a publicized humiliation of the passive partner,[13] is quite similar to the content of the much later Pompeian inscriptions and hardly seems to record a sacred act. On the other hand, they do not contain threats, as certain Roman graffiti do: "I will irrumate you" or "I will bugger you." The surviving Greek graffiti that are without question sexual in nature are also overwhelmingly homosexual. Furthermore, all of them were inscribed by the active partners only. Indeed, in contrast to many modern ones, no ancient graffiti (or literature) brag of any passive performance either anal or oral.

Believing that the earliest Greek poets and, hence, early Greek societies were untouched by Dorian influences including pederasty, Erich Bethe (1907) argued that the initiatory pederasty of the Dorians spread late (i.e., at the beginning of the seventh century B.C.) but also rapidly from Sparta to non-Dorian Hellas. He drew upon the new science of anthropology, evoking, as we have seen, ritualized initiatory pederasty in New Guinea and other primitive warrior societies, where the semen of the warrior supposedly made the youth who received it vigorous and brave.[14] Bethe maintained that the pederastic initiation of Dorian youths into manhood had a sacral character. Since rituals of manhood were holy among the Dorians, their pederastic practices did not constitute true homosexuality but a type of phallus-worship: "The love act itself, as a holy act, in a holy place, was consummated according to officially recognized usages."[15]

Although many went along with Bethe's theory about Dorian origins and the rapid diffusion from Sparta to non-Dorian areas, few accepted his thesis about anal injection. Anatol Semenov's reaction is typical: "In fact, how then was it possible for such a simple, . . . primitive folk like the Dorians already in quite ancient times to have reached such a refinement of moral corruption as to extend the protection of the state to an unnatural vice? This is patent nonsense. Rather something of this kind might have been expected of the Ionians, from early times pleasure-seeking, and familiar . . . with all the outgrowths of the ever so rich Oriental culture!"[16]

Although Semenov could admit that pure Dorian *Knabenliebe* eventually turned into buggery, Albert Ruppersberg demurred: "I admit from the outset that pederasty was a widespread vice among the Greeks, but I contest the view that boy-love, at least as Bethe understands it, was 'a publicly recognized, sacred, fundamental and life-determining element' (p. 440)."[17]

Such critiques culminated in the dictum of Ulrich von Wilamowitz-Moellendorff, the dean of German philologists, that Bethe's theory of a Dorian *Knabenliebe* involving initiatory anal penetration of the youth by his lover should not be taken seriously.[18] Nevertheless, Wilamowitz-Moellendorff recognized the military nature of Dorian pederasty, believing that it originated in the womanless conditions of their plundering bands. Unlike many of his predecessors, he warily admitted the erotic, even the sexual bond of lover and beloved, emphasizing rather "the ennobling of the sensual need":

The eros that bound the Sacred Band of Thebes, the elite of the army, and not only permitted the relationships of the pairs of friends but rather sanctified them, is another thing. To be sure only the wish that blinded the eye has caused denial of the sensual element in it that should rather be acknowledged as the root of everything. The invaders brought boy-love with them, which in their wandering hordes had the same cause as among the Celts and among many Germanic tribes of the great migrations. It was the urgency of the situation, the close intimacy on the campaigns of plunder that allowed no female camp-followers. This communal life persisted in the gymnasia and *syssitia*, and therefore also its consequences. That is not the distinctive feature (this would recur always), rather the ennobling of the sensual need. The boy who is received into the community and has so much to learn needs the older comrade who initiates and protects him, since in such a society a cruel form of hazing usually prevails. The knight has need of a page, and in a circle of members of the same social stratum this cannot be a slave. (Wilamowitz-Moellendorff and Niese [1910] 92)

Wilamowitz-Moellendorff's successor at Berlin, Werner Jaeger, implicitly appreciated the pedagogical value of Greek pederasty. He believed that by building upon the Dorians' simpler custom of training body and character, the Athenians produced through the exaltation of manly beauty a higher practice. It used Homer as a basic text to stress excellence and competition and concentrated on developing intellectual abilities as well as physical and moral qualities. He did not speculate, however, as to whether the practice was physical.[19] In 1948 his French admirer Henri-Irénée Marrou downplayed somewhat the role of Homer but articulated a similar sentiment about the pedagogical value of pederasty in ancient Greece. Aware of the attacks on Dorian theories as racist, Jaeger cagily remained silent about the origins of Greek pederasty.

No one else produced a theory of origins, not even those prolific writers on Greek pederasty of the 1920s and 1930s, the German classicist professor Hans Licht and the French aristocrat L. R. de Pogey-Castries. Both of them avoided discussion of origins altogether.[20] Like the Victorian Symonds, Licht hesitated to accept the Dorian thesis while admitting that "it was especially in the Doric states that this custom [pederasty] prevailed."[21] Licht and other homophile scholars allowed that the Dorians might have introduced pederasty to Greece but remained skeptical. They also denied that Dorian pederasty was asexual without accepting Bethe's view that it was merely a ritual.

"Lustless" Pederasty

Though disdainfully and decisively rejected by his contemporaries, Bethe's theories were revived in 1982 by Harald Patzer, a German classicist who claimed that the latest ethnographical findings summarized by Gisela Bleibtreu-Ehrenberg and her "most modern ethnological conceptual categories . . . confirm Bethe to an extent that he himself could not have suspected."[22] Patzer argued that (1) Dorian warriors, out of a sense of obligation to their society and at the request of the youth's relatives, reluctantly penetrated their *eromenoi* anally only in order to transfer their virtue to them through their sperm; (2) that the best of the classical Athenians, being highly refined and above sensuality, did not have sex with their *eromenoi* at all; and (3) that it was only in Hellenistic times that a promiscuous, sensual pederasty proliferated. To Patzer, the essential features of institutionalized pederasty were all aimed at the edification of the adolescent. Thus, they cannot have existed for the satisfaction of the *erastes*'s personal inclinations. In his opinion, the warrior, without the slightest lust, obliged the youth's anxious parents and injected his anus with semen as a social duty, perhaps only once without any enjoyment. Unlike Bethe, who did not speak to whether or not the warrior enjoyed it or how often he buggered the youth,

Patzer thus attributed to the "pure" Dorian warrior a Christian asceticism. The warrior had intercourse only to impregnate the youth with virtue. He did not enjoy or apparently have to repeat the act. The youth's family was eternally grateful to the young man who facilitated the maturity of their son by thus transmitting virtue to him.

Unable to square such a theory with, in particular, the evidence of the Theran inscriptions, I turn now to two further areas where scholars have gone in search of the beginnings of institutionalized pederasty in the peninsula: the early Greek myths and the warriors of Greece's Dark Age.

Three

Pre-Pederastic Immortals

Homeric and Hesiodic gods and heroes (the earliest Greek ones about whose
sexual life we have any details) were exuberantly and perhaps exclusively
heterosexual. Like the contemporary aristocrats in whose image they were
largely constructed, the gods had, in addition to one wife, numerous mistresses or one-time female partners whom they raped or seduced. Among
the immortals only the eternally youthful Apollo, Ares, Artemis, and Athena
remained unmarried, though Ares, whom Hephaestus entrapped with a net
in flagrante delicto with his wanton wife Aphrodite, was hardly chaste.
Zeus produced children by scores of females. Heracles fathered even more.
Those intrepid souls who persisted in preserving their chastity against the
blandishments of the gods were often punished.

The question of the place of homosexuality or pederasty in the poems
attributed to Homer, Hesiod, and other early poets is vexed. One school
of thought, to which a few ancients such as Xenophon and Maximus of
Tyre subscribed, denies that they ever referred to it in any form at all.[1] A
modified version of that theory, based in part on Pindar's sanitization of

the cannibalistic myth of Pelops, holds that after the epics became standard texts for *paideia* (education), Greek editors decorously diminished and disguised all unseemly material in them, including explicit homosexuality.[2] The other extreme, including most ancient Greek critics, maintains that the *Iliad* turned on the love between Achilles and Patroclus.

The one overarching fact in this controversy is that only in the late seventh century did Greek mythographers begin to assign *eromenoi* to gods and heroes. The epics clearly describe an old-fashioned society which had vanished long before the classical age. Neither athletic nudity nor gymnasia, both of which so characterized fifth-century Greek society, were mentioned in any of the epics, hymns, or the other early poems. Nudity before other males was an embarrassment to the Homeric Greeks, who conducted their athletics clothed. It is not present in the games described in the *Iliad*, in which, while wrestling, heroes grabbed one another by their belt-buckles (XXIII, 700–739). The shipwrecked Odysseus hid his private parts with a branch from the princess Nausicaa and her maids (*Odyssey*, VI, 128–30). Moreover, the rigorous age-class system that dominated Sparta and Crete, which supposedly preserved ancient customs (if we are to believe Sergent, Sallares, and other modern scholars) is nowhere to be found in the epics or the hymns, any more than seclusion of women, herding of boys, delayed marriages, or gymnastic exercises.

On the other hand, the Homeric question has befuddled modern scholars for almost two hundred years and may never be settled. (It puzzled the ancients over an even longer period.) Was there one blind poet, born sometime between the twelfth and the seventh century, or a committee of composers? Did one poet compose the *Iliad* and another the *Odyssey* or did someone at a later date string together a series of lays from various times and places, as Lachmann claimed?[3] Did bard teach bard an ancient song, each reciter altering what he learned to suit his interactive audience, each recital constituting a recomposition, as Milman Parry and Albert Lord have taught us? It would be presumptuous of me to claim to have the answers to these questions. I pass over them to concentrate only on those features of the Homeric text that relate to a discussion of pederasty.

Greek Love in Homer

I have already noted the absence of nude athletics, seclusion of women, delayed marriages, and gymnastic exercises in the Homeric texts. Nevertheless, when classical Greeks and those of later ages read the *Iliad*, they

saw both Achilles and Patroclus on the one hand and Zeus and Ganymede
on the other as examples of pederastic lovers. (They could not agree, however, on whether either or both couples engaged in sex.) This pederastic
interpretation is particularly intriguing because neither pairing appears in
the epic in a form which corresponds to basic features of institutionalized
pederasty. There is no indication in either of the all-important mentor-
pupil relationship, which in the case of Achilles Homer gave to the centaur
Chiron. Moreover, Achilles and Patroclus are portrayed as age-mates. Zeus
and Ganymede do fit the age-asymmetrical pattern, but the *Iliad,* unlike later
accounts, gives no indication that Ganymede was transported to Olympus
because of an interest on Zeus's part in the beauty of the youth. It was the
other gods who perpetrated the abduction. According to the poem, Ganymede was "the loveliest born of the race of mortals, and therefore the gods
whisked him away to be Zeus's wine-pourer, for the sake of his beauty, so
he might be among the immortals" (XX, 233–35). As to Zeus's feelings, in
the only other passage to refer to Ganymede, we learn no more than that
Zeus gave King Tros, Ganymede's father, some fine steeds as compensation
for his abducted son (V, 265–67).

The disparity between the letter and thrust of the Homeric text and classical Greeks' reading of Zeus and Ganymede and Achilles and Patroclus as
pederastic couples implies that mention of Ganymede and passages expressing the intense sentiments between Achilles and Patroclus may have been
introduced late into the epic. It also argues forcefully against a very ancient
pederastic tradition among the Greeks.[4] Rather, we appear to be confronted
by a social change that postdated the development of the basic story of the
Iliad and yet achieved such prominence in the culture that readers of the
poem willingly espied pederastic behavior in the chief of the gods and in
the most revered of their heroes even though the epic text specified no
such thing.

In the case of Ganymede, although the epic text does not reflect patterns
of institutionalized pederasty, the myth as it appears in the Homeric *Hymn
to Aphrodite,* which may have crystallized c. 600 or slightly later, suggests
that the story was beginning at that time to be recomposed along pederastic
lines. According to the hymn, Zeus was the abductor and he was attracted by
the boy's beauty: "Verily wise Zeus carried off golden-haired Ganymede because of his beauty, to be amongst the Deathless Ones and pour drink for the
gods in the house of Zeus—a wonder to see—, honored by all the immortals
as he draws the red nectar from the golden bowl" (203–17). Later Sophocles
was to write that "Ganymede's thighs set Zeus aflame" (fr. 320), and classical
vase paintings depicted the rape of the handsome youth (see fig. 1).

Dover noted that "the earliest surviving testimony to Zeus's homosexual desire for Ganymede is Ibykos (fr. 289), where the ravishing of Ganymede was put into the same context as the rape of Tithonus by Dawn, who did not want a wine-pourer [but a sexual partner]."[5] A notorious and indiscriminate lover of adolescents who according to Cicero exceeded his fellow poets Alcaeus and Anacreon in erotic themes (*Tusculan Disputations*, IV, 71), Ibycus (fl. c. 530) was a contemporary of the Pisistratids, who commissioned an important editing of Homer. Ibycus located Zeus's rape of Ganymede on Crete, long associated, as we shall see, with the pederastic kidnapping of youths.

Many writers, including Pindar (*Tenth Olympian*, 19), Xenophon (*Symposium*, 8, 31), Plato (*Symposium*, 180b), and Aeschylus (fr. 228), assumed that a pederastic relationship existed between Achilles and Patroclus, but, faced with the Homeric portrait, classical Greeks had a problem deciding which one must have been the older. Some assigned the role of teacher-lover to Achilles, others to Patroclus, imagining the essential difference in age required for pederastic liaisons of their own time.

Regardless of how we decide to assign the roles of teacher and pupil in the relationship, there is no missing the degree to which the *Iliad* underscores an emotional bond between the two men. Achilles' boundless grief over the death of Patroclus and his revenge on the Trojans for killing his friend are but two indications of that bond. Hear Achilles' address to his dead companion: "[N]ow you lie here torn before me, and my heart goes starved for meat and drink, though they are here beside me, by reason of longing for you. There is nothing worse than this I could suffer, not even if I were to hear of the death of my father" (*Iliad*, XIX, 314–22). Later, the ghost of Patroclus appears to his friend to ask that their ashes share one urn: "There is one more thing I will . . . ask of you . . .: do not have my bones laid apart from yours, Achilleus, but with them, just as we grew up together in your house. . . [L]et one single vessel, the golden two-handled urn the lady your mother gave you, hold both our ashes" (XXIII, 81–92). Was it this devotion between the two young males, so beautifully transcribed in books 19, 22, and 23 of the *Iliad*, that justified the transformation of warrior comrades into *erastes* and *eromenos* and prompted such a remark as "Bereaved, Achilles thought of Patroclus' thighs" (Aeschylus, fr. 228)? If so, it is interesting to note how few moderns have been led by the Homeric verses to such an interpretation.

In *Studies of the Greek Poets* (1873–76) Symonds argued that the love of Achilles and Patroclus occupied a central place in the *Iliad*.[6] A decade later he reduced their relationship to mere "heroic friendship."[7] Licht, Dover, and Boswell, among others, have complicated matters further by confusing

Greek pederasty with modern homosexuality.[8] Sergent, however, carefully distinguishing between modern androphilia and Greek age-asymmetry, denied that the relationship was pederastic: "It is not pederasty, without a doubt, but homophilia, and an intensity of emotions between two men in an expression that surpasses that which our own culture tolerates."[9] Cagily he avoided the long-debated question as to whether the two had ever engaged in sex with each other.

Even more recently David Halperin has resurrected the old view that Achilles and Patroclus had a nonsexual relationship. Maintaining that the men were only heroic "pals,"[10] Halperin further stressed the similarities between their friendship and that of David and Jonathan and Gilgamesh and Enkidu. He did not decide whether the three more or less contemporary pairs of heroes arose simultaneously as a sort of folk archetype, or whether, as has been suggested, the other two derived from Gilgamesh. In all three, the same-age subordinate fills the role of squire or servant to the dominant figure. Not bothering, except in the case of Achilles and Patroclus, to refute the theory that all these pairs of heroes loved each other, Halperin agreed with Nagy that each was modeled on the relationship between a hero and a retainer, or *therapon,* a Semitic word meaning "ally, confederate,"[11] which Nagy translated as alter ego. Halperin concluded: "In each of these narrative traditions, the friendship between the heroes appears to be an element that is crystallized relatively late in the process of formation of the transmitted texts."[12] If this is true for Achilles and Patroclus, is it not perhaps another sign that the institutionalization of pederasty, too, occurred late among the Hellenes? The relationship of Achilles and Patroclus, no doubt originally one of intense male bonding in a society that had not yet institutionalized pederasty, was, I think, recomposed by bards for recitation before a culture that had established such a practice. Their comradeship as warriors could serve as the model for lovers faithful to the death in battle, whether or not these men were originally just "pals" or pederastic lovers, but the emotions that they express in the text we read today reflect the fantasies of a pederastic imagination.[13]

Thus, although examination of the Homeric texts reveals no more evidence of early institutionalized pederasty in Greece than the other avenues we have been discussing, the fortunes of the Ganymede myth point to a break with the older (nonpederastic) treatment of the tale c. 600. In addition, the later rereading both of that myth and of the relationship between Achilles and Patroclus underscores the extraordinary influence of institutionalized pederasty upon classical Greek culture, each a point that I ask the reader to keep in mind as this study unfolds.

Hesiod and Other Early Poets

At this juncture, there remains only to emphasize that what has come down to us of the Hesiodic texts contains very little homoeroticism, pederasty, or any other form of homosexuality. Similarly, the other early epics and hymns—so far as we can reconstruct them from the fragments, summaries, commentaries, and so on that have survived—were also predominantly heterosexual. Some, composed or altered after 630, contain references to pederasty. (Laius's rape of Chrysippus is typical of the material added when the epics were reshaped in pederastic times; it appears for the first time in Peisander of Camirus, whose birth the *Suda* situated in Rhodes in the thirty-seventh Olympiad, which lasted from 632 to 629 B.C. The *Little Iliad* includes a story of Zeus compensating Laomedon with a vine as the price for Ganymede.) Moreover, even if early poetry not ascribed to Homer and Hesiod does describe some form of homosexuality, it is not the institution-alized pederasty of classical Greece.

By the same token, it must be pointed out that upper-class pederasts of the Near East did not normally train boys of their own rank with whom they were in love to become warriors. Neither did the Romans. Some Greeks living before 630 were familiar with temple prostitutes, eunuchs, servile cupbearers, and other types of effeminates much documented in the ancient Levant, as well as with Scythian shamans and cross-dressers, but the early epics and hymns, unless emended, like the early elegiac poetry ascribed to Callinus and Archilochus, do not reflect institutionalized pederasty. It was to become a system that among literate peoples is unique to the Hellenes.

Four

Situational Homosexuality and Demography

Greek pederasty was in fact one of the most obvious and lasting survivals from the [Greek] feudal "Middle Ages." Greek homosexuality was of a military type. It was quite different from the inversion which is bound up with the rites of initiation and the duties of a priesthood. . . . [L]ove between men is a recurring feature of military societies, in which men tend to be shut in upon themselves. The exclusion—the utter absence—of women inevitably means an increase in masculine love. . . . The phenomenon is more accentuated in a military milieu, for here, with the glorification of an ideal made up of masculine virtues like strength and valour and loyalty, with the cultivation of a distinctively masculine pride, there goes a tendency to depreciate the normal love of a man for a women.

—Henri-Irénée Marrou, *A History of Education in Antiquity*
(London, 1956), 27

Yet another explanation for the origins of Greek pederasty came from a professor at the University of Paris. Drawing a dubious analogy with medieval Europe, Henri-Irénée Marrou envisaged a Greek Dark Age (which he called a "Middle Age") populated by lusty knights living in crude forts or citadels. These men, he reckoned, had sexual relations with their young squires given the absence of ladies to share the rough life of the citadel. But Marrou had little evidence to support his theory; there is no indication in the sources that before 630 Greek knights were particularly given to pederasty. Aware of the lack of Minoan and Mycenean evidence, he shared the view of some nineteenth-century Germans that Homer made no mention of pederasty because the poet had been too reticent or too embarrassed to include the practice in his epic.[1] However, even if we could believe that Homer or the bards who evolved the corpus ascribed to him had such inhibitions, the argument fails to explain why for a full century and a half after the end of the Dark Age all other poets and artists depicted a society that had none of the basic concomitants of institutionalized pederasty. Terpander, Callinus, Tyrtaeus, and perhaps most significantly Archilochus, who was uninhibited in describing heterosexual acts, did not mention pederasty.[2] True, one fragment of Archilochus appears to attack someone as a "cornet player" (fellator?), but it is difficult to say that pederastic sex is being described here. It is quite impossible to extend Archilochus's metaphor to attest all the features of institutionalized pederasty.

Equally unconvincing is Marrou's apparent assumption that the situational homosexuality he posited for the Dark Age knights changed forever the sexual practices of these men and their descendants. As modern studies, notably the Kinsey report, have shown, the majority of men who find themselves in the conditions hypothesized by Marrou for Greek knights revert to heterosexuality when they regain regular access to females. This is as true of sailors on long voyages or of prisoners as it is of teenagers who have their first sexual experiences in male boarding schools.[3]

Despite the many imperfections in Marrou's thesis, it does raise one important point for our investigation: the possibility that certain situations and certain developments in Greek society which fostered close contact and bonding between males may have accustomed them to appreciate such behavior and thus prepared the way for the institutionalization of pederasty. Dover, writing about the spread and importance of pederasty throughout Greece, was brought to assume that the practice fulfilled "a need for personal relationships of an intensity not commonly found within marriage or in the relations between parents and children or in those between the individual and the community as a whole."[4] If Dover is correct, we must believe that the homosexual experiences of warriors, sailors, colonists, and others in the society would have highlighted such a "need" and underscored that gap between male-male relationships and the bonds of marriage, family, and community that Dover speaks of.

Womenless Colonists

Setting out from the Greek peninsula to flee the drought and/or invaders, colonists became a regular part of Greek history after 1000 B.C. Aeolians and Ionians fled during the Dark Age to the Aegean islands and the Anatolian coasts, and some Dorians followed later. Many of the founding bands of Greek colonists were entirely male, given the dangers and rigors that accompanied moving into enemy territory. A colony might include the wife of the founder or a priestess, but probably more colonists took native brides (or boys) rather than import females from the homeland. In any case, for long periods the original colonists remained without access to females; new arrivals in the later decades also often came without women. When the colony was well established, its inhabitants would often ask the mother city to send them wives, but evidence from the whole colonial period indicates that womenless colonists frequently took native brides, as sources say they did in Marseilles, Cyrene, Miletus, and Thasos.

Besides being for long periods without women of their own background or without equal numbers of females of any sort, the colonists were often estranged to a certain extent from their native wives. Sometimes they did not eat with them and perhaps lived apart from them more than was the custom in the homeland. Pausanias stated that "the Ionians overwhelmed the original Milesians, killed the entire male population except for those who ran away when the city fell, and married their wives and daughters" (VII, 2, 3). Herodotus said that when the Ionian immigrants to Miletus married native women after slaughtering their fathers, husbands, and sons, their wives enacted a law, which they swore to observe, "that none should ever sit at meat with her husband, or call him by his name" (I, 146). In Cyrene, where the colonists also married natives (Pindar, *Ninth Pythian Ode*), their wives purportedly declined to dine with their husbands because like the Egyptians the women refused to eat beef or pork (Herodotus, IV, 186).[5]

How often native boys or Greek youths who were part of the expedition served the sexual needs of these colonists one can only speculate, but judging from modern-day experiences situational homosexuality must have been very prevalent, both with native boys and amongst the colonists themselves. The earlier convict settlements in Australia are a case in point.[6] In 1822 a rumor circulated that women had been sent there to prevent men from committing "unnatural crimes." In 1832 and 1837 Parliament obtained evidence of the prevalence of sodomy in the Australian colonies. Convicts called each other "sods," and adolescent convicts had names like Kitty and Nancy. One chain gang prisoner lamented that his companions were "so far advanced . . . in depravity" that they openly engaged "in assignations one toward the other" and "kicked, struck or otherwise abused" anyone who dared to condemn "their horrid propensities."[7]

Mariners, Soldiers, and Their Mates

After the population explosion that began in 800, the less crowded islands beckoned to the Greeks more than ever. In addition, Greek trade was expanding exponentially. With better ships and greater skills, these intrepid mariners could undertake ever longer voyages that must have fostered not only comradeship but also homosexuality, but the *Odyssey* is silent about such activity. Even the much later *Argonautica* of Apollonius of Rhodes has no overt homosexuality other than the affair between Heracles and Hylas, which allegedly began before their expedition. Homosexual flirtations and affairs among mariners must, however, have occurred, even when voyages were somewhat short.[8] Nor could men always expect female companionship when they put into shore.

Prolonged absences from home in army service could also stimulate homosexual feelings and activities. Xenophon (*Anabasis,* VII, 4) speaks of certain commanders who allowed their troops to take boyfriends as well as women along, but many soldiers must have turned to each other for sexual relief then as now.[9]

In later times in Greece, lover and beloved sometimes fought side by side. On Crete a boyfriend came to be called *parastates* ("one who stands beside [in battle]"). In fourth-century Thebes, Gorgides organized the famous Sacred Band made up of 150 pairs of lovers. Eleans, too, often went into battle beside their lovers. How often Spartans and others fought alongside their lovers after the institutionalization of pederasty is not easy to determine. Whether a squire or charioteer might normally have become a sexual partner (presumably passive) of his superior is certainly open to question. Interestingly, some later Greeks imagined just such behavior about certain heroes of the Trojan War. Eubulus remarked about that conflict: "No one ever set eyes on a single *hetaira* [prostitute]; they wanked themselves [masturbated] for ten years. It was a poor sort of campaign: for the capture of one city, they went home with arses much wider than (sc. the gates of) the city that they took" (fr. 120). This may well reflect traditions of his own day in the army, but it is mostly a piece of irreverent humorous fantasy.[10]

Poor Farmers, Emigrants, Paupers, and Slaves

When speaking of the mariners' long trips, I mentioned how a population explosion after 800 compelled the Greeks to set sail for less crowded areas of the Mediterranean. The effects at home of such overpopulation were even

more profound. The explosion may have occurred because of the gradual
immunization of the population to diseases that had previously ravaged the
region.[11] In any case, after 800, when the climate may also have improved, a
healthier and better fed population multiplied, expanding at the fastest rate
imaginable.[12] If McNeill (1976) and the demographers and epidemiologists
that he summarized are correct, general advances and declines in population are most likely to occur because of changes in human immunity to
diseases, but these causes can and often do operate together with the more
traditional factors (such as war and famine) to bring about demographic
booms that can last for several centuries.[13]

By the middle or end of the seventh century, when good colonial
sites were running out, population pressure at home became intolerable,
threatening to impoverish the Greek upper class. The English archeologist Anthony M. Snodgrass has examined the increase in datable burials in
Athens over two thirty-year generations. On this basis he has concluded
that the population had been increasing at the rate of 3 percent annually.
Although this is not higher than the most rapidly increasing populations in
some Third World countries today, the rate yields an astonishing increase of
700 percent if extended over a century. I do not insist on such a magnitude
nor do I imagine that the increase was uniform for each year. However,
that there was a general population explosion during much of that period
is difficult to doubt.[14] It may have been achieved in ancient Greece because
the abundant food supplies that better weather and technology made possible were coupled with high birth rates due to early marriages and lack of
contraception.

Camp (1979) has strongly disagreed with Snodgrass's conclusions and
Morris (1987) has argued that the increase in population from 800 to 700
may not have been so great as the sevenfold figure postulated by Snodgrass.
Nevertheless, Sallares has strongly endorsed Snodgrass's theories, arguing
that a great and general population expansion took place more or less from
800 to 480.[15] Indeed, no one can deny that the Greek population was far
greater in 500 than in 1000.

Hesiod's *Works and Days* seems to represent hardship due to overpopulation during the early Archaic Age (seventh century). It suggested that
it was desirable for men to marry only when they approached the age of
thirty.[16] His *Theogony* enjoined against having more than one son, although
he understood the need of having children to provide for one's old age,
which he foresaw as needy. Fear of poverty owing to overpopulation lay
behind the injunction: "There should be only one son, to feed his father's

house, for so wealth will increase in the home" (*Theogony,* 376–82, 603–13). Other signs of overpopulation come from the small island of Ceos. There people who lived to sixty were purportedly compelled to drink hemlock, apparently regardless of their rank. Even Ceos's most famous poet, Simonides, was said to have fled into exile in his fifties to avoid that fate (Strabo, *Geography,* X, 486). The *Cypria,* ascribed to Stasinus of Cyprus (fl. c. 600), also speaks of the hardships of overpopulation: "There was a time when the countless tribes of men, though wide-dispersed, oppressed the surface of the deep-bosomed earth, and Zeus saw it and had pity and in his wise heart resolved to relieve the all-nurturing earth of men by causing the great struggle of the Ilian war, that the load of death might empty the world" (3).

In such a time, many small farmers and craftsmen must have been too poor to marry or even to form any permanent liaison with females at all. These people, who mingled with the paupers and indeed fell into their ranks, often had similar problems securing sexual relief and probably turned to one form or another of homosexuality, perhaps with the street boys or orphans of the day. We have, however, no incontrovertible evidence at all of their homosexuality before the Late Archaic period.

Levantine Origins

Although I have been suggesting that developments within the Greek world such as overpopulation and situational homosexuality constituted important elements in the background to institutionalized pederasty, another school of thought has implied that Levantines and more specifically Lydians corrupted the ancient Greeks. The Greeks were seen as morally upstanding Aryans, induced by the Levantines to inject a sensual, sexual dimension into what had previously been a religious ritual between males or merely a pure, asexual comradeship.[17] This perspective thrived in the nineteenth century, when European racists attributed to the Hellenes a genetic superiority encompassing both moral and physical qualities.

Search as they did, Aryan supremacists could find no evidence to substantiate their hypotheses. In spite of the fact that *kedeshim* and other forms of male temple prostitution and transgenderal homosexuality abounded in the ancient Near East,[18] the less religious Hellenes failed to build large-scale temples with permanent staffs and remained alien to the idea of male temple prostitutes. Moreover, even when Greeks institutionalized pederasty, they produced a far different custom from that practiced in the Near East. Not only was it not associated with temples, it had nothing to do with eunuchs, effeminates, transvestites, shamans, or slaves. The upper-class Greek youths grew up to be the equal of their lover-patrons. Aristocratic and athletic, they trained for war and citizenship.[19]

Not a single ancient ever argued that the Greeks acquired the institution of pederasty from any other people. Proud of their unique pederastic system, the Greeks were acutely aware that they did not borrow it from barbarians. In fact, it is worth repeating here that Plato accounted pederasty, philosophy, and nude sports as the three things that set the Hellenes apart from the barbarians (*Symposium*, 182b). Herodotus of Halicarnassus, one of the Greek cities located closest to the Near East and Egypt, claimed very specifically that the Persians "learned pederasty from the Greeks" (I, 135).[20]

Middle Archaic Innovations: A New View

If, as I have tried to suggest, it is difficult to find evidence that institutionalized pederasty arose among the earliest Indo-Europeans or even the proto-Greeks, we must now propose and justify its appearance at a later date. The correct time, I believe, was the middle Archaic Age (between 650 and 600), a period of considerable innovation in many fields.

In art a decisive change occurred after 650.[21] The geometric style associated with the early Archaic Age contained numerous silhouettes of human forms as well as of animals and other objects such as ships and chariots, but they were still more abstract than realistic in nature. Prior to 650, we see at best a trend away from the earlier linear style and toward the larger and more numerous figures that occasionally interrupted the geometric patterns once dominant on the surface of the ceramics. About 650 a precise break with the remnants of the geometric style finally takes place. The new mode emphasized human figures rather than geometric lines.

The sculpture of the early Archaic Age, too, resembles that of the Proto-geometric more than it does the art produced in the decades after 650, when the first monumental statues, strongly influenced by Egyptian art, appeared. Early Archaic statues were small and crude. The few extant life-size statues (mostly mutilated) and vase paintings, like the literature of the same early Archaic period, provide no evidence that adolescents received training from men who were approximately ten years their senior or exercised nude. None of the gods or heroes, except perhaps Orpheus and Dionysus or other imports from Thrace or Asia, were said to practice or shown practicing pederasty before the last decades of the seventh century. The earliest firm evidence of such activity comes from the seventh century, not the eighth century, despite statements by Bowra and Sergent to the contrary.[22]

Traditionalists who believe that all important classical institutions took shape either in the early eighth century or in the decades just before 480 miss not only the "orientalizing" of art (the increasing adoption of Meso-potamian and Syrian motifs) and its focus on the male body, for which we can find clear Egyptian models, at least for the earliest *kouroi,* but also the great institutional innovations in Crete and Sparta in the middle of that age which will be discussed in detail below. At that time Sparta and colonies prone to innovation and experimentation imported from Crete a number of key institutions associated with institutionalized pederasty: symposia, the seclusion of women, and gymnastic nudity. These institutions endured as long as classical civilization did.

Part Two

The Institutionalization
of Pederasty

Five

The Immortals Become Pederasts

Son of Tantalus! I will tell of thee a tale far other than that of earlier bards:—what time thy father, in return for the banquets he had enjoyed, bade the gods come to his own dear Sipylus, and share his duly-ordered festal board, then it was that the god of the gleaming trident, with his heart enthralled with love, seized thee and carried thee away on his golden chariot to the highest home of Zeus, who is honoured far and wide,—that home to which, in aftertime, Ganymede was also brought for the self-same service.

—Pindar, *Olympian Odes,* I, 37–45

Scholarly investigation into the origins of homosexual elements in Greek myth has substantiated Pindar's admission, or rather boast, that he fabricated a pederastic tale (the story of the god Poseidon and a hero, Tantalus's son Pelops) which he claimed to be older than the legend about Zeus and Ganymede. For a long time, some have argued that such elements entered Greek mythology at a relatively late date. In 1837, for example, M. H. E. Meier wrote: "Only after this institution [of male love] had been established among the Greeks did they, in accordance with their custom, transfer it through their myths to the world of their gods and heroes."[1] The Victorian W. E. H. Lecky shared this opinion about the relatively late addition of pederastic episodes to Greek myth.[2] Nearly a century later, in his celebrated *Greek Myths* (1955), Robert Graves also recognized that pederastic myths and legends were late, a thesis Dover finally endorsed only in 1988.

Reaching the same conclusion as Lecky, Rudolf Beyer's fundamental book on pederasty and other forms of homosexuality in Greek and Latin mythology (1910) emphasized other important observations as well. Beyer realized that the pederastic myths associated with the various cities were created only after their inhabitants had institutionalized pederasty. Thus he accepted the thesis that these fables showed as no other sources did from which regions pederasty spread to other corners of Greece.[3] It will be the purpose of this chapter to situate in time the institutionalization of Greek pederasty and to show how most of the legends about the pederastic gods and supposed heroic founders of pederasty lead us back to Crete as the land from which the custom eventually spread throughout Hellas.

Pederastic Gods and Heroes

The heterosexual promiscuity of Greek gods and heroes reflected and, in the ninth and eighth centuries, even surpassed that of the ruling classes, upon whom they were largely modeled. The *Iliad* lists seven mistresses of Zeus (XIV, 317–27) and Hesiod ascribed to him seven successive wives without claiming that the first wife, his sister Hera, ever died or was divorced (*Theogony*, 886ff.). Mythographers eventually mentioned 115 women that Zeus bedded.[4] Yet like their aristocratic worshipers who, though officially monogamous, often kept virtual harems of concubines and slave girls, the gods, though formally monogamous, were in fact polygamous.

Around 600 poets and artists began to introduce pederastic episodes into the old myths or to create entirely new stories about the gods and heroes. Vase painters and lyric and elegiac poets such as Alcaeus, Alcman, Stesichorus, Ibycus, and Anacreon made, as we shall see, the earliest unmistakable references to such pederastic activity. They did not challenge the overwhelming heterosexuality of the Olympians, nor did they or their classical and Alexandrian or Latin successors ever ascribe to heroes or immortals the concomitants of pederasty, that is, messes for males, symposia, athletic nudity, gymnasia, or the segregation of women. In short, they did not presume to restructure the basic society of Olympus, whose outlines had so clearly been established before 630.

However, already by the end of the fifth century perhaps, poets had assigned at least one *eromenos* to every important god except Ares and to many legendary figures. The comic poets, especially those of the Middle Comedy (c. 404 to 323), often introduced the immortals' *eromenoi* on the stage. Besides his *Adonis,* in which he depicted the love of Dionysus, Plato Comicus wrote a *Laius,* in which he apparently touched upon that king's love for Chrysippus. Strattis and Diogenes the Cynic both wrote a *Chrysippus.* Antiphanes and Eubulus each wrote a *Ganymede.* The *Scholia Laurentsiana* on Apollonius of Rhodes's *Argonautica* A 118 told how the highly renowned seer and physician Melampus became the beloved (*philtatos*) of Apollo in the *Megalai Ehoiai*.[5]

As a result of the new tales, most heroes, including Orestes and Theseus, were now portrayed as having been in their youth the *eromenoi* of gods or other heroes or, conversely, of having become *erastes*.[6] Some imagined that Orestes took his companion Pylades as an *eromenos;* others, that Theseus was Minos's *eromenos*. As an adult, Pelops had married the daughter of a king who had killed all her other suitors after beating them in a chariot race. Through his brave deeds, he became a hero (whose tomb was perhaps the oldest cult structure at Olympia). Pindar made this hero an *eromenos* who resembled Ganymede in that he, too, was abducted to become the boyfriend of a god. In a slightly different version, "Philostratus says that Poseidon fell in love with Pelops when the youth was serving wine to the gods in his father's house."[7]

Although boyfriends came late in the history of Olympus, we must not forget that the Greeks were proud of pederasty. They did not invent pederastic myths about the gods to excuse a human custom that they found immoral, as Plato and most moderns have supposed. Rather the Greeks considered pederasty an improvement over an earlier, more primitive system, comparable to the change that occurred when the handsome, lithe Ganymede replaced the lame and clumsy Hebe as Zeus's cupbearer. In Strato's words, "Every dumb animal copulates in one way only, but we, endowed with reason, have the advantage over animals in this—we invented anal intercourse. But all who are held in sway by women are no better than dumb animals" (*Greek Anthology*, XII, 245). Nowhere do we read of a late-blooming divine or heroic pederast being less pleased with his *eromenos* than he had been with the woman he deserted or neglected for the youth, unless perhaps it be Orpheus, who apparently did not love any of his *eromenoi* (unnamed by Ovid) as he did his lost wife Eurydice, taken away from him to the Underworld.

Mythological Originators of Pederasty

Indicative of the high esteem in which pederasty was held is the fact that certain gods and heroes were designated as its originators. They include Zeus, Laius, Orpheus, Thamyris, Minos, Tantalus (father of Pelops), and even Poseidon, as we have seen. Why these individuals were specified is not always easy to explain. Beautiful Apollo and the heroic Heracles had the most *eromenoi,* but they are not ever said to have begun the custom. A close association with Crete may explain the choice of Zeus and Minos. The fact that Laius and Orpheus both for different reasons gave up sex with females and took up with boys as an alternative lends some credence to Marrou's theory that situational homosexuality prepared the Greeks for institutionalized pederasty.

The most common version of the origin of pederasty traced it to Zeus's seizure of Ganymede, a very beautiful youth and the only individual living on Mount Olympus both of whose parents were mortals. The traditional account of the abduction placed the *harpagion* (literally, "the place of seizing") in the Troad, which was logical since the boy's father was the king of Troy (Athenaeus, XIII, 601f). Another version situated it on the island of Euboea, near Chalcis. The fact that Crete was so often seen as the birthplace of pederasty led some writers, however, to change the legend and to maintain that Zeus had kidnapped Ganymede from Crete. Similarly, the originator of pederasty was often said to be not Zeus but King Minos of Crete, or even his younger brothers Rhadamanthus or Sarpedon.

After Zeus, the individual most frequently associated with the introduction of pederasty to Hellas was Oedipus's father Laius, king of Thebes. While visiting King Pelops, who hospitably received him at his court in the Peloponnesus (Apollodorus, III, v, 5), Laius seized Pelops's beautiful young son Chrysippus. According to some later myths, he may have had to relinquish the youth to Zeus. Because the Thebans failed to punish Laius for the crimes of kidnapping and rape (rather than of pederasty, which was not a crime), Hera sent the Sphinx to punish them.[8]

Hesiod, who like Homer often reflected conditions of the ninth and eighth centuries, sang of Laius but not of his pederasty. The first author known for certain to have described him as the introducer of pederasty because of his rape of Chrysippus was, as I have noted, the epic poet Peisander of Camirus, whose birth the *Suda* situated in Rhodes in the thirty-seventh Olympiad (632–629).[9] According to Bowra, Peisander composed his masterpiece, the *Heraclea*, "soon after Stesichorus."[10] By my theory that would mean after the institutionalization of pederasty. Pisinus, an obscure early epic poet whose works are all lost and whom Peisander may have plagiarized, probably himself flourished after 630 in the period of pederastic mythmaking, when forerunners of Ibycus, Anacreon, and Pindar were perhaps already busily ascribing *eromenoi* to gods and heroes.

Another epic poet, Cinaethon of Lacedaemon, who supposedly flourished sometime between 600 and Hellenistic times, related in his now lost *Oedipodeia* the story of Laius's rape of Chrysippus and the curse on the house of Laius pronounced by Pelops because of so brutal a crime.[11] Both Aeschylus and Euripides dramatized the tribulations of Chrysippus.[12] Euripides first told how Laius, king of Thebes, after having been warned that a son would kill him, sought to avoid fathering that son by refraining from intercourse with his wife (who, nevertheless, finally seduced him when he was drunk, thus conceiving Oedipus). In his frustration at sexual deprivation, Laius kidnapped Chrysippus. Plato, who in his old age was hostile to sexual relations between men, assumed with Peisander that Laius was the first pederast: "Suppose you follow nature's rule and establish the law that was in force before the time of Laius. You'd argue that one may have sexual intercourse with a woman but not with men or boys" (Laws, I, 836).

Local Founders

Eventually mythographers created a fable to explain when some hero or other personage institutionalized pederasty in almost every *polis* or region. These myths and legends are distinct from those biographies and histories which purport to state who first actually institutionalized pederasty or its concomitants anywhere in Hellas. Many a city tended proudly to claim that a hero and his *eromenos* institutionalized pederasty there, and frequently the city celebrated that foundation with an annual festival. Such feasts might take place around the supposed tomb of the founder or of his beloved, much as the most famous of Greek games honored the tomb of Pelops at Olympia.

The practice of creating a legend to describe when a hero institutionalized pederasty in a particular place led Sergent to believe that he had discovered yet another means to show the prehistoric origins of Greek pederasty.[13] If it could be demonstrated that these legends reflected the Cretan system of abduction and rape, which Sergent assumed to be very primitive and very ancient, then, he assumed, the legends, too, must be extremely old (no matter how late the earliest attestation, information which he could have obtained at a glance from Beyer's 1910 study, a work Sergent did not cite). He painstakingly reviewed all extant founding myths, stating whether or not each myth was, in his opinion, very old. In the end, of the sixty-eight myths surveyed, Sergent categorized only nineteen as old and nine as perhaps of ancient origin.[14] Even more troubling, however, is Sergent's assumption that the Cretan model was an ancient one. I believe that though it involved ritual abduction and perhaps even theoretical rape as well, the Cretan system was relatively recent and that the dramatic myths of local founders of pederasty reflected the Cretan model and not some ancient prototype. If pederasty represented a very ancient practice brought to the peninsula by preliterate proto-Greeks, it is hard to understand why each region would have felt obliged at a later date to name a local founder of the custom. The very existence of the founding myths implies a need to establish something new in the society, new to each *polis,* something that had not been indigenous to the Greek or Doric *Volk.*

Six

Cretan Knights
and "Renowned Ones"

The Cretan lawgiver regarded abstemiousness as beneficial and
devoted much ingenuity to securing it, as also to keeping down
the birthrate by keeping men and women apart and by instituting sexual relations between males.

—Aristotle, *Politics,* 1272a 12

To date, researchers concerned about the origins of institutionalized pederasty have, I believe, overlooked two central points. First, there is the fact
that the majority of ancient authors who did not name some divine or
clearly legendary, ahistorical figure as the founder of the practice attributed
the institutionalization of pederasty to seventh-century Cretans. Some of
these accounts specify the role of lawgivers or "musicians," who are also
spoken of as having helped export this system to Sparta, Athens, and some
of the colonies in Italy and Sicily. Second, although pre–World War I scholars generally tried to deny the historicity of these lawgivers,[1] archeologists
are now tending to confirm the likelihood of stories related to a number
of early legends.[2] Some even see certain heroes of the Theban epics and
the accounts about prehistoric Dorian leaders as historic. Others, like Nagy,
accept as authentic some or many of the words or deeds associated with
various persons flourishing during the early and middle Archaic Age but
believe that the late Greeks attributed to one or another of those persons
the words and deeds of other individuals who names we may never know.
This chapter applies the new line of reasoning to the data about seventh-
century Crete and Cretan "musicians."

Sources

Henri van Effenterre has argued convincingly that Plato, who believed in a Cretan origin for pederasty, probably did visit Crete and knew much about its history.[3] Aristotle was as usual well informed about Cretan concerns. Other Athenians of the classical age were also closely acquainted with Cretan affairs. During the Peloponnesian War, Gortyn had favored Athens, which had a *proxenus* (diplomatic representative) there, and the Cretans bestowed a crown on Athens. Cretan archers often served as mercenaries in Greek armies, and Crete was frequently visited because it lay on the route from Athens and other Aegean ports to Sicily and from the Peloponnesus to the Levant and Egypt. A papyrus fragment in Arabic refers to a lost work of Aristotle that seems to have mentioned a Cretan member of the Platonic Academy. Interest in and knowledge of Cretan institutions among fourth-century Athenians seem in fact to have been extensive.

Detailed evidence for Dorian Crete is, nevertheless, scanty. Unlike late Minoans and Myceneans, early Dorians left few impressive ruins and no writings. No authentic writings or sayings of the Cretan "musicians" or sages of the later seventh and early sixth centuries, that is, Onomacritus, Thaletas, and Epimenides, have survived. Except for a few inscriptions, most notably the Laws of Gortyn (c. 500), we have no Cretan literary sources whatsoever after the last linear B tablets (perhaps as late as the early eleventh century) and before the third-century B.C. poet Rhianus of Bene. Mythographers from other areas provide legends, myths, and epics replete with references to Cretan pederasty. Latter-day historians, also from other regions, provide incidental details about general Cretan customs.

The number of ancient writers who support, directly or indirectly, a Cretan birthplace for pederasty is impressive. Herodotus (484-c. 420), the father of history, and Thucydides (c. 455-c. 400), often called the first scientific historian, provide incidental material about the origins on Crete of athletic nudity, a practice intimately related to institutionalized pederasty (for example, Thucydides, I, vi, 5). Plato (c. 429–347), much concerned with love between males, set his last dialogue, *Laws,* on Crete, which he considered its birthplace. Morrow argued that Plato and his contemporary academicians assembled a great many texts about Cretans and that Plato spoke accurately about them in four dialogues: *Protagoras, Crito, Republic,* and *Laws.* Morrow believed that Aristotle (384–322) used this collection for his *Constitution of the Cretans,* now lost except for fragments surviving in Heraclides Ponticus, but summarized in the *Politics.* The *Minos,* written by Plato or by someone else shortly after his death, may also have drawn on the collection as did probably Ephorus.[4] With his students, Aristotle collected constitutions for 158 Greek states, including at least one typical one from Crete, where all *poleis* seem to have adopted similar, if not identical, laws and customs. Stressing historical evolution, he was most explicit about the institutionalization of pederasty in Crete as part of a program designed to reduce birthrates.

The summary of Ephorus's lost history in the *Geography* of Strabo (X, 4, 15–22), though brief, nevertheless provides our fullest account of Cretan pederasty. Ephorus (400–340) was perhaps not influenced by his contemporary Aristotle in asserting that pederasty and its related institutions were invented by the Cretans and perfected by the Spartans (X, 4, 17). However, both of them may have used a common authority or source. An apparently quite independent Sicilian source, Timaeus of Taormina, who turned fifty about 300 B.C., remarked: "The practice of pederasty came into Greece from the Cretans first" (Athenaeus, XIII, 602f). Pederastic Cretan lawgivers or related Cretan customs are discussed or alluded to in surviving fragments by Heraclides Ponticus (fl. c. 360), Dosiadas (fl. c. 250), several contributors to the *Anacreontea,* Polybius (c. 200-after 118), Hermonax, a third- or second-century Alexandrian, and Sosicrates, possibly from Rhodes, who is deemed to have used a variety of Alexandrian sources now lost. Together with Athenaeus of Naucratis (c. 200 A.D.), an antiquarian who preserved fragments of the writings of some 1,250 authors, these men provide most of the rest of our literary information about Archaic Crete, which also produced the *kouroi* statues and other pederastic art.

Myths associate the earliest institutionalization of pederasty with Crete more than with any other locality. From the late seventh or sixth century, when they first began ascribing *eromenoi* to gods and heroes, poets placed many pederastic couples on Crete: Zeus or Minos and Ganymede, Rhadamanthus and Talos, Minos and Theseus, Minos or Sarpedon and Miletus or Atumnios, Apollo and Atumnios, Euxunthetus and Leucocomas, Leucocomas and Promachus, and Idomeneus and Meriones.[5]

Byzantine scholars add an intriguing philological footnote. In the fifth century A.D. the lexicographer Hesychius of Alexandria, who used the commentaries of such erudite Alexandrians as Aristarchus of Samothrace (c. 217–145), explained that when Greeks said "according to the Cretan way" they meant to practice anal intercourse (K, 4080). Hesychius had the entry *kretizein: epi tou pseudesthai kai apatan* "to play the Cretan: for lying and deceiving," but a separate lemma of his reads *Kreta tropon: to paidikois chresthai* "the Cretan way: to practice pederasty."[6] The tenth-century *Suda* lexicon

and the twelfth-century work of Eusthathius of Thessalonica also discuss
such phraseology.[7]

Demography

During the eighth century B.C., when the general population of Greece appears to have increased greatly,[8] the privileged Dorians of Crete may have
multiplied even more rapidly. Crete had suffered the most during the desic-
cation and lack of trade during the Dark Age. Now it benefited most with
the return of better weather and increased trade after 800. As a way station
from the Aegean to the West, Egypt, and the Levant, it rewon much of the
prosperity and leadership it had enjoyed in Minoan times.

The rapidly multiplying Cretan upper class of Doric knights would not
have been able to provide estates for its sons adequate to maintain their
aristocratic lifestyle. (They customarily divided an estate among all surviving legitimate sons, who chose by lot which of the roughly equal shares
was to be theirs.) The kosmoi (Cretan officials) decided to institute measures to curb the population explosion.[9] In his Politics, Aristotle discussed at
length the necessity for control devices to prevent impoverishment through
overpopulation, observing that "A great state and a populous one are not
the same. . . . An excessively large number cannot take on any degree of
order" (1266b 8, 1326a 5, 1326a 25). In another passage Aristotle described
the precise measures taken in Crete to deal with the population increase.
The words of such a great authority and one so crucial to my thesis bear
repeating here: "The Cretan lawgiver regarded abstemiousness as beneficial
and devoted much ingenuity to securing it, as also to keeping down the
birth-rate by keeping men and women apart and by instituting sexual relations between males" (Politics, 1272a 12).[10] As population pressure mounted,
Dorian knights all over Crete, fearful that their estates would be subdivided
among too many heirs, accepted the laws of their sage or sages, segregating
women and institutionalizing pederasty. These ordinances were presumably
first applied to one of their communities (we know not which) but soon
copied by the others.

Shamans, "Musicians," Sages, and Lawgivers

Who was the Cretan lawgiver mentioned by Aristotle? Hirschfeld thought
it was King Minos,[11] but that would put him too early. (Moreover, we cannot be certain that Minos was actually historical.) Perhaps he was Thaletas
or his teacher Onomacritus, who lived around the middle of the Archaic

Age. Whoever he was (perhaps even a committee or a succession of sages), he may have merely perfected and systematized earlier population control measures. The prestige of Cretan *kathartai* (exorcists) is attested by the legend that Apollo was purified by Karmanor the Cretan after the slaying of Python (Pausanias II, 30, 3). Onomacritus, whom Ephorus placed at the head of the list of lawgivers, sages, and "musicians," was closely associated with the introduction of the Orphic mysteries. The Cretan lawgiver Thaletas, credited with being the adviser of the legendary Spartan Lycurgus, reputedly quelled a plague in Sparta in the late seventh century (Pratinas, fr. 8 B). As a result, we can see that these charismatic figures were thought to be to some degree magicians or miracle workers.

If, as Ephorus specified, Thaletas of Gortyn introduced the Cretan reforms, it was presumably in his youth, for in old age (c. 615) he was said to have been brought to Sparta, where I presume he helped introduce institutionalized pederasty. A more reliable tradition makes Thaletas a student of Onomacritus. Thus Onomacritus rather than Thaletas would have introduced the reforms to Crete about 650. I believe that another Cretan sage of that age, Epimenides, helped Solon introduce them to Athens.

Epimenides, who purified Athens of the dangerous pollution caused by violation of the right of sanctuary during the conspiracy of Cylon, was assimilated to the type of the peri-Arctic shaman. He came from Cnossos, the site of the great labyrinth, and having grown up in the shadow of the palace of Minos, he could lay claim to an ancient heritage of wisdom, especially as legend asserted that he had slept for fifty-seven years in the cave of the Cretan mystery-god. Epimenides' supposed exchange of letters with the Athenian lawgiver Solon, though not considered genuine, shows the existence of a tradition of links between the legal minds of Crete and Athens. After Epimenides' death his body was found covered with tattoo marks, the sign of the shaman, and his long sleep can be equated with the trance state that is part of the shaman's novitiate.[12] Thus, it is not impossible that, as Dodds (1951) has proposed, the Cretan sages who, I believe, introduced the new pederastic system were influenced by Scythian shamanism, which included cross-dressing, gender inversion, and androphile homosexuality.

Whatever the exact origin or date of these lawgivers, tradition connected them all to seventh- and sixth-century Crete, without explaining explicitly that any of them established the laws that were attributed to Minos, much as Spartan laws were attributed to an oracle received by Lycurgus. Thus these traditions assigning the institutionalization of pederasty to Crete reinforce the myths and legends, most of which also support a Cretan origin for regulated, socially useful pederasty. Because no source antedating 630

mentioned or depicted institutional pederasty, it seems logical to assume
that it did not exist previously, at least not for long, even on Crete, especially since the leading sources of the fifth and fourth century state or imply
that it was at least a relatively recent establishment.

The Pederastic System of Age-Classes

All the institutions adopted by the Cretans in the seventh century—pederasty, athletic nudity, seclusion of women, all-male messes, and herds of
boys—seem to have been new to the Hellenes as such, even if all or some
may have had isolated or occasional forerunners. The Cretan system is described most fully by Ephorus (as summarized by Strabo in Book 10 of his
Geography). Formal puberty for boys (*apodromoi*) occurred at twelve. *Ebioi*
(youths between twelve and twenty) were known after the age of twenty or,
by some accounts, after twenty-six as *dromeis* (from *dromos*, a running track
where beginning at twelve or perhaps seventeen aristocrats exercised nude).
The exact duration of these age-classes, which are poorly attested and may
have changed over time, are roughly the same as the better documented age
groups in Sparta. Once a youth became a *dromeus* he ceased to belong to a
"herd" (*agele*). Presumably the youths then lived in barracks at the *andreion,*
where they ate together with older married men who, as at Sparta, lived at
home with their wives. These rites of passage began with the kidnapping
at age twelve and continued until as a husband the aristocrat went to live
with his wife. Rituals for age groups are by no means necessarily primitive
customs, as the various grades of feudal knighthood demonstrate.

All seemed to have married at the same age, perhaps at thirty, as Lycurgus supposedly decreed for Sparta. They may also have married at twenty
or twenty-six, that is, even before they left the herd, or at some other age,
varying from time to time according to shortages due to wars, famines, or
epidemics. In any case, they continued to sleep in the *andreion* from age
twenty until they set up housekeeping with wives, normally at age thirty,[13]
if we may presume from Spartan usage, while their young wives lived with
relatives. Even after marriage, aristocratic men always dined together.

A Cretan knight's ritual kidnapping of a twelve-year-old (with the boy's
relatives as accomplices before and after the fact) and carrying him off for a
two-month honeymoon in the wilderness were apparently the prelude to a
prolonged homosexual relationship that obviated the pressure for early marriage. These pairings were carefully negotiated. Indeed in Archaic Athens
and Sparta they could bind families together almost in the way that mar-

riages did. There it is documented that an *eromenos* often married a daughter, niece, or cousin of his *erastes*. In the words of Ephorus, on Crete:

They have a peculiar custom in regard to love-affairs, for they win the objects of their love, not by persuasion, but by abduction; the lover tells the friends of the boy three or four days beforehand that he is going to make the abduction; but for the friends to conceal the boy, or not to let him go forth by the appointed road, is indeed a most disgraceful thing, a confession, as it were, that the boy is unworthy to obtain such a lover; and when they meet, if the abductor is the boy's equal or superior in rank or other respects, the friends pursue him and lay hold of him, though only in a very gentle way, thus satisfying the custom; and after that they cheerfully turn the boy over to him to lead away; if, however, the abductor is unworthy, they take the boy away from him. And the pursuit does not end until the boy is taken to the "Andreium" of his abductor. They regard as a worthy object of love, not the boy who is exceptionally handsome, but the boy who is exceptionally manly and decorous. After giving the boy presents, the abductor takes him away to any place in the country he wishes; and those who were present at the abduction follow after them, and after feasting and hunting with them for two months (for it is not permitted to detain the boy for a longer time), they return to the city. (Strabo, X, 4, 21)

Upon return from the honeymoon, there was a celebration where the youth received three gifts:

The boy is released after receiving as presents a military habit, an ox, and a drinking-cup (these are the gifts required by law), and other things so numerous and costly that the friends, on account of the number of the expenses, make contributions thereto. Now the boy sacrifices the ox to Zeus and feasts those who returned with him; and then he makes known the facts about his intimacy with his lover, whether, perchance, it has pleased him or not, the law allowing him this privilege in order that, if any force was applied to him at the time of the abduction, he might be able at this feast to avenge himself and be rid of the lover. (Strabo, X, 4, 21)

Forever thereafter the *eromenos*'s participation in this institution was noted:

It is disgraceful for those who are handsome in appearance or descendants of illustrious ancestors to fail to obtain lovers, the presumption being that their character is responsible for such a fate. But the parastathentes (for thus they call those who have been abducted)[14] receive honours; for in both the dances and the races they have the positions of highest honour, and are allowed to dress in better clothes than the rest, that is, in the habit given them by their lovers; and not then only, but even after they have grown to manhood, they wear a distinctive dress, which is intended to make known the fact that each wearer has become 'kleinos,' for they call the loved one 'kleinos' and the lover 'philetor.' (Strabo, X, 4, 21)[15]

In addition to Ephorus's detailed description, three sets of antonyms in the Cretans' vocabulary provide important insights into the evolution followed by Greek youths in the system established by Aristotle's lawgiver. These antonyms, not yet fully analyzed in any previous work on Cretan customs,[16] are:

apagelos	"pre-herder"	*agelaos*	"herd member"
apodromos	"pre-racer"	*dromeus*	"runner," i.e., "gymnast" or "athlete"
skotios	"obscure"	*kleinos*	"renowned."

The last pair is particularly interesting: *skotios* is attested in the scholiast on Euripides.[17] The antonym *kleinos* is explained by Athenaeus (XI, 782c): "kleinoi legontai para Kresin hoi eromenoi, spoude de autois, paidas harpazeinz" (the beloved are called *renowned* by the Cretans, since they put much effort into abducting boys). Eustathius of Thessalonica, in commenting on Homer, gave a like explanation in his gloss on *Iliad*, XX, 280. *Skotios* designated the youth who had not yet been introduced into society, who had not acquired a lover (in Sparta the analogous term was *kryptos* 'hidden, secret'), while *kleinos* was the term applied to the Cretan boy after his *harpagmos* 'abduction' and two-month "honeymoon" in the wilds with his lover.[18] The semantic opposition accounted for the Cretan use of *kleinos* in the sense of "the youth loved (by the *paiderastes*)."

The first pair of antonyms expressed the contrast between the *apagelos* ("ho medepo synagelazomenos pais ho mechri heptakaideka" [the youth who has not yet joined an *agele,* the one under seventeen]," according to Hesychius's gloss), and the *agelaos,* who has become a member of the "herd."

The second pair opposed the *apodromos*, the youth who has not begun to practice at the gymnasium (which the Cretans called *dromos* 'track'), to the *dromeus*, whose training had started.[19]

Thus *dromeus* would be parallel to *agelaos* (elsewhere *agelatas*) in designating the male who had reached the age of joining the *agele* and participating in the military training. Cretan knights underwent it in age-classes, membership in which then made them citizens in the Cretan commonwealth. In Sparta, Boeotia, and Eretria, which like Crete grouped males strictly in age-classes, young upper-class males made similar transitions at roughly the same ages. In Boeotia and Chalcis, youths of twelve were styled *pampaides* 'fully grown boys,' for which Laconic inscriptions offer the parallel *hadropampais*.[20]

In the law code of Gortyn *apodromos* occurred only once (VII, 35ff.) and was immediately contrasted with *dromeus* (VII, 40ff.), so that it was equivalent to "minor." It is generally agreed that *dromeus* meant an adult, one who had attained his majority. The exact age at which a youth became a *dromeus* is uncertain; some place it at eighteen, others at twenty.

Strabo's account is distressingly vague as to the precise times and terms of passage from one status to another.[21] In Sparta, according to Plutarch's "Lycurgus," the life of the male child was divided into six-year periods. The third, beginning after his twelfth year of age, was marked by a far more rigorous regime: the youth no longer wore a tunic, received only one cloak a year, lived in the wild with age-mates, ate hard, dry flesh, was not allowed to bathe or anoint himself except on a few specified days, and could now have a lover. Entry into the fourth age-class amounted to a rite of passage to manhood and the rights and duties of the adult citizen.

The Cretan boy, it would seem, had four or five major transitions in his life: (1) the *harpagmos*, abduction at approximately the age of twelve by an older lover and mentor that represented his "coming out" into the society of adolescent males, which parallels a change of status at the same age in other Greek city-states and is also the time of life at which the pubescent youth begins to interest the pederast; (2) entrance at the age of seventeen into the *agele*;[22] (3) the beginning—at perhaps the same age—of his military training on the *dromos*, the open-air exercise ground for track and field events which evolved into the elaborate gymnasium of later centuries; (4) marriage; and (5) moving in with his wife, i.e., establishing his own home if this event took place after the actual marriage.

Demographic Consequences

I have suggested that the Cretan system of institutionalized pederasty spread to other parts of Greece because of its success in stemming, at least among the upper classes, the population explosion that began in the eighth century. Our evidence for that success is both theoretical and concrete. Thanks to a model prepared by Mogens Herman Hansen,[23] we can observe the general effect that the new Cretan system would have had when it changed the marriage age for males from eighteen or nineteen to thirty. Hansen's table suggests that instead of having 1,925 per 100,000 males in the eighteen- to nineteen-year-old category, one would have only 1,570 males eligible for marriage at thirty. In short, there would be about 18 percent fewer husbands to create families since such a large proportion died between the ages of eighteen and thirty. Moreover, only 54 percent of the husbands who married at thirty would be alive at age fifty, that is, twenty years after their marriage, instead of 60 percent of the nineteen-year-old bridegrooms. (Because Spartans tended to marry girls of eighteen or nineteen, but Athenians and most other Greeks married girls of fifteen, the demographic effects on Sparta of the demise of nearly half of the thirty-year-old husbands twenty years after their marriage would have produced somewhat lower reproduction rates.)

Except in Sparta, the wives of the fifty-year-old husbands would be on the average only thirty-five and therefore often still fertile when half of them became widows. Unless they remarried, during the last decades of their fertile period (35–45) they would not produce any legitimate children. If, on the other hand, they had married grooms of nineteen, when the grooms reached forty, only one-third of them would have died (1,210 surviving out of 1,920). Thus, a much higher proportion of women would have been fertilized throughout the entire period of their fertility. Consequently, delayed marriages for upper-class males from eighteen or nineteen to thirty would reduce the birthrates significantly, even if the men remained as potent at fifty as they had been at twenty, which, of course, is not the case.

One fact surrounding the effect of the new Cretan system is the absence of colonies produced by Cretan *poleis* after the middle of the seventh century. Nor do we hear of immigrants leaving Crete in significant numbers for established colonies. It gained a reputation for peace, law, and order, a further indication that the segregation of women and late marriage of upper-class males, combined with pederasty, effectively curbed the population increase that was forcing other Hellenes to emigrate, revolt, and struggle with other *poleis* for fertile lands and trade routes. The Athenian in Plato's *Laws* commented: "The laws of Crete are held in exceptionally high repute among all the Hellenes" (I, 631b).

Cretans had sent out colonists before the reform ascribed to Onomacritus and Thaletas curbed their population explosion. Until the mid-seventh century Cretans were, like other Greeks, active in trade and colonization, indicating that they had not yet instituted effective birth control measures.[24] (We must, of course, consider their enterprising spirit as well. Not all colonists sought farmland rather than opportunities for trade.) Although Cretans themselves ceased colonizing at a rather early date, evidence for Cretan influence on the western colonies of other *poleis* abounds. Daedalic architecture and sculpture had Cretan roots. Cretan cultural influence extended west even to Spain. Cretan pitchers with spouts have been found at Massilia (Marseilles) and on Minorca. The name Massilia itself is perhaps Cretan, since it was also borne by a river on Crete. At Costig on Majorca bulls' heads, today found in the museum in Madrid, have been unearthed whose great similarity to corresponding Cretan artifacts is undeniable. The cult of the bull (Diodorus IV, 18) that prevailed in ancient Spain greatly resembles the Cretan one. The catching of the bulls with nets was as customary on Crete as it is supposed to have been in Plato's Atlantis, the depiction of which was, according to Schulten's illuminating argumentation, inspired by ancient Spanish locales, customs, and historic events.[25]

Diffusion to Sparta and Other Areas

Before the end of the eighth century, Spartans, Dorian cousins of the Cretans, had settled more than one site in Crete: "well-built" Lyttos and Polyrrhenion "rich in sheep" (*Odyssey*, 293). These perhaps, along with the Spartan colony on Thera, which could serve as a way station on the route from Lacedaemonia to Crete, became conduits of customs from Crete to Sparta.[26] Following Ephorus, Strabo maintained that Spartan colonists, the Lyttians (or Lyctians), borrowed Cretan institutions (X, 4, 17). Aristotle agreed with Ephorus.[27] Perhaps, however, Thaletas of Gortyn rather than the Spartan colonists provided the critical connection. Whatever the medium, pederasty, along with its associated features, herds of boys, athletic nudity, and perhaps certain aristocratic political institutions, were imported from Crete to Sparta. As Ephorus stated: "It is said by some writers . . . that most of the Cretan institutions are Laconian, but the truth is that they were invented by the Cretans and only perfected by the Spartans" (Strabo, X, 4, 17).

Aristotle firmly maintained that Spartans borrowed the practice of seg-regating women from the Cretans (*Politics*, II, 23–25). He asserted that gen-der segregation was designed to check population growth, as was pederasty, which young aristocratic males substituted for marriage and possibly for all heterosexual contact. Crete was perhaps the only country where homo-sexuality was not only legal (as it was in all Greek *poleis*) but even embodied in constitutions.[28]

From Crete the Spartans imported not only gymnastic nudity and ped-erasty but the *syssition* (common mess), whose old Spartan name, *andreion*, was the same as that used in Crete. "This is a plain indication of its Cretan origin" (Aristotle, *Politics*, 1271b 40). There was, however, a significant dif-ference. In Crete the state furnished the meals from public lands and appar-ently the men took home from the mess food for their wives and children (*Politics*, 1271a 26, 1272a 12). In Sparta, as in the Spartan colony on Crete about whose messes we are informed, each member contributed his share and was excluded if he became too poor to do so. The senate, known as the *Gerontes* in Sparta and the *Boule* in Crete, and the ephorate of five men (*kos-moi* in Crete) came later, but both of these Spartan institutions may well have been imitations of Cretan antecedents (*Politics*, 1271b 40).[29]

Regardless of when the Spartans borrowed some of their institutions from Crete, they probably institutionalized pederasty along Cretan lines just after the Second Messenian War (which I believe came late—635–615). As has so often happened elsewhere, especially in traditional societies, these relatively late importations were in time said to be ancient. To give these radical measures authority, Spartans and others describing their history and institutions maintained that Lycurgus garnered wisdom in lawgiving on Crete before rather than after enacting his reforms. According to Ephorus, when Lycurgus arrived in Crete he studied with Thales [Thaletas] and then went to Egypt to learn about its institutions. Only later did he attempt to "frame the laws" at Sparta (Strabo, X, 4, 19).

Plutarch tells a comparable story, again insisting on Lycurgus's training on Crete under Thales.

> From Crete he sailed to Asia, with design, as is said, to examine the difference betwixt the manners and rules of life of the Cretans, which were very sober and temperate, and those of the Ionians, a people of sumptuous and delicate habits, and so to form a judgment; just as physicians do by comparing healthy and diseased bodies. Here he had the first sight of Homer's works, in the hands, we may suppose, of the

posterity of Creophylus; and, having observed that the few loose expressions and actions of ill example which are to be found in his poems
were much outweighed by serious lessons of state and rules of morality, he set himself eagerly to transcribe and digest them into order, as
thinking they would be of good use in his own country. They had, indeed, already obtained some slight repute among the Greeks, and scattered portions, as chance conveyed them, were in the hands of individuals; but Lycurgus first made them really known. ("Lycurgus," IV)

Herodotus maintained that Lycurgus introduced to Sparta laws and institutions from Crete. He, however, asserted that Lycurgus imported the
Cretan customs during his regency, not after it, as Ephorus believed (I, 65).

The pseudo-Platonic *Minos* (written apparently not long after Plato's
time) also implied Cretan pederastic origins and Spartan borrowings:

SOCRATES. Do you not know which of the Greeks use the most
     ancient laws?
COMPANION. Do you mean the Spartans, and Lycurgus the lawgiver?
SOC. Why, that is a matter, I dare say, of less than three hundred
     years ago, or but a little more. But whence is it that the best of
     those ordinances come? Do you know?
COM. From Crete, so they say.
SOC. Then the people there use the most ancient laws in Greece?
COM. Yes. (318c–d)

For Spartans, who shared with the Cretans the same dialect, some common primitive Dorian institutions such as the names of the three tribes,
and a similar problem of controlling helots, the Cretan models would be
among the first to come to mind and probably the most suitable and easi-
est to adopt and adapt. Lycurgus, or rather the authors of the Eunomia who
claimed that they were restoring the Lycurgan constitution, visited Crete,
adapted institutions needed to perfect the Spartan phalanx, and introduced
these in oracular fashion.

Removing the element of the abduction, Spartans transformed the Cretan institutions to serve a society in which heavily armored infantrymen—
the hoplites—replaced cavalry. The Spartan as well as the Cretan system influenced most of the rest of Hellas. But knights in Thessaly and Boeotia,
where cavalry reigned longer, may have imported the Cretan system un-
modified and perhaps reexported it to Chalcis on the neighboring island of
Euboea whereas others adapted it for heavy infantry training.

In the major trading city of Corinth, with its small *contado* (surrounding territory), cavalry did not play a large role. A legend holds that Archias, a man from a leading family who loved the young Actaeon, came to kidnap him. But the father and his relatives, who did not want to yield the youth, pulled him back. In the struggle Actaeon was torn apart.[30] Archias is reputed to have fled and founded Syracuse in 734 B.C., a date far too early to coincide with my theory about the institutionalization of pederasty at Crete. However, the dates advanced for the foundation of the western colonies are poorly attested and open to doubt, as is the story itself. Of interest in the legend is its evocation of the Cretan custom according to which a family, if willing, would allow ritualistic kidnapping but if not, might oppose it. The tale may indicate that Corinth, then, like Crete, a leading maritime power, borrowed pederasty directly from Crete and not through Sparta, which apparently abolished the ritual kidnapping when it institutionalized pederasty.

The brief revival that Crete enjoyed in the middle Archaic Age ended before the beginning of the classical period. By then the Persians had seized the eastern coast of the Mediterranean and cut off the trade with Ionia, Egypt, and the Levant that had made Crete central. Still, even when classical writers sought to explain the origin of their peculiar institution, they were able to ascertain that it originated in Crete and in relatively recent times.

Cretan pederasty seems more primitive than the Spartan practice or any other for that matter, if only because the ritual kidnapping prevailed only there. So did the two-month "honeymoon" of the couple in the wilds, during which the youth proved himself by hunting. Because similar initiation rituals exist among certain primitives even today, some scholars have assumed that those Cretan practices, along with the nature of the gifts provided to the successful youth upon his return to society by his *philetor,* presumed a preliterate origin for Cretan pederasty. Yet, as we have seen, no ancient authority assumed that pederasty had originally been a pan-Dorian, much less a proto-Greek, phenomenon. Moreover, most of the myths presume a Cretan origin, and although several posit Thracian or Boeotian origins for Greek pederasty, no one today imagines that it originated in Sparta. It was Sparta, however, not Crete, that became famous for heroic pederasty.

Seven

Spartan Hoplite "Inspirers" and Their "Listeners"

> At Sparta the party loving was called eispnelas and his affec-
> tion was termed a breathing in, or inspiring (eispnein); which
> expresses the pure and mental connection between the two per-
> sons, and corresponds with the name of the other, viz.: aítas,
> i.e., listener or hearer. Now it appears to have been the practice
> for every youth of good character to have his lover; and on the
> other hand every well-educated man was bound by custom to
> be the lover of some youth.
>
> —K. O. Müller, *Die Dorier* (1844), 4:4

Because of their borrowings from Crete, the Spartans established institutions before the end of the seventh century that were much closer in nature
to those of the Cretans than to the institutions of any other Dorians. So
similar were the two societies that some later authors believed the Cretans
might have borrowed Spartan institutions rather than the reverse. Although
the Spartans dropped the practices of the ritual kidnapping and the honeymoon, they made the customs that they did import more rigorous than
their Cretan prototypes, as Aristotle observed in his *Politics*.

According to Herodotus, prior to the great reconstruction of their society
(called the Eunomia) the Spartans "had been the very worst governed people
in Greece, as well in matters of internal management as in their relations
towards foreigners" (I, 65). After the Eunomia, admiration for their prowess
induced other Greeks, particularly aristocratic ones, or at least those rich
enough to serve as hoplites, to imitate their lifestyle and manners, including
pederasty and its associated customs. Spartan culture flourished briefly, just
after they made pederasty the basis of their pedagogy, but within a genera-

tion their rigid adherence to what they considered a perfect system, their overemphasis on military and physical training, and their dislike of innovation stifled intellectual and artistic progress, just as their austerity, prohibition of gold and silver money, and scorn of commerce impeded economic progress.

About Crete we know only of the system as a whole, of mythological figures, and of shadowy "musicians" or lawgivers, but prior to the appearance of Rhianus of Bene (fl. c. 275 B.C.) we do not know of any indisputably historical individuals clearly designated as pederastic or of the youths whom they loved. We do not have the names of a single historic Cretan couple. On the other hand, for Sparta, we have the names of numerous couples and to a certain extent their biographies and historical contributions.

Sources

However late, scanty, and unsatisfactory the literary sources for Sparta may be, they are the most extensive that we possess for any Greek city except Athens. Epigraphy and archeology have added less information proportionally on Laconia than on almost any other area since the Spartans did not erect many large buildings, scorned ostentation, and felt no need to wall their city. From the works produced by (or perhaps merely ascribed over time to) Late Archaic poets who visited or came to reside at Sparta little survives save tantalizing fragments and paraphrases or generally unreliable notices and critiques about them or their works. The antiquarian Sosibius (fl. c. 300) is the first indubitably Spartan intellectual from whose writings fragments have survived.

Although all the leading fifth- and fourth-century historians, philosophers, and political theorists discussed the customs of Athens's chief rival, none did so in great detail. In his *Constitution of the Lacedaemonians* and *Life of Agesilaus,* Xenophon, an aristocrat, idealized the city that during his youth had defeated his native Athens, which he deemed too democratic. Admiring Sparta only slightly less, Xenophon's contemporary Plato exaggerated its oligarchic virtues in order to contrast them with Athenian democratic decadence and excesses, whereas his rival, the orator Isocrates (436–338), criticized Spartan customs and institutions. Aristotle, who devoted much of his *Politics* to Sparta, pointed out the many similarities among the customs of Sparta, Crete, and to a lesser extent Carthage. He argued that as the Spartans borrowed from the Cretans, the Carthaginians borrowed many of their institutions from the Spartans (1272b 24–1273b 26). A pseudo-Aristotelian

Constitution of the Lacedaemonians exists in a few fragments, but the one he must have prepared for Crete does not survive. Indeed, none of the 157 others that he prepared are extant save the one for Athens. Still, the fruits of his labors are often present in the *Politics.*

The works of two of the greatest mid-fourth-century historians, Theopompus and Ephorus, are mostly lost. Rather than admiring Sparta, Ephorus seems to have somewhat denigrated it. He also attributed its central institutions to an imitation of Cretan ones. The Roman biographer Cornelius Nepos (94-c. 24 B.C.) has left us in his partially preserved *Lives of Illustrious Men* the portrait of three Spartans: "Pausanias," "Lysander," and "Agesilaus." Of Plutarch's *Parallel Lives,* written in the second century A.D., five about Spartans survive: "Lycurgus," "Lysander," "Agesilaus," "Cleomenes III," and "Agis IV." His "Lycurgus," our most comprehensive source for Spartan institutions, described conditions which probably took their final form just after the Second Messenian War and may actually have reflected what were then bold new innovations that only purported to restore the putative Lycurgan system. In his voluminous other works, including the *Moralia,* Plutarch gave many incidental details about Spartan attitudes and habits. Pausanias (fl. c. 150 A.D.) described Spartan monuments and rituals in his *Guide to Greece,* and composed the longest surviving account of the Second Messenian War. In his *Varia Historia,* the rhetorician Aelian (c. 170–235) provided some details about Spartan social customs.

Although all of the ancient sources speak of the importance, indeed of the centrality, of pederasty to Spartan society after Lycurgus instituted his reforms, most books on Sparta published in English sidestep the subject, including works by K. M. T. Chrimes (1949), G. L. Huxley (1962), and W. G. Forrest (1968). Both the old and the new edition of the massively detailed *Cambridge Ancient History* avoid discussing it. H. Michell shrank from it: "This aspect of Greek morals is an extraordinary one, into which, for the sake of our own equanimity, it is unprofitable to pry too closely."[1] An exception is P. A. Cartledge, whose general book on Laconia (1979) and article "The Politics of Spartan Pederasty" (1981) dealt directly with the subject.

Pre-Pederastic Sparta

Spartan expansion began slowly after the early eighth century. In the First Messenian War (735–715), King Theopompus inspired the Spartans to conquer and enserf the Messenians, who inhabited the valley to their west. The list of Olympic victors drawn up by the fifth-century sophist, Hippias of

Elis, seems independently to confirm the dates of the first war: no Spartan won before and no Messenian after the traditional dates for that conflict.[2] Thereafter Sparta, which soon seized Pylos and the rest of the coast of Messenia, remained by far the largest *polis* in Greece. The annexations necessitated reorganization of Spartan society and government. Apparently Spartans ceased doing any labor or business since each was assigned an estate (*cleros*) with helots (serfs) to work them. This system may have evolved gradually as the estates were acquired, bequeathed, or redistributed over a long period of about a century embracing both Messenian wars rather than all at once, as tradition alleges.

The necessity of keeping the helots in subjection and of maintaining extended frontiers put Sparta on the road to militarism by 715. During the seventh century, however, Sparta was frequently worsted, partly perhaps because her powerful Dorian rival Argos may have introduced a revolutionary, highly disciplined infantry formation—the phalanx—that rendered outmoded the old cavalry formations upon which, some suppose, Dorian superiority had formerly rested.

Scholars still debate the origin of the phalanx. Some claim that it appeared full-blown; others, that it evolved gradually.[3] Developed somewhere in Hellas and introduced between the two Messenian wars to Sparta and in due time to all other advanced Greek societies, it revolutionized warfare. It consisted of serried ranks of close-drilled, highly disciplined, and heavily armored hoplites, carrying pikes. In such formations, each man's large shield, strapped to his left arm, covered the next's exposed right flank. Through a combination of bravery instilled by example and praised from childhood on, of loyalty developed through friendship or love, and of closely coordinated teamwork engrained through constant drill, the phalanx, if it held, broke cavalry charges and overwhelmed opposing phalanxes.

The argument advanced by Forrest and H. L. Lorimer that the reorganization of Sparta's army into phalanxes took place before the Argives ambushed the Spartans at Hysiae in 669 seems less convincing than the proposition that the Spartans adopted the phalanx only after they had been defeated at Hysiae by the Argives, who used the new formation.[4] As Cartledge recognized: "Sparta had been slower than Argos to adapt to the new hoplite mode of infantry warfare."[5]

As I believe that Sparta perfected the phalanx and institutionalized pederasty only after the Second Messenian War, the correct date of that confrontation is crucial to my views about the time of the establishment of that practice in Laconia. To fix the date, a few words about the length of a generation in Greece are necessary. According to Tyrtaeus, the interval between the First and Second Messenian War, in which he himself fought, was two generations. Raphael Sealey, Forrest, and Cartledge, along with many other scholars, ascribed thirty years to Greek generations. H. T. Wade-Gery, correctly in my opinion, held out for forty.[6] The length of a generation became forty years, I suggest, when the marriage age for upper-class males was raised from twenty to thirty. Although it is true that generations often measured thirty years when men married at twenty, by the end of the seventh century, in Sparta as in most of Greece, marriage was being postponed (and would soon be forbidden in some societies) for men under the age of thirty. From Hesiod, who c. 700 wished a man to marry about thirty (*Works and Days*, 695–701), to Solon, who c. 580 advised men to marry between twenty-eight and thirty-five (*Elegy and Iambus*, I, 141), many others suggested or imposed late marriage for upper-class men, in contrast to the Homeric custom of early unions. If a man married at thirty or later, his children produced over the next twenty years would on the average be forty years younger than he. Thus in overpopulated Late Archaic Sparta and elsewhere, where upper-class males waited until thirty to marry, it is possible that a forty-year generation became traditional. As a result, the Messenian revolt may not have broken out about 655, as many modern scholars maintain, but about 635, as tradition recorded. (It is possible some later writers became confused and imposed the forty-year interval on earlier accounts, but at other times they interpreted the generation referred to by earlier historians as signifying a thirty-year period.)

The war *à l'outrance* that Spartans fought for over twenty years against the Messenian rebels shook their society to the core. Convinced after near catastrophe that they had to recast their society, they instituted the Eunomia, ascribing it to Lycurgus. After their hard-won victory, they reconstructed their dislocated society and eliminated everything that was not conducive to maintaining security abroad and supremacy at home over helots and the inhabitants of Laconia and Messenia who were subordinate to Sparta but not enserfed (the *perioikoi*). In addition to attempting to avoid the *stasis* (class struggle and class warfare) that had discombobulated Sparta earlier, Spartans also sought to limit their legitimate offspring to the number of *cleroi* (estates) that they had to give them, thereby reducing rivalry within their own ranks.

Most scholars have overlooked Aristotle's observation that some citizens had become "very poor and others very rich, a state of society which is most often the result of war as in Lacedaemon in the time of the [Second] Messenian War; this is proved by a poem of Tyrtaeus called *Eunomia*.

Crushed by the burden of war, certain citizens demanded a redistribution of land" (*Politics*, 1306b). However, as Antony Andrewes has observed, "we do not know if any redistribution was carried out then. The most that can be said is that if any redistribution had taken place later than the middle of the sixth century we should almost certainly have heard of it [because the sources become more accurate and full then]."[7] During the great revolt, all else had been subordinated to military prowess—to training the best possible hoplite for an invincible phalanx. As a result, the years immediately following the war seem the most likely for the completion and consolidation of the Eunomia, including the institutionalization of pederasty.

Lycurgus, Tyrtaeus, and Thaletas

The ancients agreed that a lawgiver had introduced pederasty to Sparta. None believed that it was instituted as a prehistoric Dorian or Indo-European custom, except perhaps by implication Pindar, who ascribed Spartan customs to the Dorian ancestor Aegimius. Although like other Hellenes Spartans came to view Heracles, the supposed ancestor of their kings, as a pederast, they usually ascribed the institutionalization to a more historic personage. Three names are associated with the customs, laws, and constitutions of Sparta and with its adoption of pederasty. Lycurgus was the name most often cited for the introduction of pederasty and of most of their other institutions. However, it seems better to assign many of them to Tyrtaeus, who at least was clearly historical. The soundest tradition makes the Cretan "musician" Thaletas of Gortyn the importer of pederasty to Sparta but also considers him a contemporary of Tyrtaeus rather than of the legendary Lycurgus.

Regarding the dates of the most famous of these three, Lycurgus, there is the greatest confusion. Herodotus believed that the Spartan system came from Crete rather than from the Delphic oracle.[8] Most classical writers followed Herodotus in ascribing the Eunomia to Lycurgus, traditionally said to have been the guardian of an early king. Ancients gave dates for Lycurgus almost as widely separated as those they assigned to Homer. Herodotus placed Lycurgus around 1000; Thucydides situated him more than four centuries before his own time, that is, in the ninth century. Even Aristotle placed him in the early eighth century. To solve the puzzle, Timaeus posited two Lycurguses: an elder and a younger, who might have flourished as late as the second half of the seventh century ("Lycurgus," 1). The contemporary poet Tyrtaeus's failure to mention Lycurgus, however, makes one doubt that anyone of that name, even a second Lycurgus, could have produced the Eunomia c. 615.

Although Terpander supposedly visited Sparta before him, the earliest Spartan writer, if indeed he was Spartan, was Tyrtaeus, the patriotic poet and national hero who is clearly and unequivocally associated with the Eunomia. In fact, one of his fragments comes from an elegy entitled *Eunomia* (*Elegy and Iambus*, I, 63). An anti-Spartan tradition depicted him as a lame Athenian invited by the Spartans to raise their morale when they were at a nadir in the war against their helots (scholiast on Plato's *Laws* [*Elegy and Iambus*, I, 53] and Pausanias [IV, 15, 6]). Repeating that claim, the Athenian Lycurgus's oration *Against Leocrates*, delivered in 330, also explicitly tied Tyrtaeus to the Spartan system of (pederastic) education: "Everyone in Greece knows that the general they took from our city was Tyrtaeus, by whose aid, with a wisdom that looked far beyond the dangers of that day, they both defeated their enemies and *established their system of education* [my italics]" (105–7). Similarly, in his last dialogue, Plato blamed Tyrtaeus as well as Homer for having "laid down evil precepts about life and institutions [or alternatively "bad rules for the conduct of life"] in their writings" (*Laws*, IX, 858), by which I believe he was referring to pederasty. At least the Athenian who speaks here is the same person who elsewhere in the dialogue censures pederasty (as well as art, poetry, and music).

If the Olympiad of 612–609 given by Eusebius[9] for Tyrtaeus's *floruit* is correct, Tyrtaeus's reference, "he has the noble bloom of lovely youth [*erate*], aye a marvel he for men to behold, and desirable [*eratos*] unto women, so long as ever he be alive, and fair in like manner when he be fallen in the vanguard" (*Elegy and Iambus*, I, 71), might indicate an institutionalization of pederasty in Sparta by that date. Licht detected homoeroticism therein as he did in Tyrtaeus's praise of the beauty of the youthful Tithonus (12, 5).[10]

Instrumental in institutionalizing pederasty in Sparta was the Cretan musician Thaletas. As an associate or disciple of the Cretan sage Onomacritus, Thaletas of Gortyn must have flourished during the latter part of the seventh century. Whoever called him to Sparta, whether Lycurgus or Tyrtaeus, he imported the "Dance of the Naked Youths" from Crete to quell a plague that followed the end of the Second Messenian War.[11] In any case, he came to Sparta after pederasty had been institutionalized on Crete. His contemporary compatriot Epimenides similarly ended a plague in Athens a decade or two later, when, I believe, Solon institutionalized pederasty there, using Cretan and Spartan models.

The importance of these individuals for the formation of the Spartan lifestyle reflects a custom among Archaic Greeks according to which foreigners were imported or foreign models studied in order to reform constitutions and help in solving crises.[12] Aelian pointed out that whenever the Spartans, with "no skill in music[,] . . . required the aid of the Muses on occasion of general sickness of body or mind or any like public affliction, their custom was to send for foreigners, at the bidding of the Delphic oracle, to act as healers or purifiers. For instance they summoned Terpander, Thales [presumably Thaletas of Gortyn], Tyrtaeus, Nymphaeus of Cydonia, and Alcman" (*Varia Historia*, XII, 50). Among others, Plato claimed that Tyrtaeus was an Athenian and that the Cretans acknowledged that Tyrtaeus's poems were well known in their *poleis*: "Yes, they have been imported into Crete from Lacedaemon; so we know them, too" (*Laws*, I, 629a). This late source implies that Crete and Sparta were in close contact during Tyrtaeus's lifetime, just when the Spartans were importing Cretan institutions. Pausanias cited a contemporary of Eratosthenes (c. 275–194), the Cretan Rhianus of Bene, as a historical source for the Second Messenian War (IV, 6, 1), suggesting again how closely connected Archaic Sparta and Crete may have been.[13]

If not the author of the Eunomia, Tyrtaeus, like Thaletas, at least contributed to the great reforms of his day. However, Lycurgus appears to have been already by then a name in Spartan legend, and during the crisis, reformers pretended that they were restoring his long neglected but inspired and equitable laws. This would help explain why we do not have the name of a single seventh-century reformer who was unequivocally of Spartan ancestry. Perhaps Tyrtaeus paraphrased a forgery. If so, such a deception was wholly successful, as were the Cretan forgeries of the laws that Minos purportedly received from Zeus. Once established, the cult of Lycurgus grew and details about his life multiplied. About the life and deeds of the actual Lycurgus, if such a person ever lived, we know nothing, and undoubtedly much of what Tyrtaeus and others did was ascribed to him.[14]

The Eunomia

From Tyrtaeus on, writers frequently spoke of the Eunomia. The phrase became shorthand for the entire Spartan system, whether it had been introduced piecemeal or not. Besides maintaining the number of men trained to serve as hoplites at the desired level of 9,000 to 12,000, the system prescribed pederasty and gymnasia with the grouping of boys into "herds," all of which ideas came from Crete. As I have already mentioned, Spartans suppressed the kidnapping and honeymoon, rituals that were replaced with public floggings and enforced theft of food by herd members. The *crypteia,* or periodic random killing of helots by the herd, also seems to have had no Cretan precedent, so that the Spartan version seems to have been the crueler of the two, although over time both appear to have been inimical to intellectual and artistic creativity. Other less direct evidence ties Spartan pederasty to Cretan models. Aelian qualified as *neanias* (youth) the male who was the hero of a pederastic adventure situated in Crete celebrating Hyacinthus, Apollo's *eromenos,* whose festival became so important in Sparta (*Varia Historia,* III 10, 12). Indicating that upper-class pederasty there may have been imported from Crete, this term (*neanias*) is also used for a member of the elite corps of the *hippeis* (knights, from *hippo* 'horse') in Sparta. Three hundred of them guarded the Spartan king, "because they think that their safe return and victory depend upon the friendship of the men drawn up" (Xenophon, *Constitution,* IV, 3–4). The *Hyacinthia,* most famous at Sparta, was also celebrated in Crete at Gortyn and Cnossus (Willetts [1962] 104–5). Like the Cretans, Spartans sacrificed to Eros before battle (Athenaeus, XIII, 561) and used *paedonomes* to supervise boys (Sergent [1987a] 57). The Spartan custom of ritually kidnapping wives (Plutarch, "Lycurgus," XV) may have been an original Dorian one that inspired the Cretan custom of kidnapping *eromenoi.*

During the decimating Second Messenian War, Spartans were forced to enlist helots and *perioikoi* as soldiers, many of whom then became citizens. When the war ended, new citizens and perhaps old ones who might have become impoverished and thereby lost full rights (as one did when he could not make the required contribution to the mess, the *syssitia*), presumably received allotments of land, no doubt most often in Messenia. This practice must have raised or returned the number of *cleroi* to 9,000 or 12,000. To avoid the subdivision of these already numerous allotments into uneconomic units, the Spartans then adopted, in addition to infanticide, the Cretan customs of late marriage, athletic nudity, seclusion of women, herding of boys, men's messes, and, I believe, pederasty, which on Crete completed this pattern of interrelated practices. These customs were designed, as Aristotle said, to limit the rapidly expanding population of Cretan landowners. The occupation of practically all the most desirable colonial sites in the west by the second half of the seventh century (Spartans do not seem to have immigrated to the Pontus, which continued to be colonized later) and increased rivalry from the Carthaginians and Etruscans for what remained to be settled limited emigration there. Overcrowding soon led other Greek states to imitate these customs as emigration was gradually becoming impossible.[15]

The Second Messenian War also brought the Spartans to institute more rigorous training for their boys in order to make perfect hoplites of them. Afterwards the Eunomia made that rigor permanent by combining such training with customs imported from Crete to produce a deliberately limited number of athletic champions and military heroes united by love and drill into a formidable phalanx whose members were expected to serve the *polis* selflessly. After the Eunomia, boys at seven were "enrolled in certain companies and classes, where they all lived under the same order and discipline, doing their exercises and taking their play together" (Plutarch, "Lycurgus"). Forbidden to wear tunics after the age of twelve, they received but one rude cloak a year, and until they attained their majority at eighteen they roamed the countryside in herds, called *agelai* as in Crete. Each was headed by an outstanding *iren*, as Spartans aged twenty to twenty-two were designated, the category just older than ephebes (18–20). These droves terrorized, beat, robbed, and occasionally even murdered helots. They exercised nude together in the palaestra and slept outdoors in groups on beds of rushes.

Although a youth does not normally become very useful in warfare much before eighteen, serious mental and physical instruction can begin at twelve, an equally crucial turning point for both mind and body when almost all educational systems promote from primary to secondary school. Spartan age categories, though stricter and more consequential, resembled those of other *poleis*.[16] The Spartans began their schooling at seven (or our six depending on how one reckons) but did not advance much beyond elementary literacy and the memorization of patriotic poetry. Incidentally, boys' competitions were apparently added at the Olympic Games only in the late seventh or early sixth century, when pederasty became dominant.[17] Other festivals came to have categories for those between twelve and sixteen as well as for those between sixteen and twenty.[18]

The most detailed discussion of the *agele* and of the age categories have used inscriptions from Roman times to analyze the internal structure of the Archaic herd.[19] Chrimes's argument that Sparta preserved its *agoge* (rigorous training for Spartiates) with only insignificant changes and brief interruptions from Archaic to imperial times is convincing. The *iren* chosen to lead the herd, the *Boagos* ("leader of the bull-calves" or, as Hesychius defined the term, "the boy who was leader of the *agele*") would regard strictly the rank of the boys' families. The *Synepheboi*, who were much rarer, may have been of higher-class families than the *Kasens*, who might have mothers of lower rank, perhaps foreigners (*perioikoi*), or even helots, or be "adopted" foreigners like Xenophon's sons. *Kasen* has the connotation of adopted brother or cousin. Training was so rough, often scarring, sometimes maiming, and even occasionally fatal, that royal heirs were exempted from it. Having successfully completed the ephebic training, the *Boagoi,* who were from the most distinguished families, could be chosen at age twenty to rule the younger males.

Spartan youths had fewer ties to the messes than did Cretan youths, in part because they were not kidnapped and brought there as in Crete. Plutarch furnished many details as to how Spartans were divided into age cohorts. They probably borrowed the actual age limits from Cretans, but, as I have pointed out above, we are little informed of the exact ages at which males moved from one age category to another on Crete.

Between the ages of eighteen or twenty and sixty, Spartiates dined in *syssitia* (or as they also called them *phiditia*), modeled on Cretan *andreia,* by which name houses for these messes were at first also designated in Sparta. These all-male messes were supposedly instituted by Lycurgus to check disobedience as well as to inculcate habits of sobriety, frugality, and good manners (Xenophon, *Constitution* V, 2–7).[20] At the proper age of eighteen or twenty, one had to be elected to the *syssition* in order to become a full citizen. Such a person was designated a Spartiate or "Equal." A single negative vote sufficed to exclude a candidate from membership. If he was not chosen, he could not exercise full citizenship despite having completed the rigors of the *agoge.*

Flogging for all kinds of misdemeanors, especially for stealing food, toughened Spartan boys. Public contests to see who could endure the longest became tourist sights in Roman times. While the youths were flogged at the altar of the temple of Artemis Orthia, a priestess held up a small statue of the goddess in her hand to indicate a religious approbation. Pausanias, relying on an idea of Euripides that Spartans once practiced human sacrifice, reported that they "used to slaughter a human sacrifice chosen by drawing lots; Lycurgus substituted the whipping of fully grown boys, and the altar still gets its fill of human blood" (III, 16, 9). Specially designated priests inferred omens from observing the effects of the blows. According to Mozonius, preserved in the fifth-century A.D. anthology of pagan writers collected by Stobaeus, "The sons of the Lacedaemonians make it very evident that stripes do not appear to them either shameful or hard to be borne, since they allow themselves to be whipped in public, and take a pride in it."

Despite such violence, hardly any writer (except Plato) disapproved of the customs that the Spartans imported from Crete. Having asserted that

Lycurgus borrowed institutions from Crete, Herodotus emphasized sworn brotherhoods and common messes as ingredients of Sparta's military greatness (I, 65). Plato's uncle Critias, another admirer of Spartan habits, observed that in contrast to the excessive drinking typical of Athenian symposia, "The Spartan way brings food and drink enough for thinking and working, but no excess; they have no day set aside for overindulgence and drunkenness" (Diels, II, 88, 6, 9ff.).

Nude athletics were perhaps as central to the Eunomia as they were to Greek pederasty in general. Pagan Greeks, like early Christians, knew that nudity encouraged pederasty. Plato described the *poleis* where pederastic love thrived as "the cities which have most to do with gymnastics" (*Laws*, I, 636c). Cicero opined: "For my part I think this practice [pederasty] had its origin in the Greek gymnasia where that kind of love-making was free and permitted." (*Tusculan Disputations*, IV, 33). Catullus had Attis remark: "I, to be a woman—I who was a stripling, I a youth, I a boy, I was the flower of the gymnasium, I was once the glory of the palaestra" (LXIII), and Plato's dialogues make it quite clear that each palaestra recognized one youth as its greatest beauty.

No literate peoples other than the Greeks ever exercised nude, though many, including the Egyptians, stripped their prisoners and kept them nude to debase them. The Lydians considered nudity humiliating (Herodotus, I, 10). As Thucydides pointed out (I, i, 6), the Spartans were the first (mainland) Greeks to strip naked in athletic competitions (probably c. 615 at the behest of the Cretan Thaletas). Against such an authority as Thucydides we cannot credit the anecdote of Pausanias (I, 44, 1) that it was Orsippus of Megara who introduced nudity (c. 720) because the accidental falling of his garment facilitated his victory in the *stadion,* the Olympic foot race. It seems far more likely that because of the Spartans' frequent victories in the Olympic games, nudity spread to the upper-class youths of other cities attending them. Thus, becoming popular, it may have infiltrated other cities even before lawgivers set up gymnasia in imitation of those at Crete and Sparta.

Demography

The traditions regarding Spartan marriage customs are as contradictory as those about other spheres of life in that *poleis*. Practices seem to have changed with circumstances. If they married before thirty, the age at which the law allowed them to set up housekeeping with their wives, Spartan men apparently had to sneak away from their comrades to see their spouses since until that age they were required to live in barracks, as was apparently the

case in Crete (Plutarch, "Lycurgus," XV). Xenophon said that Lycurgus designed this system to heighten their desire and to ensure that "any offspring
which might result would therefore be stronger than if the parents were
surfeited with each other" (*Constitution*, I, 5–6).

Sanctions against those who did not marry were probably made severe
only after decline in the population became a problem. The unmarried
could, according to a late source, be locked in a dark room with maidens, and each obliged to marry the woman he left the room with. If they
persisted in their bachelorhood, they could be thrashed until they married
(Athenaeus, XIII, 555). Public opinion (probably after 480) also chastised
those who delayed marriage unduly: "[T]hey were denied that respect and
observance which the younger men paid their elders; and no man, for example, found fault with what was said to Dercyllidas, though so eminent a
commander; upon whose approach one day, a young man, instead of rising,
retained his seat, remarking, 'No child of yours will make room for me'"
(Plutarch, "Lycurgus," XV, 3).

It appears that to compel marriage severer measures were eventually
adopted at certain times, even to the point, if one cares to believe it, of
making persistent bachelors parade around the city nude in mid-winter.
These customs help explain why for a century and a half after the Eunomia
the population remained stable. On the other hand, the sharply declining
population from the fifth through the third centuries may indicate that
Spartan birthrates were below those of the rest of Greece although the usual
explanations given are infanticide, loss of status through poverty, and failure
of potential citizens to complete the *agoge*. Nevertheless, declining fertility
rates resulting from less frequent marriages and from less frequent impreg-
nations (due in part perhaps to pederastic preoccupations of husbands or to
anal intercourse) should not be dismissed out of hand.

In Aristophanes' *Lysistrata,* in which Athenian and Spartan representa-
tives become desperate for sex after their wives have gone on strike, the
Athenian finally exclaims, "Why don't we summon Lysistrata, who alone
can reconcile us?" His Spartan counterpart retorts, "By the twin gods, summon Lysistratos too, if you like!" After the reconciliation between husbands
and wives, when the Athenian proposes, "Now I want to strip off and work
the land!" the Spartan replies, "And I want to do the manuring first!" Dover
realized the implications of such statements:

> Before drawing the conclusion that Athenians and Spartans are here
> contrasted as heterosexual vs. homosexual, we should reflect that
> Aristophanes could perfectly well have put both these jokes into the

mouth of a speaker of Athenian or any other nationality, given that
the Athenian in 1091f. has said "If someone doesn't reconcile us pretty
quick we shall have to fuck Kleisthenes!", and that heterosexual anal
intercourse was common (to judge from the vase-paintings) at Athens.
The second joke, however, has an additional point if the Spartans were
regarded as the "inventors" of anal penetration.[21]

The isolated piece of information that it was a Spartan custom "for girls before their marriage to be treated like favorite boys" (Hagnon in Athenaeus,
XIII, 602d) further suggests that anal penetration was permitted, if not encouraged. Of course, Hagnon might have been referring to intercrural sex.
Whichever activity he meant, a passage from Plutarch's "Lycurgus" shows
how fragile the distinction between homosexual and heterosexual coupling
could be in Sparta. According to Plutarch, part of the preparation for the
bride's wedding night included cropping her hair and dressing her in male
clothes (XV, 5).

Sparta, like other *poleis,* often tried to correlate marriage patterns and
birthrates with population pressures.[22] At times of population shortage, as
during the First Messenian War, absentee Spartan husbands are reported to
have requested single citizens of good character and physique to impregnate
their wives so that they might produce sturdy and virtuous soldiers (Plutarch, "Lycurgus," XV). In Early Archaic Sparta, as elsewhere, overpopulation often encouraged emigration to colonies, exposure of infants, attempts
at contraception, abortion, and delayed marriages. The Eunomia mandated
that all babies judged by the elders to be sickly and ill-formed should be exposed. The elders' decision was final, whatever the wishes of the father, who
in other *poleis* had the deciding voice.[23] The numbers of Spartiates were diminished by yet other factors. Those who could not endure the rigorous
training (*agoge*), those who "trembled" in war, and those who were unable
to provide their shares of the public messes lost their status as *Homoioi,* that
is, "Equals."

Aristotle was probably correct in saying that his Cretan lawgiver instituted segregation of the sexes and pederasty among knights in order to
diminish the number of their heirs (*Politics,* 1272a 12). It was exceedingly
difficult to provide estates large enough for the knights to support equestrian accoutrements, including fine steeds which require extensive pastures.
The Spartan lawgiver who imported the Cretan innovations apparently also
aimed at an antinatalist policy. Lycurgus delayed the marriage of females
until eighteen or nineteen (we do not know at what age Cretan girls mar-

ried), which is thought to have been the highest in Greece. With this measure the lawgiver purportedly did not seek to diminish the birthrate but to provide stronger offspring from older, more mature mothers, for which reason he also ordered women to exercise, an expedient not copied elsewhere ("He made the maidens exercise their bodies in running, wrestling, casting the discus, and hurling the javelin, in order that the fruits of their wombs might have rigorous root in vigorous bodies and come to better maturity, and that they themselves might come with vigour to the fullness of their times, and struggle successfully and easily with the pangs of childbirth" [Plutarch, "Lycurgus," XIV]). This measure undoubtedly saved the lives of certain girls because fifteen-year-olds experience greater difficulty and run more risks in childbirth than eighteen-year-olds, but delaying the marriage of fertile females by an average of three or four years must also have retarded the growth of the Spartan population. Once that growth faltered, the Spartans turned to certain measures, discussed above, designed to increase their numbers, but they did not renounce pederasty. Apparently the practice had become so deeply rooted and so respected that the Spartans were unwilling to give it up. Before 465 Sparta always succeeded in replenishing its population. Only after that date, when heavy war casualties became endemic, and disabling poverty increased, did it become impossible to reverse that decline. Homosexuality, which had abetted Sparta's greatness, did not cause its decline, and no ancient drew that conclusion.

Inspirers and Listeners

Spartans sought to produce heroes who would fight unflinchingly in the phalanx. The inspirer's primary duty was to instill courage, loyalty, patriotism, and endurance in his listener. A worthy and dedicated lover also inspired by example. During battle, the peril, anguish, din, confusion, and blood put almost unbearable strain on the hoplite. His chances of surviving the lethal clash of the phalanxes greatly increased if his fellows held steadfast, each protecting his own left and the exposed right side of his neighbor.

Perhaps because of Spartan closemouthedness and their tendency to submerge themselves in the communality of their fellows, we do not have the name of a single Spartiate identified as inspirer or listener for the whole of the Archaic period. In fact, even for classical and Hellenistic times we have identified as such only kings or other members of the royal household and their lovers or beloveds. Our earliest example of these laconic heroes comes from the very beginning of the classical age. Cornelius Nepos described the "intensely sensual" nature of the relationship between Pausanias, the victor at Plataea in 479, and his *eromenos* Argilius (4, 1), who betrayed his lover's treason to the ephors (Thucydides, I, 132). The long-lived Agesilaus (444–360), a lame bastard not originally thought of as an heir and consequently not exempted from the *agoge*, heard (as they said of listeners) the regent Lysander while still in the herd. His son Archidamus III (r. 361–338) loved Cleonymus. The last great king of Sparta, Cleomenes III, crushed with his army by the Macedonians in 222, heard Xenares and inspired Panteus. After Cleomenes' defeat, Panteus fled with his lover the king to Egypt where both heroically committed suicide following an abortive uprising against the corrupt tyrant Ptolemy IV. Cleomenes' reforms at Sparta, notably his restoration of discipline there, and his many successful military campaigns constitute the last major historical achievements of that prominent city, just as Cleomenes and his lover provide our last example of heroic lovers from Sparta, which soon sank into insignificance.

How often and in what form, or even whether the inspirer and listener normally had sexual relations, is quite impossible to tell. Between the graffiti at the Spartan colony of Thera, which date to about 600, and the Attic comedies of the late fifth century we have no clear-cut statement about anal intercourse anywhere in Hellas, however much the system would seem to have encouraged it. Most Greeks seem to have felt that after the *eromenos* had sprouted a beard physical involvement of any type was, if not improper, at least unseemly.[24] Others, but by no means all, apparently believed that men who had grown old and fat made themselves ridiculous by continuing to pursue adolescents. It was assumed that once a former *eromenos* became an adult he should no longer endure a passive sexual role. Indeed, he should, in his twenties, take an *eromenos* for himself.

Not a single literary or artistic source describing sex in the Spartan barracks or herds has come down to us, nor has any about homosexual acts between Spartans and their helots, slaves, or *perioikoi*. The Dutch scholar Jan Bremmer opined that Bethe's celebrated assumption that the Spartan term *eispnelas* should be understood as " 'in-blower' of seed . . . must remain pure conjecture. Strictly speaking we cannot but conclude that there does not exist any certainty about the Spartan way of copulation."[25] Former lovers usually remained close friends. Perhaps as adults they still engaged, at least occasionally, in sexual acts with each other. Perhaps in certain periods they also often fought alongside each other in ranks of battle. According to Xenophon, Socrates declared that Spartiates "even when arrayed with foreigners and even when not stationed in the same line with their lovers just as surely feel ashamed to desert their comrades" (*Symposium,* VIII, 35).

Xenophon and Plutarch maintained that although Spartans' love for youths depended upon the physical beauty of the male (as it theoretically did not among the Cretans), it did not arouse sensual desires in the *erastes.* These writers argued that if a Spartan coveted his *eromenos*'s body he was seen to be no different from a father coveting his son's body or a sibling his brother's. Spartans supposedly declared such a person to be forever "without honour," that is, they deprived him of his citizen's rights.[26]

The Attic comedians, however, regularly parodied the sensual character of Spartan love of youths. *Lakonizein,* like *kretizein,* meant to act as a pederast, implying anal intercourse (Aristophanes, fr. 338; Eupolis, 351, 1). Cicero rejected the assertion that Dorian pederasty had no sensuality: "The Lacedemonians, while they permit all things except outrage in the love of youths, certainly distinguish the forbidden by a thin wall of partition from the sanctioned, for they allow embraces and a common couch to lovers" (*Tusculan Disputations,* IV, 4). And, indeed, it is difficult to believe that no sexual activity ever occurred as a result of this homoerotic educational process which paired an unmarried adult at the apogee of his virility with an adolescent, still to a certain degree androgynous. Inspirers and listeners exercised and wrestled together nude and perhaps also dined and drank together, two on a couch, in a society, we must remember, that had no equivalent of the Judaeo-Christian or Zoroastrian injunction against committing homosexual acts.[27] Moreover, certain Greek vase paintings depict scenes of tender affection between the pederastic pair (see figs. 2 and 14) as well as moments in which the males prepare to engage in sexual intercourse (see figs. 11 and 12). Still, this vexing question must not overshadow the fact, so well formulated by Werner Jaeger, that "Lovers who were bound by the male Eros were guarded by a deeper sense of honour from committing any base action, and were driven by a nobler impulse in attempting any honourable deed." As a result, "The Spartan state deliberately made Eros a factor, and an important factor, in its educational system, its *agoge.* And the relation of the lover to his beloved had a sort of educational authority similar to that of the parent to the child; in fact, it was in many respects superior to parental authority at the age when youths began to ripen into manhood and to cast off the bonds of domestic authority and family tradition. It is impossible to doubt the numerous affirmations of the educational power of Eros, which reach their culmination in Plato's *Symposium.*"[28]

Cultural Efflorescence and Blight

Seventh-century Sparta saw an influx of foreign artists, artisans, poets, and musicians. Well-known for its delight in what came to be deemed traditional or old-fashioned music, Sparta attracted musicians for a generation or two. Olympus of Phrygia, a composite figure fusing Greek and eastern musicians, Terpander from Lesbos, Thaletas of Gortyn, and his contemporary Polymnestus of Colophon, Xenodamus of Cythera, Xenocritus of Locri, and Sacadas of Argos were all drawn to Archaic Sparta (Plutarch, "On Music," 9). The most famous literary figure of the Spartan cultural efflorescence, however, was Alcman, a poet who lived at the time of the Eunomia. The date, place of birth, and descent of Alcman have been disputed in modern times much as they were in antiquity. He may have been a native Spartan or a foreign slave from Sardis. Modern editors have Alcman flourishing in the thirty-seventh Olympiad (632–629 B.C.). Although other authors date him earlier, Eusebius (c. 260–340) said that Alcman flourished c. 612 (*Chronology*, 403, 14: Ol. 42, 2). This late chronology is buttressed by a date *post quem*. Alcman's allusion to the king of Sparta in 635, the likely date of the beginning of the Second Messenian War, of which, however, his fragments say nothing at all, leads me to believe that his *floruit* was just after that conflict.[29] Athenaeus placed him at the time of the Spartan victory over Argos at Thyrea in 546 (XV, 678b), so that Eusebius's date is about in the middle of those given by the other sources.

Alcman is usually cited as the chief male poetic representative of love for women (including what would now be styled lesbian love). Some ancients regarded him as the inventor of erotic poetry. He made abundant use of double entendre and subtle allusions.[30] His *Partheneia,* which constitute most of his surviving verses, show maidens unashamed of their mutual intimate attachments. Others seem to have had affairs with matrons. Nearly seventy lines are fully readable and there are also 177 fragments in the 1988 Loeb Classical Library edition of his poems (*Greek Lyric,* 2) as well as ancient commentaries about them. As Dover noted, Alcman's language is erotic, but as in the case of Sappho's monodies, it is impossible to know who is addressing whom in some of his choral odes. The relationship between the lesbianism that he described and the lesbianism that Sappho practiced on Lesbos has been noticed.[31]

There can be no doubt about Alcman's sensual glorification of beautiful Spartan girls and his description of lesbian love among them; however, no pederastic verses attributed to Alcman have survived although several

ancients listed him with others who were clearly pederastic poets.[32] A commentator on Alcman's life stated that "the Spartans . . . put him in charge
of the traditional choruses of their daughters *and young men* [my italics]"
(*Oxyrhynchus papyrus* 2506, fr. 1, col. 2).

Two of Alcman's fragments are particularly pertinent to our discussion:
"Aphrodite it is not, but wild Eros playing like the boy he is, coming down
over the flower-tips—do not touch them, I beg you!—of the galingale" (58).
The reference to the garlands with galingale led Bowra to conclude that
such a garland was particularly appropriate for a ceremony of ladies "concerned with Hera as a goddess of health and growth." Easterling found, on
the contrary, that wreaths were made from whatever was handy, as galingale
was in Laconia. He concluded, therefore, that if the allusion was to garlands, "the context is the familiar symposia," with Alcman warning against
a dangerous passion, Eros, irresponsibly playing with human affections. The
distinction Alcman made between Aphrodite, whose type of love was common, and Eros, whose love was wild, might explain the claims of Athenaeus
and the *Suda* that Alcman invented love poetry. Thus we see interconnec-
tions between Alcman's concepts and those of the overtly pederastic poets,
as indicated by a second fragment: "At the command of the Cyprian, Eros
once again pours sweetly down and warms my heart" (59a).[33] Whatever
these fragments signify, it must be noted that no lines unequivocally discussing male pederasty by Alcman have survived.

For a generation at least after the enactment of the Eunomia, Sparta enjoyed cultural prominence. As late as the mid-sixth century the Spartan
Gitiadas erected the celebrated Bronzehouse. Not known for other monumental buildings or stone statuary, Archaic Spartans nevertheless managed
to build this glittering temple on their acropolis. There, to the right of the
Bronzehouse, stood "a statue of Zeus the Highest, the oldest of all bronze
statues, not cast in bronze in one piece, but each part made of beaten
bronze and then fitted together and all held in place with bolts" (Pausanius,
III, 17, 6). Over time, however, the fundamentally anti-intellectual bias of
the Eunomia blighted the Spartans' cultural efflorescence. Thereafter they
began to cling to their old songs and dances, rejecting innovation. Conscious anachronism rendered Sparta and Crete increasingly anomalous, as
most of the rest of the Greeks rapidly evolved intellectually and socially. The
Ionians were the first to deny magic and miracles and to seek only rational
explanations for the origins of the world and the workings of nature. Many
moderns have gone so far as to claim that the east Greeks, these settlers of
the Aegean Islands and the Anatolian coasts, were the first individuals, the

first fully conscious humans who saw themselves as distinct from all others, even those in their own immediate society. For two centuries Ionians and Aeolians had profited from their fortuitous location to engage in a rich cultural exchange between the Hellenic and Near Eastern civilizations. From their magnificent harbors they had sent forth merchants and colonists all over the Mediterranean, who returned home laden with knowledge as well as profit. But it was only after they adopted pederastic institutions from Crete and perhaps from Sparta also at the very end of the seventh century that their creative impulses burst forth.

Part Three

Diffusion

Eight

Gymnasia, Symposia, and Pederastic Art

That sexuality played a decisive role in pederasty and does not
stem from the lustful imagination of a few scholars is clear to
every unprejudiced observer when he sees the archaic vase paintings on which a man, an erastes, gropes the genital organs of
a youth, an eromenos. This gesture, which in early Greek art
also appears in heterosexual eroticism, becomes more concrete
in later, red-figured vase depictions.

— Carola Reinsberg, *Ehe, Hetärentum und Knabenliebe*
(Munich, 1989), 189

Within a generation after 600 most Greeks had followed the Cretans and
Spartans in institutionalizing pederasty. Tradition credited the introduction
of the practice to "sages," that is, counterparts of the Cretan "musicians" who
had invented the new pederastic system. Of the so-called Seven Sages, all
except the legendary Lycurgus lived in the seventh and sixth century.[1] I follow tradition in this matter, recognizing fully that these sages, like Lycurgus,
may in truth have been committees of lawgivers or citizens whose laws and
reforms were later ascribed to a particular individual. However we choose to
speak about the agency for the institutionalization of pederasty in the varied
Greek *poleis,* I appreciate that some readers may question the possibility that
one sage or even a few lawgivers could have imposed upon the populace of
any city the far-reaching social changes we have been discussing.

Nevertheless, without endorsing the theories expounded so passionately
by Thomas Carlyle in *The Hero in History,* we can see from more contemporary evidence how a few individuals are quite capable of effecting the transformation of numerous, particularly congruous societies. I refer to Hitler
and Mussolini, who remodeled their own countries and were then imitated

by others in eastern Europe, and to the Communists who did no less after 1945. That none of these modern experiments lasted more than a few decades may indicate only that the reforms instituted by the Greek sages were more workable and more beneficial.[2] Dover, too, I must add, does not dismiss out of hand the notion of a single individual "inventing" pederasty: "The Greeks had the right end of the stick, at least, in regarding innovation as having precise location."[3] He is also quick to provide discussion of a quite different nature on why pederasty spread so quickly among the Greeks and why it appealed to their society, citing, for example, "deficiencies of familial and communal relationships." This two-pronged presentation highlights both the complexity of our subject and the fact that the origin and diffusion of pederasty need not be explained in the same fashion throughout all Hellas.

Of note also is the relationship between pederasty and certain tyrants, that is, individuals whose ability to set standards during their dictatorship cannot be gainsaid. A number of those tyrants were themselves distinctly fond of adolescents and collected around themselves courts heavily populated with pederasts and beautiful pages. Although little is known about the earliest tyrants, by the time of Polycrates, Hipparchus, and Hiero, we can identify not only the artists and poets they supported but also some of the comely youths so admired at their courts.

The ensuing chapters in Part 3 will chart the spread of pederasty region by region. There the accent must fall upon those contemporary figures, notably poets, whose surviving works record the intense outpouring of sentiments associated with pederastic relationships. But the new mode established by the "sages" involved along with the mentor-pupil bond of *erastes* and *eromenos* new ways to prepare the youth's strength of body (the gymnasium) and mind (the symposium). To understand something of these all-important institutions is to grasp much that is essential to the world of *erastes* and *eromenos*.

Sources

The Late Archaic poets, whose numbers include the nine canonized by the Alexandrians, provide our primary literary sources for their age. The earliest of the nine, Alcman, Sappho, and Alcaeus, represented local values rather than pan-Hellenic traditions. Of the middle poets (chronologically speaking), some believe that at least Stesichorus was, like the earliest three, perhaps no more historical than Homer, and that these four were merely names applied to corpora that had evolved over time. Ibycus and Anacreon, however, associated with tyrants of the day about whom we possess substantial biographical information. These two poets must be considered true historical personages. Because the final members of the canon, Pindar, Simonides, and Bacchylides, lived into the classical age, we are better informed about their lives.

Of the works of these poets and their contemporaries, few survive. The Theognidean corpus (1,388 lines) is the longest by far to come down to us in manuscript. Even it is not complete and much included in it may have actually been written by predecessors or by imitators who lived as late as Hellenistic times. Pindar of Thebes (518–438) has left a corpus of sufficient length to fill a slim modern volume, though it is but a fraction of what he actually composed. Ibycus of Rhegium, Anacreon of Teos, and Simonides of Ceos are known to us through far fewer lines.

Scholiasts on other peoples' works give us some data. Literary critics from Aristotle to Cicero, Seneca, and Quintilian as well as some of the Christian Fathers, especially Clement of Alexandria, provide more information. Byzantine lexicographers such as Hesychius, Stephanus, Photius, the compilers of the *Suda,* and Eustathius of Thessalonica also help. The biographies of both poets and philosophers, all of which are late, are highly anecdotal and clearly contain deductions about the authors from their works rather than from actual facts. Like today's tabloids, the *Lives* penned by Diogenes Laertius, Iamblichus, Eunapius, and others are full of gossip.[4] No one is more useful, however, than the much neglected Athenaeus, whose discursive dialogues contain many gems drawn from early works.

History was first developed by Herodotus of Halicarnassus, who digressed but briefly into the Archaic period. His successor Thucydides attempted to summarize that age in a few passages. Their information is, nevertheless, invaluable regarding the spread of pederasty and its concomitant institutions. At various times local writers, especially Herodotus's contemporary Hellanicus of Lesbos, traced the history of cities back to their foundation. Strabo, Diodorus Siculus, and Plutarch relied heavily upon Ephorus, who often used those logographers and other early sources with discrimination. Pausanias, Aelian, and even certain Byzantine compilers often reported accurately on ancient traditions and preserved fragments of lost authors by citing them. Inscriptions and papyri (including a manual for wrestling), as well as statues and drawings, greatly increase our knowledge of early Greek athletics.[5]

Innumerable vases provide revealing scenes from gymnasia and symposia. Like the homosexual graffiti at Thera, explicit pederastic art also first ap-

peared in the late seventh century.[6] Dover mentioned the oldest pictorial
evidence of Cretan homosexuality, a late seventh-century bronze plaque
that depicts the return from the hunt of a *parastates* (*eromenos*), whose sexual
organs show under his tunic. Armed with a bow and carrying a goat, he
seizes the forearm of his *philetor.*[7] Soon thereafter a flood of art and poetry
celebrated a new lifestyle, so different from that of the epics.

Gymnasia

Athletics rendered the Greek adolescent more desirable as an *eromenos*. It
was not merely the beauty and flexibility of his body that they improved
but his endurance and *sophrosyne* (self-control). If, as theory supposed, many
Archaic Greeks loved their boys for their good character and virtue—in the
original sense of manliness—nothing could more clearly demonstrate this
than athletic success. The discipline and endurance that prepared a youth
for athletics could also prepare him for war, the most essential duty of a
citizen. Thus exercise in gymnasia could inspire love as truly as flirtation at
symposia. An anonymous late epigram says it more succinctly, if less elo-
quently than Pindar's odes: "When Menecharmus, Anticles' son, won the
boxing match, I crowned him with ten soft fillets, and thrice I kissed him
all dabbled with blood as he was, but the blood was sweeter to me than
myrrh" (*Greek Anthology,* XII, 123).

Gymnasia were originally no more than open spaces on the outskirts
of cities, preferably near a source of water for bathing. Pederastic scenes as
shown on the black-figure vases of the mid-sixth century were still set in
such outdoor locales, whereas scenes on the later red-figure vases from c. 520
were frequently set in or near enclosed and even slightly built-up gymnasia.[8] Often located near temples, the gymnasia might themselves contain
statues of patron deities and heroes. These statues indicated that the gods
took an interest in athletics; they also emphasized important links between
the gymnasia and pederasty.

The statues which predominated in gymnasia were not of the handsome youth Apollo but of the boy Eros, the young Hermes, and the mature
Heracles. They seem to have personified the three stages of physical development: Eros, the prepubescent end of boyhood; Hermes, the ephebic
stage; and Heracles, the fully developed adult ready for marriage. Eros further represented friendship and concord, Hermes eloquence, and Heracles
physical strength (Athenaeus, XIII, 561d).

As Plutarch and Aelian testified, Eros inspired military victory.[9] On the

Figure 1. Zeus attempting to abduct Ganymede (Museo Archeologica
Nazionale, V. P. T. 212). Reproduced by permission of the Museo Archeologica
Nazionale, Ferrara.

Figure 2. Two males about to kiss (Musée du Louvre, G 278, photo
M. Chuzeville). Reproduced by permission of the Musée du Louvre, Paris.

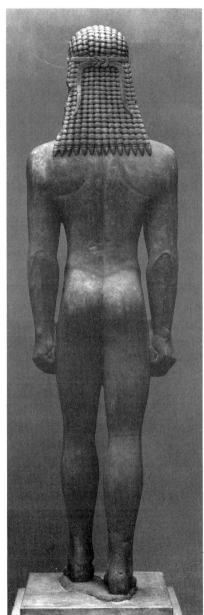

Figures 3–4. Kouros, c. 615–590 B.C. (The Metropolitan Museum of Art, Fletcher Fund, 1932, 32. 11.1). Reproduced by permission of the Metropolitan Museum of Art, New York. All rights reserved.

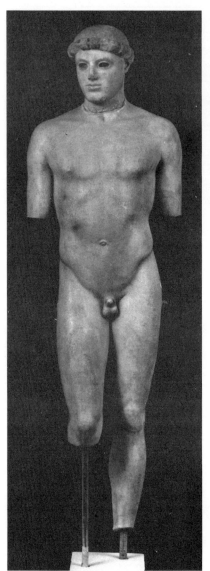

Figures 5–6. Kouros, the "Kritios Boy," c. 485–460 B.C. (Acropolis Museum, 698). Reproduced by permission of the Acropolis Museum, Athens.

Figure 7. Two males at a symposium (Musée du Louvre, G 81, photo
M. Chuzeville). Reproduced by permission of the Musée du Louvre, Paris.

Figure 8. Male reaches for the genitals of a youth (Staatliche Antiken-sammlungen, 1468). Reproduced by permission of the Staaliche Antikensammlungen, Munich.

Figure 9. A suitor offers a hen to a prospective *eromenos* (Ashmolean Museum, 517). Reproduced by permission of the Ashmolean Museum, Oxford.

Figure 10. Youths being courted (Staatliche Antikensammlungen, 2655). Reproduced by permission of the Staatliche Antikensammlungen, Munich.

Figure 11. Youth prepares to copulate with an older man (Ashmolean Museum, 1967, 304). Reproduced by permission of the Ashmolean Museum, Oxford.

Figure 12. Youth prepares for anal copulation by sitting on the lap of another male (British Museum, F 65). Copyright British Museum, London.

Figure 13. A youth, brandishing a lyre, rejects a suitor (Aegisthus painter, 470–460 B.C., Fitzwilliam Museum, 37. 26). Reproduced by permission of the Fitzwilliam Museum, Cambridge.

Figure 14. Two males prepare to kiss (Attic red-figure psykter, detail, c. 510 B.C.; attributed to Smikros, terracotta, H. 33 cm, D. 25.5 cm.; Getty Museum, 82. AE. 53). Reproduced by permission of the Collection of the J. Paul Getty Museum, Malibu, California.

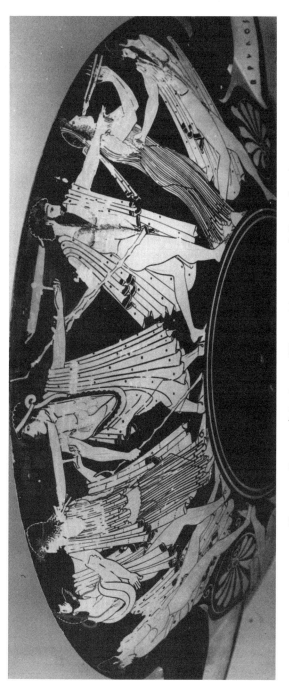

Figure 15. Comasts (Martin von Wagner Museum, 479). Reproduced by permission of the Martin von Wagner Museum, Würtzburg.

eve of battle, Spartans and Cretans sacrificed to him. The Sacred Band of youths at Thebes was inspired by him. At Samos a "Festival of Liberty" (*Eleutheria*) honored Eros as the god who bound men and youths in the struggle for freedom and honor. For all these reasons, Eros's presence in the gymnasium was entirely appropriate. But Plutarch also said that inspired by the god, a man was " 'ready' *for his friend* 'to go through fire' " (*Eroticos*, 760d, my italics), and Eros fulfilled the additional function of inspiring love between males. To quote Flacelière: "Eros presided primarily over the passionate devotion of a grown man to a boy; Aphrodite over the sexual relations between man and woman."[10] The pederastic tyrant Pisistratus or his beloved Charmus erected a statue of the god and built an altar to him at the Academy, the premier gymnasium in Athens; Athenians worshipped him as their liberator, in memory of the tyrannicide lovers Harmodius and Aristogiton.

According to one legend, Heracles, the most popular of Greek heroes, founded the Olympic Games. He supposedly fathered so many offspring during his travels that nobles from almost every *polis* claimed descent from him. In addition to all his heterosexual activities, Heracles had some celebrated affairs with boys, most prominently Hylas and Iolaus. Cynics and Stoics underscored his virtues in the service of humanity, that is, the very hardiness, austerity, and bravery that the palaestras hoped to instill in boys.[11]

Already in the sixth century Athens had three gymnasia. Eventually seven existed there. A number of other cities had more than one even before the rise of the great Hellenistic metropolises. The only Athenian gymnasia known by name are ascribed to the sixth century by tradition: the Academy, Lyceion, and Cynosarges. The location of the Academy is certain, that of the other two somewhat less so. Aristophanes alluded to races run below the sacred olive trees in the Academy (*Clouds*, 1005–8), and Plutarch recorded that Cimon provided the Academy with a well-watered grove, running tracks, and shaded walks ("Cimon," 13, 8).

In the sixth century gymnasia and palaestras proliferated,[12] but literary sources about them become numerous only in the fifth. The gymnasium and palaestra could be public or private, as pseudo-Xenophon related: "Some of the wealthy [in Athens] have private gymnasia, baths, and dressing rooms, but the public constructs for its own use many palaestras, dressing rooms, and baths" (*Resp. Ath.* 2, 10). In the *Lysis* Plato described a newly erected palaestra. Socrates asked his young friend Hippothales, "What place is this and how do you pass your time here?" Hippothales responded: "It's a palaestra and we pass our time there in discussion." The answer reveals the development of the palaestra into a school and locus of instruction in philosophy.

Gymnastic training was designed in large part to perfect the hoplite and was probably long limited to that class and to their betters, the knights. Philostratus's remark about the great gymnasts of the past, "They made war training for sport and sport training for war" (*Peri gymnastikes*, 9, 11, 43), underlines the usefulness of gymnastic training as a preparation for war.[13] We never hear of a Greek city even under the late Roman Empire that did not have at least one gymnasium. The closing of gymnasia by various tyrants and the Persians in the sixth century may imply that they had already assumed a political function. At the very least, the action underscores the importance of the institution in the *poleis* ruled by those tyrants.

That courting, sex play, and even sexual acts occurred in and near palaestras and gymnasia is clearly attested. The inscriptions from Thera were probably scrawled near a gymnasium on the outskirts of the town. Athenians reputedly forbade adults under forty from entering the boys' palaestras. The scenes from palaestras or gymnasia depicted on red-figure vases often show foreplay or horse play rather than anal or oral sex.

The "undressing room" (*apodyterion*) which Socrates and his circle so loved to frequent was not merely a locker room. Many had benches where one could relax and talk comfortably. The athletes rubbed themselves there with oil and then used the strigil to scrape it off after they finished. Here all awaited the special twelve-year-old beauty that each palaestra seemed to spawn. This was the cruising area par excellence of the athletic complex.[14] Aristophanes mentioned "hanging around *palaistrai* trying to seduce boys" (*Peace,* 762f) and a character of his foresees meeting a beautiful youth who has "left the gymnasium, after a bath" (*Birds,* 139–42). Compare also this opening scene from Plato's *Charmides:* "I marvelled at his stature and beauty, and I felt everyone else in the room was in love with him; they were thrown into such amazement and confusion when he came in, and there were many other *erastai* following after him too" (154c).

Despite such evidence, Poliakoff, like most of his predecessors, managed to devote an entire book to Greek athletics without mentioning pederasty or any other form of homosexuality. Now that so much has come to light about homosexuals in modern American athletics, the absence seems more pronounced than it might have been before the 1980s. Books on symposia have less frequently avoided the topic of pederasty, perhaps because Plato's dialogues made it difficult for them to do so. Even Becker's *Charikles* included an excursus, albeit homophobic, on pederasty (omitted without a word from the English translation). But both institutions were as important to institutionalized pederasty as they were to Greek culture in general.

Nudity in Athletics

Everyone agrees that nudity in gymnastics, even when performed before a male public, began among the literate rather than the preliterate Greeks. Although the Homeric heroes contended mightily against one another at the games for Patroclus, they neither frequented gymnasia nor exercised nude. Rather, the very word *gymnasia* implies that the spread of the phenomenon probably reflected the extensive adoption of athletic nudity. Absent from the epic language, the term *gymnasia,* first attested in Pindar, signifies "exercises in the nude"; and *gymnasion,* "the place of nudity." The verb *gymnazomai* "to exercise in the nude," appears in Herodotus and Theognis.[15] Significantly *gymnasion* replaced the older term *dromos* "track" that survived in Crete.

Tradition assigned the introduction of nudity in athletics to Orsippus (or Orhippus) of Megara who dropped his loincloth—whether by accident or design is not clear—while running in an early Olympiad, most commonly the fifteenth in 720.[16] "Until recently," Thucydides wrote, "even at the Olympic games the athletes wore loincloths." He then went on to stress that in his eyes athletic nudity was progressive, civilized rather than savage behavior. Noting that the barbarians, especially in Asia, still wore girdles while boxing and wrestling, he mused that "one might show many other points in which the old Greek ways are like the barbarian customs of today" (I, 6). If the tyrants' closing of gymnasia shows the growing role of this facet of Greek culture in their political life, Thucydides' observation about nude athletics signals an even deeper interaction between certain new practices and the Greeks' perception of themselves, an interaction quite comparable to Plato's equation (cited at the outset of this study) between barbarians and a denigration of pederasty, nude sports, and philosophy.

The sources assure us that athletes and other males were sexually aroused by nakedness. Visiting the palaestra of Taureas, Socrates saw inside Charmides' clothes. Overcome at that moment by a sort of "bestial appetite," he said that he could no longer control himself (*Charmides* 155c–d). In *Clouds,* Better Argument goes into detail on the techniques used by gymnasiarchs to reduce sexual arousal: "And at the gymnastic teacher's, the boys had to sit with one thigh forward, so as not to show anything tortuous to those outside. And when a boy got up again he had to brush the sand over and be careful not to leave an imprint of his youth for his lovers. And no boy then would anoint himself with oil below the navel, so that the dew and down bloomed on his genitals as quinces" (972–78).

Although these passages have their place in this study—adding their own weight to the inescapably sexual reality within institutionalized pederasty—we would be wrong to think of nudity only in such terms. It dominated Greek art and, as Licht noted, fostered a remarkable reassessment of the human body: "far from being ashamed of these organs, the Greeks rather regarded them with pious awe and treated them with an almost religious reverence as the mystical instruments of propagation, as the symbols of nature, life-producing and fruitful."[17] The art historian Adolf Furtwängler even went so far as to insist that "Greek art is unthinkable without Greek gymnastics. . . . In the whole of Egyptian plastic art one seeks in vain for a display of strength, tension and energy,"[18] the very qualities that the training upper-class Greek males obtained in gymnasia sought to encourage. No little wonder that Greek sculpture reflected in its way the same new-found interest in the disciplined male body. Indeed, art historians preceded other scholars in recognizing that the crucial frontier between periods in Greek culture appears in the second half of the seventh century. By 620 a new synthesis of foreign and local influences resulted in a trend away from abstraction toward realism and the natural portrayal of the human body. Nothing illustrates this fact better than the nude male statues called *kouroi*.

It cannot be determined exactly when the Greeks first sculpted *kouroi* or where. No life-sized Greek *kouroi* exist prior to the one dated 610 at the Metropolitan Museum of Art.[19] Perhaps under Egyptian influence, which became great after 650 and often came to Greece via Crete, sculptors began with belted figures. Early *kouroi* certainly resemble their Egyptian proto-types, stiff, with clenched fists held down at their side (see figs. 3 and 4). If the first statues did wear belts, they were soon abandoned, and it is not impossible that even the earliest *kouroi* were totally nude. Even Egyptian artists at least occasionally depicted fully nude figures. However, nude or belted, the earliest *kouroi* remain highly stylized.

Formerly called "Apollos," *kouroi* were once thought to represent that deity. In truth, we do not know the uses of these figures. Some appear to have been grave markers; others, perhaps, idols. Because none of the statues name the boy depicted (in the fashion of some vase paintings which identify various *eromenoi*), we cannot establish beyond doubt that the *kouroi*, too, represent *eromenoi*. However, that possibility can hardly be dismissed, especially in light of the demonstrable evolution in the form of the *kouros* away from the early stylized figure and toward a singularly physical (if idealized) male body (see figs. 5 and 6). It is the same body that, as we have seen, poets praised in their verse about handsome athletes, the same body that gymnasia were designed to develop. Thus, however imprecise our knowledge may be about the function of the *kouroi,* these statues, nude sports, the gymnasia, and institutionalized pederasty shared the same values, and each lent luster and meaning to the others.

Symposia and Schools

As tradition associated pederasty with the Seven Sages, so the Seven Sages were in turn associated with the symposium "which was later considered to be their meeting-place."[20] Whatever truth there may be to this story, it remains that the symposium was almost as central to Greek pederasty as the gymnasium.[21]

Bremmer and other recent writers have argued that symposia evolved during the seventh century as successors of "the common meal of the archaic warrior clubs . . . [of] Doric Sparta and Crete."[22] However, they felt the influence of luxurious Near Eastern customs as well, notably with respect to the addition of couches, borrowed perhaps by Ionians even before the institutionalization of pederasty from non-Greek Anatolians or other "Orientals."[23] We cannot suppose that in general it was women who decided to eat alone, although legends tell of this in Cyrene and in Ionia. I have already mentioned that the native wives of the Greek colonizers of Miletus supposedly declined to dine with the men who had killed their fathers and brothers when capturing the site (Herodotus, I, 146). Herodotus also observed that the women of Cyrene refused to dine with their men because "the women think it wrong to eat the flesh of the cow, honoring in this Isis, the Egyptian goddess, whom they worship both with fasts and festivals. The Barcaean women abstain, not from cow's flesh only, but also from the flesh of swine" (IV, 186).

Archaic men's dining rooms seem to have had seven couches: two along each wall with one missing to allow entry. In classical times the number was sometimes expanded to three benches along each wall with one missing, making a total of eleven. Thus, they accommodated fourteen or twenty-two males, instead of the fifteen in the Spartan *syssitia.* Normally of stone or wood, the couches had pads and pillows for the guests.

In their original form in Sparta and on Crete, these eating clubs voted admission only after careful consideration, and it was often confined to relatives or *eromenoi* of existing members. However, as is confirmed by later evidence from Athens such as the *Symposium* of Xenophon and the work of the same title by Plato, hosts in that city (and presumably in others not so

regimented as Sparta) could invite whomever they wished. There seems to
have been no fixed rule as to the age at which an adolescent could be ad-
mitted to a symposium. The guiding principle was whether or not he was
old enough to drink heavily. In the *Laws,* Plato said, "we shall absolutely
prohibit the taste of wine to boys under eighteen" (II, 666a). But his ideas
were not followed and do not reflect common practice. In Xenophon's
Symposium, the sixteen-year-old Autolycus "nestled close against" his father
Lycon (III, 13).[24] Excluding adolescents from symposia would have pre-
vented the participants from using their discussions to educate the youths,
clearly one of its functions.[25] Moreover, these gatherings provided an opportunity to court and flirt with youths, if one was so inclined.

After pouring libations to the gods, the guests began to drink wine di-
luted with various amounts of water. Sipping wine with his young friend
while exchanging love poetry or ribald songs, a gentleman might flirt with
him and even kiss and embrace him (see fig. 7). Going farther with one
another in public was considered improper although slaves of both sexes
who served the guests were often pinched and pummeled during the symposia. Physical sexual acts were not unknown but must have occurred
almost exclusively when the guests were in their cups. Ladies, shut away
in the *gynaeceum* (women's quarters), could never attend these parties in the
men's chamber that each greater house possessed. One of the more popular games was *cottabos* (wine-throwing), in which, reclining on their left
elbows on the couches, the guests threw the last drops of wine from the
calices into a basin set in the middle of the room or sank saucers floating in
the basin with the thrown wine.

Some sang songs (*scolia*) to the lyre, extemporizing or altering traditional
verses. Often the songs praised an *eromenos* who might be present. Indeed,
except for choral odes, which were designed for public occasions, and certain
martial elegies composed to be sung by soldiers on campaigns or to inspire
the young, all elegies, iambs, and lyrics may have been intended or adapted
for symposia.[26] After games played during drinking bouts, *hetairai,* flute
players, and other entertainers, of either or both sexes, sometimes entered.

Sixty-two drinking songs written in the manner of Anacreon survive.
Though they were long thought to have been composed by the poet himself, research has shown that none of them can be earlier than the late
Hellenistic Age and that some may have been composed as late as the sixth
century A.D.[27] Thus, for a full millennium symposia provided elite youths
with a sort of school for intellectual pursuits as well as for manners and
morals. Nevertheless, by the sixth century B.C. formal schools for boys also

appeared in some *poleis*. The relationship between schools and symposia and between schools and gymnasia is problematic, though no one claims that schools came before either gymnasia or symposia. They may, however, have begun soon after the institutionalization of pederasty.

The earliest evidence of a school for boys is for 496, when one collapsed in Chios, crushing 119 pupils (Herodotus, VI, 27, 492; Pausanias, VI, 9, 6). Aristocratic conservatives from Theognis to Pindar (c. 518–438), who believed that blood mattered more than training in the molding of human nature, scorned schoolmasters—a clear indication that they were flourishing long before Aristophanes described schoolboys thronging the streets on their way to and from their classes (*Clouds*, 961–79).

Although, of course, the very rich could afford tutors for their children, most of them may early on have opted for the savings of a private school. Even if aristocrats perhaps preferred teaching their children at home, the hoplites were unable to afford such a luxury. We must therefore suppose that schools began when the hoplites felt that their children needed them. This may have occurred around 600, when so many other great changes were transforming Greek life. Whether invented for the aristocracy or not, schools, like gymnasia, came to serve the hoplite class, whereas symposia, at least those held in special men's dining rooms, remained a greater luxury. They were not restricted to the aristocracy to be sure, but they were available only to those who could afford them or to those who could get themselves invited.

Erotic Vases

The erotic vases alone would prove that Late Archaic Greeks routinely practiced pederasty without shame or inhibitions, as Dover demonstrated.[28] Originally, however, Greek vases did not depict pederastic scenes. At about the same time that, according to many, the Greeks borrowed the alphabet from the Phoenicians (c. 725), they also imported and began to imitate Near Eastern figured vases which soon crowded out the late geometric ones. Circa 650 Corinthian potters, often exporting to the western colonies, dominated Greek ceramics. They continued the trend away from the late geometric style, which downplayed living objects, and portrayed more realistically human and animal figures as well as griffins, sphinxes and the like. With the introduction of black-figure vases c. 570 scenes painted on vases began to portray pederasty.[29]

Although almost all of these erotic vases were manufactured in Athens, they became popular throughout Hellas. Like sculpture, they emphasized the sexual attractiveness of young males when either nude or undressing, sometimes even including inscriptions saying that the youth was beautiful (*kalos*). At Athens, after 570, black-figure vases and, after 530, red-figure vases (where the background is painted black) also portrayed "courting scenes," often with erections and intercrural sex, as well as caresses or gifts for the *eromenoi*. Vase paintings, thousands of which survive, are thus one of our principal sources for Late Archaic Greek pederasty and indeed for Greek sexuality in general. A small portion of them portray heterosexual activity.

The Athenian vases with pederastic courtship scenes were not systematically studied during the nineteenth century. Indeed, at that time many had not yet been unearthed. As early as 1927, John Beazley claimed to be able to identify, often by name and date, the most important Athenian vase painters. His work is still being updated.[30] He classified the pederastic vases, of which he identified over one hundred examples, into three groups. In the alpha group, the *erastes*, standing with bent knees, reaches with one hand for the chin and with the other for the genitals of the *eromenos* standing opposite him (see fig. 8). In the beta group, the *erastes* presents the *eromenos* with a gift of a small animal or some other trivial present (so as not to seem to be buying the beloved's favor) (see figs. 9 and 10). In the gamma group, the standing lovers are entwined, with the *erastes* apparently intending to climax by rubbing his phallus between the thighs of his *eromenos*, who remains flaccid, apparently submitting out of affection but without reciprocal excitement. I would add a delta group, in which the *erastes*, seated with an erection, is approached by his *eromenos*, who sometimes is climbing up on his lap as if to prepare for anal intercourse, quite in the manner that on other vases some women were shown mounting seated erect males for vaginal sex (see figs. 11 and 12). Curiously, there is never oral-genital contact between *erastes* and *eromenos*, and anal penetration is much less frequent than in heterosexual scenes. Some vase paintings show the youth rejecting the suitor (see fig. 13).

Dover and Gundel Koch-Harnack have shown that earlier authorities underestimated the extent of the pederastic vase paintings. Older scholars did not, for example, understand that many scenes of gift giving (or what they described as wrestling) between a man and a youth were in fact courting scenes.[31] From the pictures alone one could not know that gift giving was necessarily a prelude to pederasty, but in conjunction with the literature, that fact becomes irrefutable.

Jiří Frel used Beazley's collection, plus a few other exemplars, to assign twelve pederastic courtship scenes to the period 575–550 (mostly after 560), fifty to 550–525, fifty-seven to 525–500, and nine after 500, with a very few in the 470s. After 510 they diminished in favor of heterosexual scenes.[32] The *eromenoi*, fully grown but unbearded on the black-figure vases, became younger and smaller, and even the *erastai* often became younger on the red-figure ones (see fig. 14). Knud Friis Johansen noted that after 520 a beardless *erastes* often courted a very young, barely pubescent *eromenos*. Often, but not always, both were partly draped on the red-figure vases in contrast to the older black-figure depictions which almost always show nude forms: a bearded *erastes* and often a fully grown, mature, but still always beardless *eromenos*.[33]

In the 1930s other scholars besides Beazley studied the erotic vases. David M. Robinson and Edward J. Fluck (1937) published a list of the youths described on the vases as *kalos* (beautiful). They showed that the adolescents adored and idolized by Athenian society were not mere "pin-ups." Rather, many of them appeared later in the annals of Athenian history as statesmen, generals, and admirals. In Athens, as earlier in Crete, to be a *kalos* was thus perhaps a first and important stage in what was a lifelong career in politics and public life. We have always known that in theory Greek pederasty was part of the process of selection and advancement of worthy boys by a prominent lover and patron. The work by Robinson and Fluck assures us that the Socratic ideal attested in the *Symposium* was realized in practice. While poets like Ibycus and Anacreon celebrated only the erotic side of loving adolescents, the testimony of the vases proves that the youth was chosen and promoted not merely for his physical beauty but for his moral and intellectual qualities also.

And what of the youth's attitude? With the exception of a few vase paintings depicting affectionate *eromenoi*, very little in the story of pederastic pedagogy hints at the feelings of the younger member of the pair. Still, Martin Kilmer's meticulous investigations in his *Greek Erotica on Attic Red-Figure Vases* (1993) have added a small yet significant point to the preceding discussion. Concluding that olive oil was very likely used as a sexual lubricant in the Late Archaic period, Kilmer wonders aloud in his book whether this fact may explain the presence of containers of oil in a number of scenes of pederastic courtship. If that is the explanation, then in the case of one youth portrayed on R196, the boy "is in fact so ready for anything that he has even supplied his own little jar of oil" (16).

To be sure, pederasty did not go unchallenged. Greek tyrants in the sixth century appear to have been the first to criticize pederasty. But their opposition was political rather than moral: they feared tyrannicidal pederastic couples and plots originating among elite groups of lovers in symposia or gymnasia. The Persian overlords of Ionian tyrants seem to have encouraged them to repress pederasty out of a similar concern over the heroic friendship and fellowship which pederasty was supposed to instill (cf. Plato, *Symposium*, 182c).

Their concern was well justified. The lovers Harmodius and Aristogiton assassinated the brother of Hippias, tyrant of Athens, and intended to slay Hippias himself (Athenaeus, XIII, 561). Phalaris, the tyrant of Agrigentum, first condemned and then not only released but praised his would-be tyrannicides (two lovers) when he saw how brave they were (Aelian, *Varia Historia*, II, 11; Athenaeus, XIII, 602b). None of the writings of those tyrants who criticized pederasty during the sixth century survive but Athenaeus is explicit regarding their distrust of pederastic bonding: "Because of these love affairs, then, tyrants, to whom such friendships are inimical, tried to abolish entirely relations between males, extirpating them everywhere. Some even went so far as to set fire to the wrestling-schools, regarding them as bulwarks in opposition to their own citadels, and so demolished them; this was done by Polycrates, the tyrant of Samos" (XIII, 602a–b, d).

When we leave the perspective of the tyrants, we discover that if the *erastes* was young enough and the *eromenos* properly coy and discreet and there was no payment, no Archaic figure seems to have censured their love-making. In fact, no one before Plato and Xenophon is known to have done so. Oral sex, it is true, seems to have been condemned from the beginning, as it was to the end. A vase painting reproduced in Dover (R1127) shows one male satyr fellating another, and fellation was indeed more frequently practiced than was once believed. H. D. Jocelyn's brilliant article proved that Greeks even had a word for it: a form of the verb *laikazein* 'to lick'.[34]

Such then are some of the broad features of Archaic pederasty. However, after the various societies, regions, cities, and ethnic groups of Hellas embraced the practice, they adapted it to suit their particular temperaments and interests. Aeolia, Ionia, and Magna Graecia, for example, each institutionalized different types of pederasty. Thus, it is to a closer study of those variations on the institution that we turn next.

Nine

The Mainland:
Athletes and Heroes

Again, here [Athens] and in Lacedaimon the law about love is confusing, but that in other states is easy to understand. In Elis and Boeotia, and where people are not clever speakers, it is simply laid down that it is right to gratify lovers, and no one young or old would call it ugly; as I think they wish not to have the trouble of convincing the young, because they cannot argue.

—Plato, *Symposium,* 182b

. . . though sharing common beds [the Thebans and Eleans] nevertheless assigned to their favorites places alongside themselves in the battle-line.

—Xenophon, *Symposium,* VIII, 34

At the Isthmus of Corinth began an array of coterminous cities: Megara, stretching its territory across the isthmus from sea to sea; then, to the southwest, Corinth itself, with its two harbors, one on each side of the isthmus; to the west, Sicyon, separated from Corinth by a fertile plain; and to the east the various *poleis* of the Argolid. All spoke Dorian dialects. In the western Peloponnesus, Triphylia, the Pisatid, and the more spacious and powerful Elis, like the Achaean cities to its east, spoke Aetolian, or as it is now more commonly called, Northwestern Greek.[1]

Although some Dorians may have settled in the central Greek province of Doris, most emigrated south to the Peloponnesus and southerly islands, including Crete, Melos, and Rhodes, as well as to the southeast coast of Asia Minor. Branches of Northwestern Greek speakers apparently overran Boeotia and Thessaly, but they did not settle there in sufficient numbers to alter the basic Aeolic dramatically. Thus, except for backward, landlocked Arcadia, sophisticated maritime Attica, and Euboea, lying so close offshore that it might almost be considered part of the mainland, Dorians and speakers of Northwestern Greek dominated almost all of the rest of southern and central Greece. Both groups often enserfed the natives that they had overrun. Containing about 45,000 square miles, their states, which except for Corinth and Megara lacked good harbors, concentrated on agriculture, often of an almost subsistence form. Some, especially in the more northerly areas, had, like Arcadia in the center of the Peloponnesus, not yet even formed *poleis* by the beginning of the classical period. Only semi-hellenic Epirus, Macedonia, and Thrace, however, clearly failed to adopt pederasty by the end of the Archaic Age.

Whether the lords were rural knights, as in Thessaly, or urbanized hoplites, as in Argos, the typical upper-class Dorian or Northwestern Greek speaker was an unsophisticated athlete and warrior. The pederasty that they institutionalized remained close to their Cretan and/or Spartan models. Like the Spartans, the Thessalian and Boeotian knights did not retain the ritualized abduction and honeymoon of the Cretans, nor did the hoplites of Elis, Achaea, the Argolid, or Boeotia follow the severe rigor of their Spartan model. They had no obligatory common meals, herds of boys, public floggings, or *crypteia*. Yet one can discern a lifestyle almost as common as the dialects throughout all these regions.

By 480 B.C., everywhere that these dialects prevailed *erastai* trained *eromenoi* in gymnasia and at least sometimes fought alongside them in battle when they grew up. Courtship may have been much less sophisticated than in Ionia. Doubtless their symposia, too, were less elegant and less intellectual. It has often been remarked how few intellectuals there were among the Dorians, and their absence among the less-advanced Northwestern Greek speakers is even more apparent. Plato's Pausanias may not have been far off the mark when he said that Boeotians and Eleans were too rustic and inarticulate to court boys properly. However, Xenophon's claims that couples cohabited like husband and wife in Boeotia and that lovers won over boys in Elis by favors are, like Plato's disdainful judgments, not confirmed by independent testimony that has survived from natives of those regions.

Since high culture was relatively absent even from the wealthy commercial metropolises of Megara and Corinth, this lack cannot be explained solely by the rural and agricultural nature of most Dorian and Northwestern Greek–speaking societies. It must, I believe, be attributed largely to the type of pedagogic pederasty that they institutionalized, contrasting markedly with the one practiced among the more widely traveled, open-minded

Aeolians, Ionians, and Athenians, whose *poleis* were almost all heavily involved in commerce. Lasus and Cydias, two Dorians from the small Peloponnesian port of Hermione, have left us some trace of their achievements
(to be discussed below). Pratinas the playwright appears to have been the
most prolific of early Doric composers, and Eumulus of Corinth composed
epics. Still, it can be maintained that there were few Dorian intellectuals
of the first rank from the mainland before Pindar. Even Tyrtaeus may have
been an Athenian by birth, and in any case he was more famous for instilling courage than for demonstrating intellectual prowess. However much
the insistence on Dorian mental sluggishness among other Greeks may
be the result of Athenian propagandist denigration of their Dorian enemies, in the west, too, omitting the mad genius Empedocles of Agrigentum,
whose ancestry may not have been Doric, and the shadowy Epicharmus of
Syracuse, few Dorians, except perhaps for the obscure Cretan sages who
flourished before 600 and for Pindar, seem to have achieved intellectual distinction during the Archaic Age.

   Throughout the seventh and early sixth century, with the flourishing
of its orientalizing art, Doric Corinth and its colony Syracuse attracted
intellectuals and artists, but they apparently failed to produce comparable
geniuses of their own before the Persian invasions. Of course, the Dorians developed their severe temples and produced in a most traditional style
distinctive, fetching, if austere *kouroi* and *kourai*. In certain areas of the Peloponnesus they became famous for their bronzes and other metalwork, in
part because they had a plentiful supply of ore. However, although choral
odes were always composed in Doric in deference perhaps to their having
originated in that tongue, in poetry, and even more in philosophy and science, the Dorians long remained insignificant. Nearly all early intellectual
progress of note was, as far as we can tell, achieved solely by Ionians and
Aeolians.

Sources

For the mainland north of the Isthmus of Corinth, with the exception of
Pindar's poems, no real historical records exist before the classical period
outside of Athens, whose history is discernible from the time of Draco on
(c. 620). In his *Geography,* Strabo devoted three books out of seventeen to
Greece. Pausanias in his *Description of Greece* discussed Attica, Corinth and
the Argolid, Laconia, Messenia, Elis, Achaea, Arcadia, Boeotia, and Phocis
but left out the backward northern regions. Besides his life of Pelopidas, the
Boeotian Plutarch supplied in his other works certain information about
his native land as well as about other areas, as did Aristotle.

Of modern studies on the subject of mainland Greece before the rise
of Thebes in the fourth century we have on the one hand only general
histories that include—in fact overemphasize—Athens and Sparta to the
detriment of the other localities in question, and on the other, some specialized monographs on particular cities or areas. These works and their
scanty original sources will be referred to below as we come to the city or
area in question. It should be noticed, however, that not every area has even
today received a book-length study. In addition, few modern general histories or monographs discuss pederasty at all and none in depth. Because of
this double lack, I have used later data, including when possible the first recorded incidence of pederasty in each area. We are thus forced to speculate
about the spread of pederasty to central and northern Greece mainly on the
basis of legends and artifacts and to reconstruct conditions retrospectively
in the light of the history of later periods.

Athletic Elis

Eleans won fame as athletes perhaps in part because they took control of the
Olympic Games from their closely related neighbors the Pisatans, whom
they incorporated into greater Elis. Athenian intellectuals scorned them as
what we would call "dumb jocks" and berated them for grossly buying their
boys with favors instead of decorously persuading them with eloquence, of
which Eleans were deemed ignorant. Although their region may not have
formed any native cities before 470, these ethnically unified Northwestern Greek speakers developed early on distinctive religious festivals, by far
the most important of which were the Olympic Games. So far as we can tell
from the unreliable victory list drawn by Hippias of Elis, the Eleans regularly won until the Spartans began to surpass them in 720.

Pausanias's two books of his travels in Elis consist principally of a description of Olympia, where there were far more statues of Elean victors,
both youths and boys, than of any others. Doubtless no assemblage of statues so exalted male beauty as those, to which almost all the most famous
sculptors contributed. Indeed, the worship of the male body, which perme-
ated Greek culture from the sixth century on, could be said to have been
centered at Olympia in Elis. Although the males of the region were noted
for physical and athletic prowess, not for intellectual attainments, two exceptions, both of whom flourished in Athens rather than on their native
soil, are Hippias of Elis, our authority for the history of the Olympics, and
Phaedo (b. c. 417). Socrates instructed Phaedo after he had his friends pur-
chase the exceptionally beautiful youth out of a bordello in the Piraeus in

which Phaedo was working as a slave (Diogenes Laertius, II, 31). Afterwards, he supposedly founded a philosophical school in his native *polis*. His own teachings seemed to have centered on ethics. Gymnasia, in which all Olympic athletes were required by law to train for a month, dominated the city of Elis. Athletics was its main business and its chief claim to fame. Athenaeus recorded that "Elis became famous for its male beauty contests: Theophrastus . . . says that there is a beauty contest of men in Elis, that the trial is held with all solemnity, and that the winners receive weapons as prizes; these, says Dionysius of Leuctra, are dedicated to Athena, and the winner, beribboned by his friends, leads the procession which marches to her temple. But the crown given to the winners is of myrtle, as Myrsilus records in his Historical Paradoxes" (XIII, 609f). Maximus of Tyre, too, implied that the Eleans prized male beauty above all else (*Dissertations*, xxxix).

Maxims about the crudeness of Eleans abound, though none that survive were recorded before the classical period. When the Athenian musician Stratonicus (fl. c. 410–360), famous for his wit, "was asked whether the Boeotians were perhaps more uncivilized than the Thessalians he replied, 'the Eleans'" (Athenaeus, VIII, 350b). Xenophon repeated what Pausanias's statement in Plato's *Symposium* may have implied about Thebans and Eleans: "though sharing common beds they nevertheless assigned to their favorites places alongside themselves in the battle-line" (*Symposium*, VIII, 34). "I say nothing of the Eleans and the Thebans," declared Cicero, "among whom, in the loves of free-born young men, lust is actually allowed free rein" (*De Republica*, IV). Josephus alluded to "the unnatural vice so rampant among" the Eleans and Thebans (*Against Apion*, II, 273). Plutarch warned that "the sort of love prevailing at Thebes and in Elis is to be avoided, as well as the so-called kidnapping in Crete" and added, "that which is found at Athens and in Lacedaemon is to be emulated" (*On the Education of Children*, 12a). Maximus of Tyre censured the Eleans: "While I find the laws of the Cretans excellent, I must condemn those of Elis for their license. I praise the Cretans out of necessity, [but] I reprove the licentiousness of the Eleans" (*Dissertations*, xxvi, 8). Even in the fourth century the rhetorician Libanius echoed the traditional censures (II, *Oration* 19).

The earliest known Elean involved in a pederastic relationship was Phidias's *eromenos* Pantarkes, victor in boys' wrestling at the eighty-sixth Olympiad (436). In a relief under the feet of his greatest statue, the seated Zeus at Olympia, the sculptor apparently represented that *eromenos* tying a ribbon around his head (Pausanias, V, 11, 3). Generally thought to be the finest Greek sculptor, Phidias was perhaps better qualified than anyone to judge male beauty. The fact that he chose an Elean testifies to the outstanding beauty of those athletes who took such great pride in their bodies that they paraded them in their beauty contests. As we have seen, another, perhaps an even greater, connoisseur of boyish beauty, Socrates himself, chose an Elean youth, Phaedo, who devotedly attended him even in prison as he was dying from the effects of the hemlock. Do the censures of Plato and Xenophon against the Eleans countervail the refined taste of Greece's greatest sculptor and greatest philosopher?

Backward Arcadia and Achaea

In the mountainous center of the Peloponnesus, east of Elis and north of Sparta, lies Arcadia. The most backward region in southern Greece, so poor that during the classical period its young men often enlisted as mercenaries, Arcadia remained a land of villages until the fourth century. The Spartans, nevertheless, always worried how to keep their Arcadian frontier quiet if not subordinate. From the mid-sixth century, occasional attempts there to form cities and further democratic aspirations may have been related to outbursts against Spartan hegemony. We may well wonder whether the Arcadians were the last Hellenes to institutionalize pederasty.

The myth of Arcadia developed later amongst Hellenistic city dwellers who pined for the simple country life.[2] The naive shepherd lovers that they associated with this region give no evidence of an interest in training each other in gymnastics or in character. Sophisticates like Theocritus and Virgil imagined them to be easily aroused *ingénus,* bisexual or pansexual in their orientation.

Without any good harbors of its own, Achaea did not become important until the Hellenistic Age. Plutarch devoted two of his twenty-four surviving lives of Greek statesmen to Achaeans. One, the biography of Philopoemen of Megalopolis, suggests the presence of pederastic pedagogy there, for Philopoemen was educated by his *erastes* Craugis, who may himself have been the *eromenos* of Philopoemen's father.

The Dorian Argolid

The traditional rival of Sparta was Argos, located at a crucial juncture of roads in the northern part of the Peloponnesus.[3] Very proud of its Mycenean heritage, Dorian Argos reached prominence under Pheidon, whom some consider to have been in fact, if not in name, the first tyrant in Hellas.

Scholars have dated him anywhere between 895 and 600 or even later, but he seems actually to have flourished in the 670s.[4] Officially a king, he apparently restored the power of that ancient office which was everywhere else losing power to aristocrats and being relegated to a sort of high priesthood or judgeship. The heyday of Argos ended not long after Pheidon's death, though it continued to resist Sparta fiercely for centuries.

Although the Argives vengefully abetted the helots in the Second Messenian War, Sparta's total victory in that conflict and its reorganization soon thereafter finally allowed it to eclipse Argos. The city thus flourished before rather than after the institutionalization of pederasty, which it apparently adopted in a somewhat relaxed form. It produced no poets of note except Sacadas, one of the "musicians" who was credited with introducing the "Dance of Naked Youths" at Sparta (Plutarch, "On Music," 8). The abundance of metals in its territory encouraged its artists to produce sculptures of bronze. Polyclitus of Argos, perhaps Phidias's as well as Ageladas's greatest pupil, produced the Doryphoros ("youth holding a spear"), which over the ages inspired other sculptors. As he worked in bronze, none of his statues have survived, but a fine copy of the Doryphoros in the Naples museum seems to embody his theories about bodily rhythms and proportions (Pliny, *Natural History*, XXXIV, 55). Numerous copies of his Diadumenos (youth binding his hair) also survive. Both have been considered as attempts to depict the perfect male form. Even more than Phidias and Praxiteles, Polyclitus idolized the beauty and calm serenity of the athlete.

In the Late Archaic period Sicyon was already famed for pottery and painting (Pliny, *Natural History*, XXXV, 151–52). Although most no longer attribute proto-Corinthian vases to Sicyonians, the early flowering of the arts there may have established a tradition that led to the fourth-century apogee with some leading painters and their outstanding sculptor Lysippus, who emphasized sinewy and curvaceous male nudes.

Like other *poleis* in the Argolid, which was well supplied with metals, Sicyon was more famous for sculpture than for literature. However, it did produce Praxilla (fl. c. 451), one of the nine in the Hellenistic canon of women poets. She supposedly rivaled Pindar and like him sang of male pederasty. Her high reputation indicates that among some Dorians the tradition of educated, valiant females noted by Aristotle and praised by Alcman continued. She was known as a merry poet, a composer of drinking songs, and particularly of a hymn to Adonis, Aphrodite's favorite. One of her poems related Laius's abduction of Chrysippus. It made the Thebans the first lovers

of youths (Aelian, *Varia Historia*, XIII, 5). Elsewhere (fr. 7), she mentioned
Apollo's love for Carnus.[5]

We have evidence that at least one of the Argolid *poleis* was associated
with mythological and heroic pederasty: Troezen was the supposed site of
the love of Apollo for Hippolytus. Another city, Hermione, produced Lasus,
a learned rival of the pederastic poet Simonides at the court of the Athenian pederast Hipparchus. Perhaps the greatest Dorian scholar from the Archaic period, he composed hymns and pioneered the dithyrambs at Athens.
Hermione also produced the poet Cydias. Socrates called him "the wisest
man in matters of love" for his warning that someone who might fall in love
with a beautiful youth should be careful "in case like a fawn you come up
against a lion and are seized as his portion of flesh" (Plato, *Charmides*, 155de).[6]

Philistine Corinth

The Bacchiads, an aristocratic clan numbering about two hundred persons, ruled Corinth for ninety years until Cypselus (c. 657–625) overthrew
them. Like many other tyrants, Cypselus, whose dynasty lasted until c. 584,
rose to power on the turmoil caused by overpopulation and perhaps also
by the extension of military power from the knights to the heavily armed
infantryman. During the reign of his son and successor Periander (c. 625–
585), one of the Seven Sages of Greece, gymnasia and pederasty were, if not
first introduced, at least adjusted in the Spartan fashion in order to perfect
the hoplites. He became, if Aristotle is right, the first to anticipate the later
Persian practice of undermining pederastic tyrannicide by preventing males
from congregating at their traditional meeting places. According to the
Politics (1313b), Periander prohibited "common meals and club-fellowship"
out of a fear of sedition among the aristocracy. Ambracia, perhaps founded
by Gorgo, another son of Cypselus, saw its own tyrant Periander, a contemporary of Cypselus's son Periander of Corinth, murdered by his *eromenos*
in 581, allegedly because "when he was drinking in company with his eromenos he asked the lad whether he was yet with child by him" (Aristotle,
Politics, V, 1311a 36).

As the consequence of a revolt against Corinth by its colony of Corcyra,
Periander shipped to Sardis three hundred aristocratic youths whom he had
captured when he put down the rebellion so that his friend the Lydian king
Alyattes could have them castrated. On the way they were intercepted by the
Samians, who freed them (Herodotus, III, 48–49). The incident—very likely

an apocryphal tale—shows how familiar Archaic Greeks were with the Near Eastern preference for eunuchs, but it could also indicate Periander's growing fear of the tyrannicidal courage that pederastic relationships might inspire in aristocratic youths for, stripped of their virility, they would no longer suit the tastes of *erastai* and would be less likely to revolt.

Although Corinthian institutions were not so rigorous as those in Sparta, their symposia and other aspects of pederastic pedagogy do not seem to have given rise to an intellectual life. Corinth did become noted for its talented artisans. Corinthian vase painters, famous for about a generation or two for orientalizing ware before Athenians upstaged them (in part by stressing pederastic scenes on vases), were outstanding among other craftsmen of luxury items. The ornate Corinthian column, whose date of origin is unknown, may be considered another of its artistic contributions. The destruction of Corinth by the Romans probably caused a disproportionate loss of Corinthian manuscripts, but the lack even of references to Corinthian intellectuals in the surviving texts that often do speak of lost works by great Aeolians and Ionians indicates to what degree the classical Athenians, our main source of such knowledge, either did not know of any Corinthian writings or did not think them worthy to be mentioned, much less preserved.

Sober Megara

Situated at the other end of the Isthmus, Megara was less successful commercially than its rivals Corinth and Athens. Megara is, however, extraordinarily important to us because more complete verses from its pederastic poet Theognis survive than from all of his Archaic rivals combined. Except for Pindar, whose allusions are so subtle that many argued in the past that he was not pederastic, Theognis was the only other early writer of pederastic poetry of whom we have a more or less complete medieval manuscript.

Megara won fame for its spring festival featuring kissing contests between boys and youths. It was named the *Diocleia* for an Athenian youth, Diocles, who while living in exile in Megara sacrificed his life in battle to save his *erastes,* thus exemplifying the courage that so many Greeks thought typified pederastic lovers.[7] About 580 Susarion, another citizen, created the Megaran farces, which may well have been homoerotic. At least Theognis often put down the mercantile nouveaux riches, whom he thought bumptious in their efforts to imitate the ways of the landed gentlemen, including pederasty.

This aristocrat taught ethics and statecraft through his verses. In particular, his so-called Cyrnus poems, dedicated by Theognis to his young beloved, revealed the seriousness of the responsibility that the *erastes* took on when he became mentor to his *eromenos.* Some moderns call him the father of gnomic poetry and many view him as a lawgiver like Solon and Lycurgus. We know little else about him except that he fled into exile (vv. 1197–2000), believed in and expounded traditional aristocratic principles, and did not lack practical wisdom gained from political experience. One of his *scolia* reflects his emphasis on character and restraint: "In the fire the experts test silver and gold, but the mind of a man is laid open by wine, even the mind of an understanding man, who drinks beyond measure; so he is disgraced even if he was wise before" (499–502).

Although most now assign the poet to the mainland, certainty about where he wrote still eludes us almost as much as does the date at which he wrote. Plato, well aware of the poetic traditions from Sicily and having sojourned at the court of the Syracusan tyrants, believed that Theognis was a Sicilian (*Laws,* I, 630a). By assigning Theognis to Megara Hyblaea, a Megaran colony in Sicily, Plato may have meant to indicate that he found Theognis' verses recited there and regarded them as local.[8] The enormously erudite Didymus of Alexandria (c. 80–10) criticized Plato for assigning the poet to Sicily (scholiast on *Laws* I, 630 a). Like Plato, the *Suda* claimed that Theognis came from Sicilian Megara ("Theognis"). Perhaps Theognis emigrated from the original Megara to its colony in Sicily.

Of all the pederastic poets, Theognis was the most negative about this world: "the best lot of man is never to have been born" (425). Depressed about the brevity and unpleasantness of human life, he distrusted and scorned his fellow humans. In short, this cantankerous aristocrat who shunned wealth and praised self-control and piety had an attitude that in some respects foreshadowed that of the Stoics, if not the early Christians. Christian writers probably recopied Theognis's platitudinous maxims more readily than those of the livelier, more salacious poets because they deemed them to contain good advice and salutary exhortations. Inevitably, the pederastic themes caused difficulties. Whoever reedited Theognis's corpus appears to have tried to separate them out and relegated the pederastic poems to a separate, second book.

That said, Theognis was often indirect and intentionally vague when describing his effort "to attain what one loves." Characteristic are these images: "A lion trusting in its strength, I seized in my claws a fawn from under a hind, but did not drink its blood" (1278c–d). But he did somewhat crudely compare a youth to a horse "sated with barley" which has returned "to our stable seeking a good charioteer" (1249–52). Such ambiguity aside, no less an authority than Cicero tells us that the Archaic Greek poetry lost to us but known to him was lustfully pederastic (*Tusculan Disputations*, IV, 71).

It is impossible to know how many of the verses ascribed to Theognis stem from his predecessors, contemporaries, or later imitators. Among them are passages written by others or only slightly altered from those written by Mimnermus (795–96, 1020–21), Tyrtaeus (935–38, 1003–6), Solon (227–32, 315–18, 585–90, 1253–54), and Eunus (465–98 and perhaps also 667–82, and 1345–50).[9] Gregory Nagy has opined that on internal evidence the *Theognidea* could be attributed to the years between 640 and 479, that is, between the Homeric and the classical age. If so, they clearly were composed over several lifetimes.

Theognis's verses may have prevailed over all rivals at Athenian symposia, but that is only a deduction based on their survival. By his time, symposia certainly flourished in Megara (*Suda*, "Theognis"). He even furnished the names of members belonging to his club.[10] Through Theognis, Megaran symposia clearly influenced those of Athens. One of his verses also reflects the presence of gymnasia in Megara. In an elegy reminiscent of one by Solon, Theognis was in fact the first to use the term *gymnazein*:[11] "Happy is he who loves as he *exercises himself* and upon going home sleeps all day long with a fair boy" (1335–36). *Paiderastia* thus clearly constituted an essential dimension of aristocratic education in Megara,[12] and Theognis's poems to his chief *eromenos* Cyrnus became enormously popular.

The amorous verses are frequently joined with pessimistic considerations on the ingratitude and fickleness of *eromenoi*:

> I know well enough thou didst cheat me, lad: for I can e'en see through thee. (1311)

> On the neck of the lad-lover there ever sitteth a galling yoke that is a grievous memorial of love-of-strangers. (1357–58)

But he also said: "A boy shows gratitude, whereas a woman has no steady companion; she loves the man of the moment" (1367–68).

The mixture of moral platitudes and pederastic feeling that we find in Theognis may well surprise a modern reader, and yet it is through just such a conjunction of sentiments that we obtain insight into the social behavior that has inspired this study. The *Theognidea* includes moral precepts and songs to beautiful boys because pederastic pedagogy embraced the same spectrum of concerns. The multiple functions of Eros—god of love, god of honor and courage—reflect no less an amalgam of features. Entering this perspective of a continuum from moral rectitude to aesthetic perfection to physical pleasure may not be easy for a twentieth-century person, but it is essential to an understanding of the customs in question here. Werner Jaeger understood and as a result formulated this telling commentary of Theognis and his society:

> Cyrnus, the young man to whom the poems are addressed, was bound to Theognis by Eros. The poet obviously considers that bond to be the basis of the educational relationship; and it was meant to make man and boy a typical couple in the eyes of the class to which they both belonged. It is very significant that the first time we have an opportunity of studying Dorian aristocracy closely we should find that homosexual love is a ruling motive in their character. . . . It must be recognized that the love of a man for a youth or a boy was an essential part of the aristocratic society of early Greece, and was inextricably bound up with its moral and social ideals.[13]

Knightly Thessaly and Boeotia

Full of fertile fields, Thessaly and Boeotia resembled Crete in having bounteous pastures that supported a ruling class of knights. The knights of these northern provinces apparently adopted early on a Cretan type of pederasty. United under its *tagus* (head magistrate), Thessaly could field 6,000 cavalry and 10,000 hoplites, according to the boast of its militaristic leader Jason, tyrant of Pherae, who reigned from c. 385 until his assassination in 370 (Xenophon, *Hellenica*, VI, 1, 7).[14] In the first clearly datable instance of pederasty in Thessaly, the wife of Alexander, one of Jason's successors, apparently fell in love with his *eromenos*, whom the jealous tyrant imprisoned (Xenophon, *Hellenica*, VI, 4, 37).[15] The Thessalians were reputed to be as uncivilized as the Eleans and Boeotians, to whom they were compared (Athenaeus, VIII, 350b).

Farther south and more advanced was Boeotia, about two-thirds the size of Thessaly, which it resembled in climate and topography. Boeotia played a far greater role in the history of pederasty than did Thessaly. Its outstanding *polis*, Thebes, became on the mainland the legendary font of Greek pederasty. Boeotia itself was the locus of some of the pederastic legends of Heracles and Iolaus as well as of those of Laius and Chrysippus, of whom we have already heard.

Boeotia also figures in the legend of Philolaus and Diocles, who came to Thebes when Diocles fled Corinth to escape his mother's incestuous passion. Aristotle reports that at Thebes "Philolaus became their lawgiver, and among his measures there are some relating to the begetting of children. These the Thebans called 'laws of adoption.' They consist of an enactment, peculiar to Philolaus, which was designed to keep fixed the number of estates" (Aristotle, *Politics*, II, xii, 1274a 31). This law seems to have aimed at limiting the population and may well have, among other things, encouraged pederasty. Perhaps Philolaus was the anonymous lawgiver who, according to Plutarch, institutionalized pederasty there.

Thebes served for long periods as the effective capital of Boeotia. It possessed two gymnasia, one dedicated to Heracles, the other to Iolaus, often regarded in antiquity as his *eromenos*. To celebrate their love, the Thebans instituted the *Iolaeia* (Pindar, *Olympian VIII*, 84 and scholiast), a festival involving equestrian and gymnastic competitions in which victors won weapons and brazen vessels.[16] (Such behavior typified Dorian militaristic pederasty.) A shrine honoring Iolaus stood before the gate of the Proetidae in Thebes as late as the second century A.D., when Pausanias noted it (IX, xxiii, 1). There pairs of male lovers pledged their troth (Plutarch, *Pelopidas*, XVIII, and *Eroticos*, XVII).

About three miles outside the city walls stood the *Kabeirion*, the shrine of a mystery cult which arose in the sixth century, revolving around the immortal Kabeiros. *Kabeiroi* were non-Hellenic deities who promoted fertility and protected sailors. Phallic rites indicate their chthonic nature. The center of their rituals in historic times was Samothrace, but they existed in Lemnos and in Anatolia. Archeologists have unearthed votive offerings portraying a man and a youth holding an animal, a traditional courtship gift.[17] How this strange and poorly documented cult related to Greek pederasty is not clear.

Like the Eleans, who sponsored the Olympic Games, the athletic Boeotians incurred the displeasure of Xenophon and Plato: "In Elis and Boeotia, and where people are not clever speakers, it is simply laid down that it is right to gratify lovers, and no one young or old would call it wrong; as I think, they wish not to have the trouble of convincing the young, because they cannot argue" (*Symposium*, 182c). Plato and Xenophon notwithstanding, Boeotia became famous for heroic pederastic couples in the fourth century, when the Sacred Band composed of 150 pairs of lovers triumphed over Sparta. There is no parallel case in all of history of such extraordinary heroism among so many homosexually bonded couples, though the Carthaginians imitated it, and the Spartans may at times have placed lovers side by side in battle.[18] At Chaeronea in 338, all of them died heroically facing the invincible Macedonian phalanx and cavalry. Philip himself cried out when he saw their corpses: "Let no man speak evil of these heroes."

Pindar

Boeotia also produced the greatest of ancient Greek lyric poets. Although Pindar lived well into the classical period, this apologist for the Dorian aristocracy was, in spite of his cosmopolitan sophistication, the last of the poets of the old Doric tradition, of which Theognis is the only other whose works survive in significant quantity. His works and *scholia* on them, which date back to informed Alexandrians, and an ancient life of the poet supply the main biographical details. A birthdate of 522 is perhaps more likely than 518, but here we are dealing with a clearly historical personality and there are no serious questions about the authenticity of his poems.

Boasting of some Spartan ancestors, Pindar claimed to come from one of the noblest families of Cynoscephalae. He studied first at Thebes, then at democratic Athens under the musician Lasus of Hermione, who taught him to write for choruses. Because Corinna's criticism drove him to use more mythological allusions and because he subsequently defeated another woman poet, Myrtis, in competition, he was quite familiar with accomplished women, but he did not celebrate them in his surviving verses which to an overwhelming degree praised handsome, athletic youths.

Sicilian tyrants welcomed Pindar. He was brought to Syracuse by Hiero and to Agrigentum by Theron. He also visited the courts of Amyntas, king of Macedon, and of the noble clan of the Aleuadae in Thessaly, who gave him his first commission in 498. Like his rival Simonides, Pindar traveled over much of the Hellenic world. The two of them were the first lyric poets to compose for all the Greeks, not just for a certain locality or two, and the language of both contained a mixture of dialects that was more cosmopolitan than that of their predecessors.

Pindar purportedly died at the advanced age of eighty, and the gods granted him the greatest happiness—a marvelous death. Supposedly, while attending a contest at the theater in Argos, he died with his head resting on the shoulders of his beloved youth Theoxenus (Valerius Maximus, 9, 2). Pindar's tombstone was placed in front of the gate of the Proetidae at Thebes, where his ashes were interred.

Unable to reconcile morality with sodomy, Wilamowitz-Moellendorff initially insisted on speaking of Pindar's pederasty (as well as that of Socrates and Plato) as a sublimated love that uplifted its object:

> It is sensuality, to be sure, when Pindar as an old man admits that at the sight of young and handsome boys' bodies he melts like wax in a flame. But the old man who speaks thus has for the length of a lifetime been instilling the highest duties of male honor into the youth. A human being has achieved much if his soul has felt the need for love and the growth of the soul of his beloved forms part of his happiness. Certainly, the sin against nature one should not judge less mildly than did Euripides and Plato; but it is exactly Plato who teaches how the Socratic doctrine, mastering the desires of the senses, but freely confessing the pleasures of the senses, is rooted in that love which satisfies one's own longings when it instructs a fair soul in the path that leads to the highest.[19]

After the First World War a wiser, perhaps less inhibited Wilamowitz-Moellendorff quipped that those who did not appreciate Pindar's unreserved love of adolescents could not understand him: "The Delphic god never took offense at boy-love. Pindar's entire poetry can be understood only when one takes this presupposition without the slightest reserve into account."[20]

While not addressing directly the subject of Pindar's pederasty, Jaeger did describe the poet's relationship to sculpture, particularly to the *kouroi*. Competitive athletics developed the physique that Pindar and the sculptors idealized until a later period when "the Greeks began to feel that the spirit was distant from or even hostile to the body." Bodily beauty seemed to imply spiritual superiority, as in the case of Achilles and other heroes and of Pindar's victors, whom he compared to those models. Pindar thought "of himself as rivaling artists and sculptors,"[21] a point he made clear at the beginning of the *Fifth Nemean*: "No sculptor am I, that I should carve statues doomed to linger only on the pedestal where they stand. No! I would bid my sweet song speed from Aegina, in every argosy, and in every skiff, spreading abroad the tidings that the stalwart Pytheas, son of Lampon, hath won the crown for the pancratium at the Nemean games, ere ever he showed on his cheeks the hue of summer, the soft harbinger of youthful bloom."

The long-lived Pindar did apparently have several *eromenoi*. He nevertheless regretted not having sacrificed enough to Eros when he was young.[22] During his youth he supposedly fell in love with Thrasybulus, with whom he formed a lifelong friendship. From a prominent family of Agrigentum and a nephew of the tyrant Theron, that youth won the chariot race at the twenty-fourth Pythian games in 490. At that time Pindar was perhaps twenty-eight, about ten years older than the victor, whose grace and reticence he celebrated in one of his first epinicians. Twenty years later Pindar composed another (*Isthmian II*) to Thrasybulus's father Xenocrates, whose chariot won after the family had fallen from power when the democrats seized Agrigentum after Theron's death in 472. Other *eromenoi* seem to have been the flute-player Diodorus and a certain Agathon, mentioned only once in a fragment of a *scolion* preserved by Athenaeus (X, 427). Pindar apparently also loved Boulagoras of Phanagoreion until the youth reached age twenty-four, that is, some years beyond the age at which *eromenoi* were normally, at least in theory, given up (Ptolemy Chemnus, *History*, 7, in Photius, Codex 190).[23]

Even in his old age Pindar loved ephebes, whom he seemed to have preferred to younger adolescents. We know nothing more of his magnificent last boyfriend, Theoxenus, than what a surviving fragment tells us: he came from Tenedos; his father was called Hagesilas and his brother was an athlete. It was in a *scolion* addressed to Theoxenus that Pindar wrote what Magnus Hirschfeld has called "one of the most perfect love songs in the Greek language":[24]

> Meet it were, my heart, to cull the flowers of love in due season, in thy prime; but whosoever, once he hath seen the rays flashing from the eyes of Theoxenus, is not tossed on the waves of desire, hath a black heart forged, in cold flame, of adamant or of iron, and having no honour from Aphrodite of the quick glance, he either toileth brutally for wealth, or else through some woman's boldness his soul is borne along on every path while he serves her. But I, to grace the goddess, like wax of the sacred bees when smitten by the sun, am melted when I look at the young limbs of boys. (Athenaeus, XIII, 601c–d)

Although little is known of his life, more of Pindar's whole poems survive than of all earlier elegiasts, iambographers, and lyricists combined. A quarter of the seventeen books into which the Alexandrians collected Pindar's works celebrated with great force and exuberance the beauty as well as the character of athletes and the distinction of their ancestry and *polis.* Whether Pindar himself wrote out and collected his own works, which were too complex to be transmitted orally, and how the corpus may have been altered over the centuries we cannot know.[25]

The myths which dominate Pindar's epinician odes tend mostly to revolve around gods or heroes to whose stories he or others had appended homosexual episodes: Zeus, Apollo, Poseidon, and so on. In addition, many of the victors were described homoerotically. The *Eighth Olympian,* dedicated to Alcimedon of Aegina, said of him: "Comely was he to look upon, and verily he did not belie his beauty of form, when, by his victory in the wrestling match, he caused Aegina with her long oars to be proclaimed as his fatherland." To honor Agesidamus for his crown at the Olympics, Pindar described the youth in all the éclat of the beauty which won Ganymede immortality through the love of Zeus: "I, the while, who am eagerly lending a hand of help have taken to my heart the famous tribe of the Locrians, while I besprinkle with honey a city of noble sons; and I have praised the beauteous son of Archestratus, whom, on that day, beside the Olympic altar, I saw winning victory with the might of his hands,—one who was fair to look upon, and was graced with that bloom which, in olden days, by the blessing of Aphrodite, warded from Ganymede a ruthless fate" (*Tenth Olympian,* 97–105) In addition, he alludes to the life of symposia: "and [may I delight in] the graces of Aphrodisian Loves, that so, drinking deep with Cheimarus, I may fling the *cottabos* in a contest with Agathonidas."

Harmony marked Pindar's thought and expression. His nobility and profound religiosity gained him unreserved admiration among ancients. Unlike Theognis, the other great Dorian poet whose aristocratic ideals and belief in the inheritability of virtue he shared, Pindar radiated an Ionian enthusiasm for the cheerful enjoyment of life: "The first of prizes is good-fortune; the second falleth to fair fame; but, whosoever findeth and winneth both, hath received the highest crown" (*First Pythian,* 99–100). With due appreciation of restraint and moderation and devotion to religion, Pindar's verses were more pious than those of the frequently irreverent and unrestrained Ionians. This last great poetic defender of the dying aristocratic ethos lived removed from the statism, plutocracy, and democracy that were coming to the fore in his day.[26] Yet, like many of his predecessors as well as Plato and the poets of the *Greek Anthology,* Pindar did not doubt that Eros was irresistible.[27]

Phocis, Doris, and the Northern Marchlands

Phocis, to the west of Boeotia, along the north shores of the Corinthian Gulf, was most famous for Delphi, with its oracle. Phocians tried to control the shrine of Apollo, which in honor of the most beautiful of the gods contained almost as many statues idealizing male nudes as Olympia did. To the north of the numerous little Phocian towns lay the territories of Doris and Dryopis, which consisted of four small towns. Thucydides called Doris "the original homeland of the Spartans" (I, 107). Ironically and perhaps significantly, surviving sources say nothing at all about pederasty there. This fact further undermines the theory of a Dorian origin for pederasty and supports my theory that institutionalized pederasty spread from Crete to Sparta at first only to advanced areas that had *poleis*, which Archaic and even perhaps classical Doris did not.

The wildest and most mountainous region, Epirus, which lay in the northwest, had a cold climate with winter snows. It long remained primitive, without cities or Greek-style pederasty until the fourth century, although, as we have seen, Periander, the tyrant of the Corinthian colony of Ambracia on the coast of Epirus, was assassinated by his *eromenos* c. 581 (Aristotle, *Politics*, 1311a 36). Likewise, in the beautiful green Ionian islands off its coast and at Corcyra and other Corinthian colonies, with their harbors serving as stepping-stones between Greece and Italy, pederasty flourished early on, introduced by Corinthian merchants or colonists.

East of Epirus, Macedonia, a plateau broken by mountains, advanced sooner, especially because of its frequent contacts with the colonies that the Chalcidians established on the peninsula along its southern coast. It was not until the end of the fifth century, however, that the hellenizing kings of Macedonia introduced institutionalized pederasty to the natives. There it apparently had to compete with a native type of age-symmetrical homosexuality, in which adolescent noble boys loved one another, as we hear regarding Alexander and some of his companions (cf. Aelian, *Varia Historia*, VIII, 8; XII, 7).

Having an even colder climate than Macedonia because of the winds from the steppes, Thrace remained "barbarian" longer and imbibed more deeply the culture of the Scythians to whom it was so proximate. Unlike the Macedonians and even the Epirotes, the Thracians were clearly not Greek; and in fact they did not fully hellenize until Roman times. Nevertheless, they played a prominent role in the legends of homosexuality. The stories of Orpheus and Thamyris were set in Thrace. The Thracians, who seem, like the Macedonians, to have countenanced love affairs between adolescents, did not practice Greek-style pederasty in Archaic or classical times but probably had shamans. Thracian shamans may have influenced the "musician" Onomacritus, who, as we have seen, probably played a role in introducing pederasty to Crete. Anacreon, one of the most pederastic of poets, helped found Abdera c. 540, a city on the Thracian coast which became famous for its intellectuals, most notably Democritus.

Premature Euboea

Stretching some one hundred miles along the coast of central Greece from southern Thessaly to Attica, Euboea was so close to the mainland—only seven miles at the closest point—that it virtually formed a part of it. At the northern end of the straits that separate it from Boeotia, Chalcis rivaled the other main Euboean *polis* Eretria for control not only of the rich Lelantine plain that lay between them but also of Aegean trade. Each planted colonies in the west as well as in the Aegean and Pontus and each entered into a system of alliances that involved other major Hellenic ports. Only a bit before 600, when they had worn themselves out by their centuries-long rivalry, did Corinth in the west and Miletus in the east emerge as their commercial successors.

Euboeans may have played a crucial role in adapting the Phoenician alphabet to the Greek language and in the consolidation and transmission of the Homeric epics from Aeolia and Ionia to the mainland.[28] Their cultural contributions are, however, uncertain, in part probably because their early decline obfuscated whatever achievements they had made and because they sank in importance just as pederastic pedagogy was beginning to spark the Greek Miracle.

The long voyages of the Chalcidians may have accustomed them to situational pederasty from an early date. A strange tradition had a Thessalian cavalry officer, Cleomachus, introduce heroic pederasty to Chalcis:

> When the war between the Eretrians and Chalcidians was at its height, Cleomachus had come to aid the latter with a Thessalian force; and the Chalcidian infantry seemed strong enough, but they had great difficulty in repelling the enemy's cavalry. So they begged that high-souled hero, Cleomachus, to charge the Eretrian cavalry first. And he asked the youth he loved, who was by, if he would be a spectator of the fight, and he saying he would, and affectionately kissing him and putting his helmet on his head, Cleomachus, with a proud joy, put himself at the head of the bravest of the Thessalians, and charged the enemy's cavalry with such impetuosity that he threw them into disorder and routed them; and the Eretrian infantry also fleeing in consequence, the Chalcidians won a splendid victory. However, Cleomachus got killed, and they show his tomb in the market place at Chalcis, over which a huge pillar stands to this day. (Plutarch, *Eroticos,* 760e-761a)

It is just as likely, however, that frequent contact with Crete may have facilitated a direct importation. These Ionian islanders apparently institutionalized pederasty toward the end of their secular war around 600, before Solon brought it to Athens, as the use there of "chalcidize" attests. The Athenians later used *chalkidizein* interchangeably with *lakonizein* and *kretizein* to mean "to bugger."[29] Hesychius defined *chalkidizein* as "to pedicate" and added that "the male Venus was widespread" on Chalcis.[30] Athenaeus summed up a persistent tradition: "The Cretans, for example, as I have said, and the people of Chalcis in Euboea, have a marvellous passion for such liaisons [with boys]" (XIII, 601e). The Chalcidians, vying with the Cretans for the honor, claimed that the handsome Ganymede was abducted from a myrtle grove near their city.[31] Throughout their vast network of commercial and military alliances and colonies, the Euboeans may have been the most instrumental of all Greeks in spreading pederasty and its concomitant institutions as well as common weights and measures, monetary units, maritime laws, and hoplite tactics.[32]

No work of even a single Archaic or classical Euboean survives. We know too little about the pederasty of the region to see how, in being adopted, it came to differ from that of other lands, but we can presume that the Euboean colonies in the east and west followed their mother cities in institutionalizing their particular forms of pederasty, presumably less rigid and less oriented toward training the body than those of Crete and Sparta and more similar to that in Ionia. Perhaps the Euboeans may have first emphasized the *eromenos*'s need for intellectual training since he was likely to sail and trade all around the Mediterranean as an adult. Athens ultimately inherited the commerce, and perhaps also the pederastic system, of the Euboeans.

In this chapter I have tried to stress what evidence we possess for the diffusion of pederasty throughout sizeable areas of the Greek peninsula. Now we shall turn to the Aeolians and Ionians and to the developments that they brought to the same Cretan and Spartan innovations, even though, because of Persian invasions and occupation, Aeolia and Ionia were not able to profit from them over time.

Ten

Amorous Aeolia

Drink and get drunk, Melanippus, with me. Why do you suppose that when you have crossed the great river of eddying (?) Acheron you will see again the sun's pure light? Come, do not aim at great things. . . . Let us drink! Why do we wait for the lamps? There is only an inch of day left. Friend, take down the large decorated cups. . . . Mix one part of water to two of wine, pour it in brimful, and let one cup follow another at once.

— Alcaeus, fragments 38 A and 346

Some say a host of cavalry, others of infantry, and others of ships, is the most beautiful thing on the black earth, but I say it is whatsoever a person loves. It is perfectly easy to make this understood by everyone: for she who far surpassed mankind in beauty, Helen, left her most noble husband and went sailing off to Troy with no thought at all for her child or dear parents, but [love] led her astray . . . lightly . . . [and she?] has reminded me now of Anactoria who is not here; I would rather see her lovely walk and the bright sparkle of her face than the Lydians' chariots and armed infantry.

— Sappho, fragment 16

On the fertile belt of coastland that they occupied and on the large island of Lesbos, their center, the Aeolians profited early from their advanced neighbors. Interacting first with the precocious Phrygian kingdom and then with its Lydian successor, the Aeolians toward the end of the seventh century took the lead in culture over their fellow Greeks who lived in areas more remote from those civilized monarchies. But because the rugged hills greatly diminished commerce and other contact with the natives of the interior, the only Aeolian metropolis, Mytilene, turned to maritime commerce. It traded around the Aegean with other Greeks and also established contacts with Egypt and even Babylon before the end of the seventh century.

Sources

We do not have enough evidence on which to base a continuous narrative about the political, diplomatic, or military affairs of the east Greeks during the Archaic Age, nor indeed during the classical period either. On the other hand, we know a good deal about their culture, character, and intellect. Early poets as well as later prose writers attest their luxury. Fragments from and commentaries on Ionian philosophers shed light on their science and logic, but Aeolians seem to have eschewed intellectual analyses in favor of the emotions.[1] Sensuous, same-sex love seems to have been sung about first in Aeolia in all-male symposia and in rather mysterious female circles. Smaller and less populous than Ionia, Aeolia nevertheless apparently played a greater role in the development of Archaic and classical ideas of love.

No poet of love perhaps throughout all history has excelled or even equaled Sappho. Greek and Roman critics repeatedly extolled her verses. Her male contemporary Alcaeus, the first, according to some, to compose erotic poems, also won renown. Both of them inhabited Mytilene. The remarkable recovery of more and more of their verses—sadly only scanty fragments—from papyri has necessitated a reevaluation of these poets.[2] Since the 1950s, and for the first time in modern history, almost everyone has recognized them as having written unambiguously about same-sex love.

According to tradition, Sappho and Alcaeus began composing verses accompanied by the lyre around 600.[3] Today, we possess only one or perhaps two complete poems by Sappho. She was so subtle, one might even say coy, that even in antiquity, when all of her works were still extant, legends sprang up that she had addressed her poems to males rather than to the aristocratic girls to whom she is now believed to have written them. Though we do not have even one complete poem by Alcaeus, ancient testimonies, that is, comments of critics and other scraps of information about the lives and works of the lyric poets, and the exiguous fragments, particularly those about symposia, now prove almost beyond a reasonable doubt that he loved adolescent males. Modern scholars have also established the lesbian intent of Alcman's choral odes. Thus ironically two out of the three earliest erotic poets presumably referred to female homosexuality, which was hardly to be mentioned again not only during the Archaic but even during the classical period, when it may have become a taboo subject in Athens. In fact seldom thereafter did Greeks write about lesbianism, although male pederasty was destined to play an integral if not preponderant role in Greek culture as long as it remained pagan.

Mytilene

Mytilene possessed an excellent double harbor commanding the straits between its island and Anatolia. Despite factional strife, it rose sometime before 600 to become a major emporium. It developed commercial connections with Egypt, where it was one of the twelve partners in the Greek emporium at Naucratis, but during the mid-sixth century it lost ground to the rising power of Miletus, Athens, Phocaea, and Samos. After the Persians conquered it, Mytilene failed, like the other Aeolian *poleis,* to produce any literary figures of note before the historian Hellanicus in the fifth century and Ephorus of Cyme in the fourth. Thus its brief new pederastic culture and poetry of love had to take more permanent root elsewhere.

As in Athens, the first aristocratic conspiracy at Mytilene failed. A second one killed the last king, about 620. The sense of loyalty among its nobles was heightened by the *hetairiai,* clubs modeled on the Spartan *syssitia* where brothers, cousins, and more distant kin bonded through drinking bouts into courageous, if disruptive, factions and fighting bands. Alcaeus sang about the tight bonding and heroism within such a group: "It is a fair thing to die for Lord Ares" (400). During peacetime, though, the club members would harass and even fight rival groups.[4] While Solon mentioned gymnasia specifically but not symposia, Alcaeus described symposia at length with approbation, but did not mention gymnasia or palaestras.

Civil strife at Mytilene called forth Melanchrus, a tyrant who imitated the rule of the former kings. Created and maintained by an unstable alliance of clans, that aristocrat was assassinated about 612 as a result of a conspiracy that arose within Alcaeus's clan. Pittacus, who carried out the assassination, became a hero and, in time, ruler of Mytilene. He apparently did not violently alter the constitution (Aristotle, *Politics,* 1274b 18). He did have his new laws "painted up on wood."[5]

Pittacus was named as one of the Seven Sages in virtually every list. He won a high reputation for boldness, heroism, cleverness, sagacity, and success. But Alcaeus denounced him violently. Alcaeus's viewpoint and tone resemble the passionate condemnation of the new men and regret for the overthrow of the old aristocratic order expressed by Theognis, who was probably slightly younger than Alcaeus.

It seems probable that just as Solon and Periander institutionalized pederasty in Athens and Corinth respectively, so their contemporary Pittacus included it among his new laws for Mytilene. Thales of Miletus, another of the sages, who is dated by his foretelling of the eclipse in 585, never married, according to some, "and adopted his sister's son" (Diogenes Laertius, I, 26). Highly respected by his fellow citizens, he seems a likely candidate to have brought the system into Ionian Miletus.

Alcaeus

The earliest lyric poet of whom any works at all survive, Alcaeus was born c. 620 and died after 580 (Diogenes Laertius, "Heracleitus"). Greek testimonia are, with one exception, not very explicit about Alcaeus's pederastic love of youths. They do speak about his *scolia;* indeed, although Theognis first used the word for symposium, Alcaeus used a form of it (*sympotes*). The most pertinent of Greek testimonia about Alcaeus's *scolia* and their long-lasting and widespread influence comes from Athenaeus: "Most [of the dinner-guests] made mention of the well-known 'scolia' or drinking-songs of Attica, which are worth recalling to you because of the antiquity and simple style of their composers, especially those who have won praise for this form of poetry, Alcaeus and Anacreon, as Aristophanes shows in the [lost] *Banqueters:* 'Take and sing me a scolion from Alcaeus or Anacreon'" (XV, 693f-694a). Aristophanes bracketed Alcaeus with the extremely pederastic Ibycus and Anacreon, thus suggesting that Alcaeus, too, praised and practiced pederasty (*Thesmophoriazusae,* 161–63).[6]

Latin critics were more explicit about Alcaeus's pederasty. According to Cicero, "Alcaeus was a brave man and eminent in the state to which he belonged, and yet what extravagant things he says of the love of youths!" (*Tusculan Disputations,* IV, 71). He also mentioned a curiosity about the poet. It is possible that the following line referred to Alcaeus the poet, though some have conjectured that it alluded to an Epicurean philosopher of the same name: "Alcaeus 'admires a mole upon his favourite's wrist'; of course a mole is a blemish on the body; but Alcaeus thought it an ornament" (*On the Nature of the Gods,* I, 79). Horace said of Alcaeus: "Come sing me a Latin song, thou lyre first played by a citizen of Lesbos, a gallant warrior who, alike amid the very fight or when his storm-tossed ship was moored to the wet shore, sang of Bacchus and the Muses, of Venus and her inseparable boy, and of the beautiful Lycus so dark of eye and hair" (*Odes,* I, 32, 3–11). In the early 1980s, as the papyrus fragments were being studied, several scholars proved beyond a reasonable doubt that Alcaeus was a pederast.[7]

Already in the mid-nineteenth century, when so little of Alcaeus's corpus had been recovered, the poet's editor, Theodor Bergk, perceived Alcaeus's pederastic efforts in fragments 346, 386, and 397, in addition to fragments 366 and 368, whose pederastic content has not usually been contested. All of these fragments show a pattern: in sharp contrast to practices in early Crete, Boeotia, and Sparta, elsewhere apparently a man might have several boyfriends over his lifetime instead of the one who would remain a close friend and even fight alongside him in battle.

Alcaeus and his boon companions seem to have banqueted together whenever possible, even during peacetime, and his drinking songs were directed to such a group[8] and were perhaps preserved and recomposed by them orally for some generations before being written down. (Even new songs by others may have entered the collection attributed to him.) Sanctifying their mutual fealty with wine, food, garlands, and common cults, the symposiasts amused one another with hymns, riddles, jokes, invectives, and love songs. Reminding his *hetairia* that they met in the presence of arms (140), Alcaeus by turns praised them ("You are splendid: be what you are!") and berated them ("You are despicable: change!"). He lampooned Hermes and Dionysus and praised Apollo in three hymns, now lost, which were "all marked by motifs of youth." Alcaeus's Eros was "quick, bright, soft . . . and inconstant." He said to his lyre: "Child of rock and foaming sea! . . . You soften the wits of boys, oh sea-born tortoise shell!" (359).[9]

From Book 7, in which the Alexandrian editors placed the erotic poems, several fragments, some of which seem to be sympotic, survive. Addressed to Melanippus and Menon, they attempted perhaps to mentor those beautiful youths. Verses addressed to Menon, one of Alcaeus's *eromenoi,* invite the lad to dine and enjoy the pleasures of flirting with him as an interlude of relaxation from civil strife and encounters in arms.[10]

The usually thorough Burnett overlooked the possibility that two fragments suggest that Alcaeus had another *eromenos:* "You used to be a friend— someone to invite to kid and pork: such is the custom in these matters" (71). A scholiast on the margin of the papyrus that contains this verse said that it refers to "the boy whom Alcaeus loved." Fragment 73 refers to "being young in company with you all, and together with Bycchis to . . ." It may be that Bycchis was another of Alcaeus's *eromenoi.*

Fragment 374 may refer to a comast, the serenader of boys in the street or at their homes (see fig. 15). (Presumably the adolescent was still too young to frequent a symposium.) It has been translated variously:

Pray, pray receive, receive your serenader. (version in Loeb *Lyra Graeca* [1928], 1:399)

Welcome me, the reveller, welcome me, I beg you, I beg you. (version in Loeb *Greek Lyric* [1982], 1:401)

The main function of drinking for Alcaeus was to bond the comrades in the *hetairia*. Alcaeus praised drink almost as much as Anacreon did: "For wine was given to us by the son of Zeus and Semele, so that we might put all our cares to sleep. Pour it out double strength—to the brim!" (346). Wine could also consecrate pledges and reveal character (as well as make boys more willing to give in). Alcaeus constructed a dilemma. The youth who had drunk lightly so as to enhance his charm would resist advances and might become surly if pushed, but one who had become inebriated to the point of being willing and available was no longer very desirable or able: "But if the wine once soaks into his wits, he isn't worth the chase. His head hangs down, he blames himself repeatedly and takes back all he's said, but—that certain thing is gone, and can't be had!" (358). Despite such complexities, Eros could make one forget the worst disasters and the symposium could console one for life's dangers and disappointments.[11]

Sappho

Although this study is concerned with (male) pederasty, Sappho's poetry must be mentioned since it represents such a clear parallel in the world of females to cardinal features of Greek pederastic practice. The fragments that bear Sappho's name depict not only the familiar age-asymmetrical relationship of pederasty but also the pattern of temporary loves repeated with new individuals. In addition, the verses convey the impression of a mentor-pupil bond focused on communicating to the younger person a reverence for the Muses and instruction in manners and character.

More pertinent still to our investigation is the widespread recognition among the ancients of the intensity of feeling in Sappho's poetry. Consider Plutarch's remark:

Sappho speaks words mingled truly with fire; through her song she communicates the heat of her heart,

"With sweet-voiced Muses healing her love,"

as Philoxenus says. Now Daphnaeus, if through the influence of Lysan-
dra you have not completely forgotten your old loves, recite for us
the ode in which the fair Sappho describes how her voice is lost and
her body burns; how she turns pale, reels, and grows giddy when her
beloved appears. (*Eroticos*, 763a)

In pseudo-Lucian's *Erotes* (Loves), which praised Eros, the pederast Callicratidas seized on fragment 31 to argue that women could be as eloquent
in poetry as men were in the forum. Apuleius, too, saw the power in this
poetry: "Sappho has written passionate and sensual verses, certainly wanton, but yet also so graceful that the wantonness of her language captures
the reader's favour by the sweet harmony of words" (*Apology*, 9).

Here again a love that modern society has censured and denounced
emerges as the wellspring of once admired literature, a literature, moreover,
that like Theognis's *scolia* prospered for generations among the ancients. To
be sure, there was no consensus in antiquity about Sappho's sexual orientation.[12] My contention in this book, however, is not that the success of
institutionalized pederasty should be equated with a universal acceptance in
ancient Greece of that custom, but that for those whom it touched, whether
directly or indirectly, as in the case of the voice in Sappho's verse, the ca-
pacity to inspire was considerable and remarkably enduring. Unfortunately,
the east Greeks could not continue to mold their accomplishments. In the
mid-sixth century they were overrun by the Persians.

Eleven

Insouciant Ionia

Come my boy, bring me the cup, that I may drink bottoms up.
I'll mix ten measures of water with five of wine, for I do not
want to carouse again with a lack of decorum. Let us not again
behave like drunken Scythians with roaring and stamping of
feet, but drink politely to each other with fair song.

— Anacreon, fragment 43

Ionians deserve even more credit than Aeolians for laying the foundations of classical culture. Their poets — carefree Anacreon, Mimnermus, and
the gnomist Phocylides — continued the traditions begun by Alcaeus and
Sappho. In their elegant symposia, Ionians discussed physics and philosophy
as well as politics, heroism, and love. When the Persians overran this precocious civilization in the second half of the sixth century, émigrés took their
lifestyle and their worldview not only to Athens but to Ionian colonies in
Magna Graecia and Sicily. These refugees took with them a belief in ratio-
nality that is the foundation for science and philosophy, Aeolian ideas of
love which they had imbibed, and a fondness for the symposium as a plea-
surable, yet intellectual and, at times, political, institution.

More numerous than the Aeolians, the Ionians settled the middle Anatolian coast and its offshore islands. Enriched in mind as well as purse by contact with the Phoenicians and Egyptians, the Ionians soon surpassed their
mentors. Prudence and knowledge became the first object of instruction in
their maritime societies. These qualities were more valuable to merchants
and sailors than the traditional brute strength and courage exemplified by
Achilles and the other aristocratic heroes or the loyalty and discipline perfected by Spartan pederastic pedagogy, so essential to the hoplites of the
phalanx. Of all the pederastic heroes from tyrannicides to partners in battle,
few cases can be cited from Aeolia or Ionia proper or, for that matter, from

their colonists in Sicily and Magna Graecia or around the Propontis and the
Black Sea. Aeolians and Ionians, though hardly craven, produced explorers
and geniuses rather than invincible athletes and warriors.

In the late seventh and sixth century, as the love of youths spread rapidly
throughout all the advanced areas of Hellas, new literary forms evolved and
old ones may have been written down for the first time. With the exception
of Tyrtaeus and Theognis, all the early elegists were Ionians.[1] In their poems,
often erotic *scolia* to be recited at symposia, Ionian poets sang of their multiple love affairs. If the Ionian iambics and elegies and Aeolian lyrics, along
with Doric choral odes did not completely displace the epics, at least in the
lighter moments of the symposia they rivaled their popularity.

In spite of their trading connections to Crete, the Ionians may have
adopted pederasty from Sparta or from Euboea rather than from Crete. Ionians had no ritual kidnapping, for example, and no herds. They apparently
transformed Spartan or Cretan pederasty from a compulsory, initiatory
obligation into a more voluntary and intellectually oriented relationship,
perhaps like that which evolved in the ports of contemporary Euboea, also
Ionian-speaking and mercantile. In any case, before their annexation by the
Persians, the inhabitants of Greater Ionia—including the Aegean islands—
acquired a reputation for the unmeasured love of adolescents and of luxury,
as well as for philosophy and physics. Speaking of his own time, Plato, however, denied that the Ionians sanctioned pederasty, ascribing its suppression
there to local tyranny. We have hardly any of their laws and none on pederasty, nor any comprehensive description of their customs, which clearly
varied from *polis* to *polis* and changed as tyrants and aristocrats, vying for
power, frequently altered the constitutions of individual *poleis*.

Sources

Fragments and testimonies are our main source for pederasty among the
Archaic Ionians. In addition, similar but fewer fragments and testimonies
about their pre-Socratic philosophers help us understand more about symposia and other institutions related to pederastic pedagogy. Unfortunately,
we have no comprehensive accounts of Ionian pederasty comparable to that
of Ephorus for Crete and Xenophon and Plutarch for Sparta. Many scattered
references to "Lydian" or "Ionian" luxury, which both the Church Fathers
and nineteenth-century German classicists often used to imply homosexual
indulgence, induce one to conclude that Ionian pederasty, if more intel-

lectual, was also perhaps more effete, if not more sensual, than the Dorian type seen in Elis and Boeotia or in Crete and Sparta.

Tragically, not a single Ionian poet or philosopher had his works preserved in manuscript. Also, there are few surviving statues (*kouroi*) and no erotic vase paintings or graffiti from Ionia itself or anywhere in the east, if one excepts those from Dorian Thera. Neither Plutarch nor Cornelius Nepos wrote a life of a single Ionian or of any other east Greek who lived during the Archaic or classical age. Thus we do not have even one extant biography of an Archaic east Greek save those in the brief *Lives of Eminent Philosophers* of Diogenes Laertius. Herodotus and Thucydides did not say a word about the pederasty of any Archaic Ionians, except for Polycrates and his court. We have, therefore, to rely heavily here on deductions about the interrelation of pederasty with palaestras and symposia and with the Seven Sages.

Although the appreciative Alexandrian scholars (and perhaps before them some Athenian compilers) edited the works of the Ionian poets as carefully as they did the other works which have survived from Homer to Aristotle, almost all of the compositions of the pre-Socratics, who were predominately Ionian, have perished. Fortunately, since the late nineteenth century some papyri containing lines of those pederasts have been recovered from the sands of Egypt. Parts of others were quoted in works that did survive. Roman imitators or translators preserved the sense of still more verse. In addition, Greek and Latin commentators described their lost masterpieces and often ranked them in order of excellence or of salaciousness.

Miletus

The greatest of all the Greek cities in Anatolia, Miletus, called itself "First Foundation of Ionia, Metropolis of numerous great cities in the Pontus and Egypt and many other parts of the World."[2] Its name is said to have come from that of a Cretan youth, for whose affections Cretan kings were fighting. According to Apollodorus: "Now Asterius, prince of the Cretans, married Europa and brought up her children. But when they were grown up, they quarrelled with each other; for they loved a boy called Miletus, son of Apollo by Aria, daughter of Cleochus. As the boy was more friendly to Sarpedon, Minos went to war and had the better of it, and the others fled. Miletus landed in Caria and there founded a city which he called Miletus after himself" (III, 1, 2).

Despite this reputed link between Miletus and pederasty, there is no proof that the city's greatest poet, the gnomic elegist Phocylides, was pederastic. As with other Archaic Ionians, we can espy in the poet's surviving fragments attitudes and themes reminiscent of pederastic writers, but no concrete evidence of his or their sexual attitudes. Thus, although we can say that Phocylides certainly endorsed symposia and club life: "When the cups go round at a drinking-bout we should quaff our wine quietly amid pleasant talk" (Athenaeus, X, 428b), it is impossible to say more than that he confirms the presence in his city of an institution that elsewhere played a central role in pederastic verse.

Colophon

Inland some ten miles north of Ephesus, near the temple of Clarian Apollo, stood Colophon. Ionians colonized the Carian and Cretan settlement there. The sack of Colophon by Gyges of Lydia in 665 and a second sack during the Cimmerian invasion may explain the paucity of information about it. Although never a *polis* of the first rank, it did produce two outstanding intellects.

Whereas the *Suda* said that Mimnermus flourished in the thirty-seventh Olympiad (632–629), the Ionian elegist seems actually to have written a few decades later. He referred to an eclipse which seems to be that of 585 because the alternate possibility of 648 would place him too early to have corresponded with Solon. He adopted the elegiac couplet developed for patriotic and gnomic poems to verses about the love of women (and perhaps also of boys) and the joys of drinking.

Of Mimnermus's elegies, edited by the Alexandrians in two books, one of which was called Nanno after the flute girl whom he is said to have loved,[3] Horace quipped: "If, as Mimnermus believes, there is no joy without love and jests, then you should live in love and jests" (*Epistles,* I, 6, 65). According to Mimnermus, one should gratify one's own soul and pleasure lies in the enjoyment of love, for which youth grants the possibility. For this reason youth is worthwhile, old age worthless, hated and dishonored, and therefore worse than death (1–3). Mimnermus was equally quick to praise joie de vivre and pleasures of the body. His poetic quality impressed even Propertius: "In love Mimnermus is worth more than Homer. Tender are the songs that peaceful love demands" (I, ix).

The love that Propertius refers to is heterosexual. Did Mimnermus write also of the love of male adolescents? Like the pederastic lyricists, he definitely lamented the evanescence of youth and of love-inspired happiness: "But we, like the leaves that come in the flowerly Springtime when they grow up so quickly beneath the sunbeams, like them we enjoy the blossoms of youth for a season" (Stobaeus, *Florilegium*, 98, 13). Two other excerpts speak about the rapid waning of youth in a male. Their suggestion that with the loss of youth vanish both honor and love would have particular meaning for a world of institutionalized pederasty, but neither poem expresses amorous feelings for a beautiful youth. "However fair he may once have been, when the season is overpast he is neither honoured nor loved, nay, not by his own children," says one (ibid., 98, 116). The other declares that "to boys [an old man] is hateful, to women contemptible" (ibid., 63, 16). In each instance Mimnermus's lines reflect an atmosphere entirely consonant with a pederast's concern and as such are no less instructive here than the overtly pederastic words of Theognis.

The other important Colophonian, the skeptical philosopher Xenophanes, was said to have lived almost a hundred years (c. 570-c. 470). Like so many Ionians, he fled to the west to escape the Persians and apparently long sojourned in Elea, an Ionian colony south of Naples. He also tarried awhile in the Sicilian *poleis* of Zancle and Catana before perhaps visiting the court of Hiero of Syracuse. Like Plato, whom he undoubtedly influenced, Xenophanes condemned the "useless luxuries" of his fellow townsmen and deplored the elevation of athletic prowess (as distinct from training for war) over mental cultivation: " 'Tis very unconsidered, the custom of man in this matter; it is not right that strength should be judged worthier than most hold skill. For not though a city had a good boxer, nor a five-event-man, nor a good wrestler, not yet a good runner—which of all the deeds of man's letter ordered; and but little is the joy a town would get in a man's victory beside the banks of Pisa, for a city's treasure-houses are not fattened so" (Athenaeus, X, 413f-414c). Is this not clear testimony of Ionian reaction against undue (Dorian) emphasis on athletics?

The Aegean Islands

The island of Chios, supposed home of Homer, is located at the northern end of Ionian settlement, just south of Lesbos. Between the Homeridae and the multifaceted tragedian Ion (c. 490-c. 421), the island produced no major writers, but Ion did reflect in the following elegy a long-standing sympotic tradition on the island: "Let the wine-bearers mingle us a bowl and pour out into the cups of silver, while another with a golden jar in his hands sets it on its base . . . let us drink, let us play, let song rise into the night, and someone dance a fling, and do thou begin good fellowship with a will" (Athenaeus, XI, 463b).

Ceos nurtured Simonides, but such a small society could not provide adequate scope or re . . . for this important talent. Simonides and his nephew Bacchylides emigrated to Syracuse. As a result, they will be discussed later in connection with that city.

Samos

As the Persians exacted tribute from, besieged, and annexed the Greek cities of Anatolia, Samos emerged as the commercial and intellectual center of Ionia. Raising that island to its peak between 540 and 522, the brilliant tyrant Polycrates, said to have collected a library which became central to the island's culture, patronized eminent intellectuals and artists. With his proverbial wealth, Polycrates enticed the physician Democedes of Croton by offering him twelve times more salary than he was earning in Pisistratid Athens and hired the Megaran engineer Eupalinus to build his famous tunnel (Herodotus, III, 60, 133). Rhoecus and Theodorus of Samos are named as the inventors of large-scale bronze statuary, which began in this period. Rhoecus was also said to be the architect commissioned by Polycrates to build the Heraion, one of the first large-scale temples using the Ionic order.

Although we have only a few fragments from the Samian historians, the isolated facts available to us leave no doubt that Polycrates was pederastic. Athenaeus records the astonishment of a certain Alexis, a participant at one of his dinners: "the tyrant is nowhere recorded as having summoned to his court women or boys, although he was passionately devoted to liaisons with males, so much so as to be a rival of the poet Anacreon; at that time he even cut off his *eromenos'* hair in a burst of temper" (XII, 540e–f). Indeed, the best documented advance toward the creation of classical pederasty with its emphasis on pedagogy and creativity occurred on Samos.

Polycrates created a sort of intellectual hothouse for philosophers, poets, and artists that anticipated the atmosphere of classical Athens. It may well be that his circle was the first such gathering of pederasts in all history that we can document, because the group that his slightly younger contemporary Hipparchus formed in Athens was a bit later and the Pythagorean clubs in Italy, which seem to me to be pederastic, are less clearly attested in the sources. Despite charges in antiquity that the tyrant led a dissolute life, the *Paulys Realencyclopädie* gives a more positive appraisal of his regime:

Polycrates was undoubtedly a born ruler, gifted as much with a sharp eye for real political power relationships as likewise with outstanding comprehension for economic matters; under his regime Samos experienced its first and only efflorescence. . . . Remarkably touching in this regard is again a trait of social welfare: thus he cared for the mothers of soldiers who had fallen in his service by assigning them to a well-to-do citizen who had to provide for their maintenance. (Duris in Zenobius V, 94; *Paroe-miographi graeci*, I, 146)

However we judge Polycrates, the relationship between his court at Samos and the poet Ibycus is clear.

Ibycus

Polycrates or rather, according to the *Suda,* his father, who was also tyrant, attracted to his court Ibycus, the most licentious and promiscuous of the pederastic poets. Like his contemporary rival Anacreon, Ibycus continued to lust after youths well into old age, as Plato noted: "Parmenides replied, I cannot refuse, although I feel like the old race horse in Ibycus, who trembles at the start of the chariot race, knowing from long experience what is in store for him. The poet compares his own reluctance on finding himself, so late in life, forced into the lists of love" (*Parmenides,* 137a).

Ibycus came from a noble family of Rhegium at the toe of Italy. The *Suda* said that he flourished in the fifty-fourth Olympiad (564–561). Eusebius-Jerome, however, gave the sixty-first (536–533). He was probably too early to have been the son of a Pythagorean because Pythagoras himself stayed in Samos at least until Polycrates seized power c. 540 (Porphyrius, *Vita Pythagorae* 9; Diogenes Laertius, VIII, 3) and did not found his Italian brotherhoods until later. Nor is it likely that Ibycus visited another poet of pederastic love, Stesichorus (c. 630–c. 554) of Himera in Sicily, to whom he may nevertheless have been poetically indebted.[4] With abandon, he sang the praise of beautiful youths and symposia as well as sometimes of flirtatious women. His admissions of the power of love over him are particularly poignant: "In the spring the quinces, watered by the river streams, bloom in the unspoiled garden of the maidens; and the first shoots of the vine, guarded beneath shady leaves, grow and blossom; but for me love—that, like the Thracian north wind, blasting beneath the lightning and rushing, dark and fearless, from Cypris with scorching madness—is never at rest, and holds possession of my mind throughout my life" (Athenaeus, XIII, 601b).

In another statement of Love's sway, we encounter the earliest and most elaborate occurrence of a topos that later became commonplace: the lover captivated by the eyes of his beloved: "Yet again will Love eye me tenderly from beneath dark brows and cast me with manifold magic into the hopeless net of Cypris. I swear his approach makes me tremble like an old champion-horse of the chariot-race when he draws the swift car all unwillingly to the contest" (*scholia* on Plato's *Parmenides* 136e). The idea that love flashes forth or drips from the eyes of the beloved and the image of prospective lover as an object to be snared ("the hopeless net of Cypris") were extremely widespread throughout classical antiquity. Through its verse the images went on to inspire the love poetry of the Renaissance.

Ancients testified to Ibycus's lasciviousness and devotion to boys. One anonymous contributor to the *Greek Anthology* honored Ibycus by placing him in the company of the greatest pederastic poets:

> Pindar, holy mouth of the Muses, and thou, Bacchylides, garrulous Siren, and ye, Aeolian graces of Sappho; pen of Anacreon, and thou, Stesichorus, who in thy works didst draw off Homer's stream; honeyed page of Simonides, and thou, Ibycus, who didst cull the sweet bloom of Persuasion and of the love of lads; sword of Alcaeus, that didst often shed the blood of tyrants, defending his country's laws, and ye nightingales of Alcman, singing ever of maidens; look kindly on me, ye authors and finishers of all lyric song. (IX, 184)

Ibycus's sixty-seven fragments in the 1924 Loeb edition were preserved by scholiasts, grammarians, and antiquarians. Unfortunately, only one fragment comes from a papyrus (*Oxyrhynchus Papyrus*, XV 1790). Of the others, most are merely words and phrases. The longest by far (forty-eight lines, not all of which are complete), the papyrus fragment is the dedication of a collection of poems to Polycrates. It begins with a series of allusions to Helen and the Trojan War but concludes by lauding the beauty of "Troilus, for loveliness of form" likened to "gold, thrice refined." The conclusion links Polycrates to the "beauties" of Homeric legend and then to the poet who immortalizes him in song. The historical setting of the poem is disputed. Some see in it a work composed toward 564–560, when Ibycus would have arrived in Samos if invited by the elder Polycrates; others prefer to assign it to the years 536–533, and would make the Polycrates glorified by the poet the younger of two tyrants by that name. What is indisputable about the text is its unabashed glorification of youthful male beauty, one of the hallmarks of the pederastic mentality. Cicero perhaps best summarized the poet's talent: "What extravagant things Alcaeus writes on the love of youths! and as for Anacreon, his poetry is erotic from beginning to end. Yet to judge from his works they all were surpassed in this matter by Ibycus of Rhegium. And the love of all these poets was the sensual love" (*Tusculan Disputations,* IV, 71).

Anacreon

A rival to Ibycus in promiscuity, but perhaps more delicate and light-hearted, was Polycrates' other favorite poet, Anacreon (c. 570–c. 485). Describing Athens in the second century A.D., Pausanias reported: "But Pericles' statue is on one side, while near Xanthippus stands Anacreon of Teos, the first poet after Sappho of Lesbos to make love his main theme. The statue represents him as a man singing when he is drunk" (I, 25, 1).

The chronology of Anacreon is debated. He was born in Teos on the Anatolian coast. It is generally agreed that he lived to the ripe old age of eighty-five (Lucian, *On Longevity,* 26), by which time he may have seen the early works of Aeschylus, who won his first prize in 484. Who brought Anacreon to Samos is not entirely clear. Himerius reported that the poet was engaged by Polycrates the Elder to tutor his son (*Oration* 29, 22). Others, however, say that when the Persians threatened Teos c. 545, the young Anacreon and some of his countrymen emigrated to Abdera, which he helped found, in Thrace (Strabo, *Geography,* 644). From there he was summoned to Samos by Polycrates the Younger.

The lovable, normally cheerful Anacreon, who even as an old man could not give up wine and youths, declared that "the dice of Love are madness and uproar" (398). Ovid's *Tristia* (II, 363) and many epitaphs contained in the *Greek Anthology* testify to his amorousness. For example, Antipater of Sidon (fl. c. 120 B.C.) declared: "Anacreon, glory of the Ionians, may you among the dead not be without your beloved revels or your lyre; but gazing amorously with lascivious eyes may you sing clear-voiced, shaking the garland on your perfumed hair, turning towards Eurypyle or Megisteus or the Ciconian locks of Thacian Smerdies, as you spout forth sweet wine, your robe quite drenched with Bacchus, wringing unmixed nectar from its folds; for all your life, old man, was poured out as an offering to these three — the Muses, Dionysus and Eros" (VII, 27).[5] The *Suda* stressed his devotion "to the love of youths and women and to song," adding, "He composed drinking songs and iambics and the so-called Anacreontea."

Anacreon's verses not only substantiate the portrait of the *Suda,* they also give us ample references to the life of the symposia:

Bring water, boy, bring wine, bring me garlands of flowers: fetch them, so that I may box against Love. (396)

and let the mixture be poured in a clean bowl, five [of wine] and three [of water]. (409)

and let us place garlands of celery on our brows and celebrate a rich festival for Dionysus. (410)

Unlike the dour Theognis, Anacreon reveled unabashedly in the pleasures of the symposium (although Athenaeus took pains to dispel the impression that the poet was a drunkard).[6] But through the influence of the east Greeks, the symposium evolved into more than a mere banquet or the drab messes of Sparta and Crete. More sumptuous, it was often—or at least occasionally—followed by serious conversation and even discussion of the most elevated subjects, as well as by saucy songs and flirtation. In contrast to earlier poets, Anacreon scorned the epic tradition with its images and reminiscences of war. If the heroic age had not been left behind absolutely, at the very least a different mentality was now finding its voice in song.[7]

Blithely and wittily, Anacreon sang of hedonistic pederasty: "O lad with eyes of a maiden, I seek for thee, but thou heedest not, not knowing that thou holdest the reins of my heart" (360). A *scholion* on Pindar reported "that when Anacreon was asked why he did not write hymns to gods but to boys, he replied, 'Because they are my gods'" (*Isthmian* II, 1b). Still, Anacreon did not disdain women: "I dined by breaking off a small piece of thin honeycake, but I drained a jar of wine. Now I tenderly strike my lovely lyre in a serenade to my dear girl" (373). His love for Eurypyle went unrequited: "Fair-haired Eurypyle is in love with that litter-rider Artemon" (372). It was ephebes, however, who captured Anacreon's heart and inspired most of his verses. We know the names of several of them.

Aelian described a scene of jealousy (*Varia Historia,* IX, 4) involving our poet. Smerdis had won the hearts of Polycrates and Anacreon, who could never behold the youth's magnificent hair enough ("shaking [your] Thracian locks" reads fr. 422). His verses celebrated their dark abundance. The conceited youth enjoyed intensely the praise so lavished upon him. In a fit of pique, Polycrates ordered the boy's hair shorn. The poet did not allow his irritation to show. Behaving as if Smerdis had willingly cut his locks, the poet ironically reproached the vain youth for his foolishness: "You have cut off the perfect flower of your soft hair" (414). Of the extant fragments

at least four address Smerdis. Anacreon passionately confessed to him that
Eros had again overwhelmed him. The poet also made a perhaps obscene
reference to "thrice-swept Smerdis" (366).

Fragments of Anacreon's love songs to Cleobulus survive as well. "I
love Cleobulus," Anacreon declared, "I am mad about Cleobulus, I gaze at
Cleobulus" (359). Anacreon offered this prayer to Dionysus: "Lord, with
whom Love the subduer and the blue-eyed Nymphs and radiant Aphrodite
play, as you haunt the lofty mountain peaks, I beseech you: come to me
with kindly heart, hear my prayer and find it acceptable: give Cleobulus
good counsel, Dionysus, that he accept my love" (357).

Another of Anacreon's favorites was Bathyllus. He delighted the poet by
his mastery of the flute and cithara as well as his outstanding beauty. According to Horace: "Not otherwise, they say, did Anacreon of Teos burn for
Samian Bathyllus: often with hollow lyre he sang his sad song of love in no
elaborate meter" (*Epodes*, 14, 9). Polycrates had a statue of Bathyllus set up in
the temple of Hera, perhaps the first large-scale bronze ever cast by Greeks.
To Bathyllus Bergk related a beautiful fragment. When Bathyllus played the
flute, it ran, no one could dance to the music, because none could divert his
gaze from the enchanting figure. But the name of Bathyllus appears neither
in this nor in any of the other indisputably authentic fragments.[8]

The *Greek Anthology* mentioned Megistes as another of the poet's favorites. In one fragment, addressed to him, Anacreon depicted the youth at a
symposium, wreathed with a thin willow wand: "The kindly Megistes has
for ten months now garlanded himself with willow and drunk the honey-
sweet must" (352). In another fragment he told Megistes that he had known
him as a quiet and open-hearted youth in contrast to the sullen and un-
friendly people that he hated: "But I hate all who have sullen and difficult ways. I have learned that you, Megistes, are one of the quiet ones"
(416). Other fragments do not contain the names of the comely youths to
whom they were dedicated. Anacreon mentioned older men courting adolescents, as he himself and other Archaic poets did: "Once again bald Alexis
goes wooing" (394b). He also distinguished between "to marry" and "to
get married," that is, the active/passive dichotomy. About an effeminate
he remarked: "and the chamber in which he did not marry but got married" (424).

The erudite Aristarchus of Samothrace edited Anacreon's poems in six
books, three times the length of the poems that editors assigned to Theognis.
The compilation ascribed to him by the Byzantines in the tenth century,

the *Anacreontea,* faithfully reflects his style, content, and erotic mood, but includes verses by many imitators, who date from Hellenistic, Roman, and even Byzantine times. These selections are characteristic of the collection.

> Anacreon, the singer from Teos, saw me and spoke to me in a dream; and I ran to him and kissed him and embraced him. He was an old man but handsome, handsome and amorous; his lips smelled of wine, and since he was now shaky Love was leading him by the hand. He took the garland from his head and gave it to me, and it smelled of Anacreon. Fool that I was, I held it up and fastened it on my brow — and to this very day I have not ceased to be in love. (1)

> I want to love, I want to love. Love urged me to love, but I was a fool and was not persuaded. So he immediately took up his bow and golden quiver and challenged me to a fight. I hung my corslet from my shoulders, like Achilles, and took my spears and ox-hide shield and began fighting with Love. He shot and I ran; when he had no arrows left, he was distressed; then he hurled himself for a javelin, pierced the middle of my heart and loosened my limbs. My shield (and spears and corslet) are useless: why hurl weapons from me when the fight is within me? (13)

From the second century B.C. until the fifth century A.D., Latin poets also imitated Anacreon, but the Romans, who enjoyed their slaves and male prostitutes, did not ever collectively institutionalize pederasty. In contrast to Sappho's delicate verses, those of Ibycus and Anacreon with their greater lasciviousness may have been expressing the taste of their patron Polycrates, or simply the more pronounced coarseness and directness of male sexuality, but they certainly responded to the mentality of many upper-class males of the sixth and fifth centuries and of many later Greeks and Hellenized Romans as well.

Persian Oppression

Whatever their attitude toward homosexuality may have been, the Persians' oppression caused thousands to flee Anatolia, especially the upper classes. Simultaneously, their apparent suppression of pederastic institutions on which Greek education had come to rest further weakened Ionic creativity. The fairest days of Ionia thus ended with the first Persian occupation in 546. The Persians' destruction of Polycrates' brilliant pederastic court in 522 was a further blow. Lastly, their sack of rebellious Miletus in 494 gave the coup de grâce. Ionia's loss was the gain of the rest of Hellas and enterprising artists and intellectuals from the region tended to gravitate to Athens or the west.

Still, among the meager sources and surviving fragments of Ionian literature, whether openly pederastic or not, the signs of a verdant culture are clear. Polycrates' court demonstrates the establishment of at least one center to foster its growth. Phocylides assures us that the symposium flourished; Mimnermus that regret over beauty's fleeting nature had entered the poetry of a people so proud of its gods and heroes. Ibycus and Anacreon reveal an unequivocal pederastic presence singing of love and wine. The *Anacreontea* testifies to the potency of those themes which, in the manner of the *Theognidea,* persisted well beyond the Archaic Age. Ionia's flowering was brief, but it was also brilliant.

Twelve

Outré Tyrants
and Eccentric Philosophers
in the Archaic West

> Learn when you look that this is Theognetus, boy winner at
> Olympia, skilled driver of the chariot of wrestling, most hand-
> some to look at and no less impressive as athlete, the boy who
> garlanded the city of his excellent fathers.
> —ascribed to Simonides in *The Planudean Anthology*
> in *Greek Lyric,* 3:549

Not a single book or article in any language has ever been devoted to pederasty or to any other kind of homosexuality among the western Greeks. In
fact, before the 1940s only the Greeks of Sicily had been the object of any
specialized study at all. Whereas the eastern Greeks' contribution to Archaic
culture is so essential and so directly tied to ephebophilia and corophilia
that general histories have been obliged to discuss these subjects, scholars have routinely neglected the pederastic intellectuals, tyrants, and heroes
of the Archaic west or omitted references to their homosexuality. Nevertheless, pederasty seems to have played as great a role among the western
Greeks as among any others.

Lawgivers among the western Greeks seem to have copied institutionalized pederasty from Cretan and Spartan models. Its introduction into
Magna Graecia and Sicily almost two centuries after the establishment of
the first permanent Greek colonies there apparently had nothing to do
with Minoan, Mycenean, Carthaginian, Etruscan, or native customs. Nor
was its acceptance directly dependent upon the situational homosexuality
routinely practiced by sailors and colonists. Rather, the colonists' behavior, including their adaptations of pederastic pedagogy, reflected their own

character, deemed a bit outré, too lavish and physical or too mystical for the folk of the homeland who touted the golden mean. The small Mycenean trading posts in Italy, Sicily, and the Lipari islands had collapsed and apparently died out totally during the Dark Age. Probably no Greek speakers west of the Ionian Sea, which was to receive its name from the Ionian merchants and colonists who began to traverse it after 800B.C., survived from the Mycenean era. When Greeks reappeared along the shores of Sicily and Italy during the mid-eighth century, they displaced the small, scattered Phoenician trading posts from all but westernmost Sicily. Although trading with both the Phoenicians and the Etruscans, the Greek settlers saw them as barbarians and seem to have borrowed from them as little as they took from the backward tribes of the interior. Over the centuries they assimilated most if not all of the natives on Sicily and many of those in south Italy. Each of the peoples whom they hellenized adopted institutionalized pederasty, which the descendants of the original colonists had imported from their homeland c. 600. By Roman times, the Greek speakers of south Italy and Sicily had become famous for luxury.

In general, the *poleis* of Magna Graecia and Sicily were founded by three groups: the Chalcidians, Achaeans, and Dorians. Almost all of their colonies, however, attracted immigrants from places other than their mother city, both at the time of their foundation and later. Still, with few exceptions, each tended to regard itself as Dorian, Ionian, and Achaean and preserved the culture and pederasty peculiar to that ethos. Seeking out sites with good harbors and other features promoting trade, the Ionians who settled the west tended to remain merchants, whereas the Dorians and Achaeans generally picked sites that lent themselves to agriculture as well. Whether coming from various *poleis* or from one, colonists had to draw up constitutions for their foundations. Often they would simply borrow that of a neighboring colony. Like many Greeks in the motherland during the Late Archaic Age, they also often looked to Crete for models. Possibly the first imitation of Cretan pederasty occurred in the west rather than in Greece. In antiquity one tradition said that pederasty was first institutionalized in the western colonies by Zaleucus in Locri on the toe of Italy. Another tradition attributed the same action to Charondas at Catana in Sicily.[1]

We do know that the original settlers and their descendants took all the best land in the territories of the western *poleis*. After 600 it became almost as hard to acquire good lands in the west as in Greece itself and in Ionia. By that time Carthaginians and Etruscans were surging in power and rivaling the Greeks in Sicily, Sardinia, and Corsica as well as in Spain and the Balearic Islands, even if their fleets forced Greek settlers to evacuate Corsica only in 535. In 480 Gelon of Syracuse narrowly foiled a Carthaginian attempt to conquer all of Sicily.

The oligarchs in the west decided to limit their own landowning population shortly after, or possibly even before, the knights and hoplites of the homeland had institutionalized pederasty. To this end, around 600 they too adopted the population control devices that evolved on Crete and in the homeland. Where land was not as scarce, the west Greek oligarchs managed to stave off tyranny longer than did their counterparts on the more-crowded mainland. But as the uninhibited lower classes continued to multiply, eventually the oligarchs lost control even in the west. Once established there, tyranny lasted longer than in the homeland. In Sicily in particular attacks by the Carthaginians enhanced the role of tyrants as saviors of the *poleis*.

In the main, the Greek colonists kept their Hellenic customs. More than foreign influences, it was the easier material conditions, the rich land, broad fields, and subject races that distinguished the life of colonials from the existence of those who stayed at home. Before the Carthaginian onslaught, life was less intense among these pleasure-loving, carefree athletes and sportsmen. They excelled, it is true, in such practical subjects as medicine, engineering, and rhetoric. It was they, for example, who invented the rectangular street grid because "the new land had to be subdivided in more or less equal lots among the colonists, an easily resolved task as long as there was enough space and the surveyor applied to his operation the straight line and the right angle."[2] Philosophy and the higher arts were in time brought to them by Ionians refugees.[3]

Wishing to denigrate the Sicilians on the eve of the attack he planned against them in 414, Alcibiades doubtless expressed an old prejudice of the mainlanders when, addressing the Athenians, he called the Sicilians politically fickle and disorganized (cf. Thucydides, VI, 17, 2–4). Regardless of Alcibiades' jibes, Sicilian and Italian Greeks contributed to Hellenic culture both in art and architecture and in literature and philosophy. In their lands at Agrigentum, Paestum, and Selinunte are located the finest of the extant Doric temples. Diogenes Laertius devoted most of books 8 and 9 of his *Lives of Eminent Philosophers* to their philosophers: Pythagoras, Xenophanes, Zeno of Elea, and Empedocles.

Sources

For information we have to depend heavily on the small bits and pieces scattered through Herodotus and Thucydides. Lost to us are the works of the earliest historians of the west, that is, Antiochus of Syracuse, author of a history of Italy and of one of Sicily to the year 424; Philistius (c. 430–356), also of Syracuse; and Timaeus of Taormina (c. 356–260), who emigrated to Athens. Diodorus Siculus, who wrote in the late Roman Republic, pre-served, however, significant fragments and summaries of their works. For details of pederasty we are often dependent on Athenaeus and Dionysus of Halicarnassus, both of whom, like Diogenes Laertius, tirelessly preserved rumors and tidbits from older accounts. As one can readily see from the concentration of historians there, Syracuse, under its series of tyrants be-ginning with Gelon (r. 485–478), was the greatest cultural, commercial and, political metropolis not only of Sicily but for a time of all the western Greeks. Six of Plutarch's *Lives* deal with those involved in west Greek af-fairs: "Nicias," "Alcibiades," "Dion," "Timoleon," "Pyrrhus," and "Marcellus." The greatest contemporary account to survive was by Polybius (c. 200–after 118), who described the rise of Rome in the Mediterranean from 264 onward for his patron Aemilius Scipio. The lives and fragments of various poets and philosophers who either hailed from the west or sojourned there add further to our otherwise sketchy knowledge.

Magna Graecia

Magna Graecia, if we exclude Sicily from this term, consisted mainly of colonies founded around the Gulf of Taranto and their subcolonies on the Tyrrhenian Sea, to which they transported goods overland to avoid travers-ing the dangerous Straights of Messina. But there were also two other lesser clusters of colonies, one around the Bay of Naples, and the other on the toe of Italy, known today as Calabria. Because only Sicily produced his-torians of note, we are less informed about the south Italian Greeks than about most other Greek-speakers during the Late Archaic Age. The history of Magna Graecia was not satisfactorily recorded by the ancients, nor has it been studied in-depth by moderns. There is not, in fact, any standard account of it. Bérard's *La Colonisation grecque de l'Italie méridionale et de la Sicile* (Paris, 1941), along with Dunbabin's *The Western Greeks* (Oxford, 1948), come closest to being authoritative.

Cumae, traditionally the earliest colony in the west, was founded by

Chalcis c. 750. Its first known hero, Aristodemus (d. 492), who twice repulsed the Etruscans and broke their power in Latium, acquired the nickname "the Effeminate." In 524, building upon popular antagonism against
the nobles, he made himself tyrant. Subsequently, he closed the gymnasia
and forced "all the youths who were being reared in the city" to wear robes
and keep "their hair long like the girls" (Dionysius of Halicarnassus, *Roman
Antiquities*, VII, 9). The measure recalls other efforts by tyrants to discourage
the formation of pederastic bonds (such as Periander's closing of all-male
dining clubs), thereby reducing the danger of assassination by pederastic
tyrannicides.

Along the Adriatic littoral, the colonies were small and poor, as were
those facing them across the sea in Epirus and up the Dalmatian coast.
About them we have very little general information, and none at all on
pederasty. In the much greater, predominantly Achaean settlements around
the Gulf of Taranto, the Greeks enserfed the natives and established, except
for the self-indulgent Sybarites, a type of pederasty similar to that of the
Peloponnesus with a physical and military orientation. Along the coast of
Campania the Ionian and Aeolian colonists conducted symposia, and their
artistic achievements rivaled or surpassed those of their mother cities.

The pederastic pedagogy of Croton especially gained fame for its emphasis on the creation of athletes. The city was known also for its its Pythagorean Brotherhood. The Pythagoreans formed mostly all-male groups,
scorned reproduction, and like Christian monks may have experienced
situational homosexuality. Because of its political activities, the brotherhood was eventually suppressed in Croton and elsewhere in southern Italy.
Indeed, the plot of the Pythagorean Phintias against the tyrant Dionysius
of Syracuse gave rise to one of the great stories about (male) friendship in
antiquity.

About to be put to death for his plotting, Phintias asked for time to settle
his affairs. He told Dionysius that he could offer a friend as surety for his
death. Another Pythagorean, the philosopher Damon, willingly accepted
the role. "When the hour [for Phintias' execution] drew close and all were
giving up hope, Phintias unexpectedly arrived on the run at the last moment, just as Damon was being led off to his fate. Such a friendship was in
the eyes of all men a thing of wonder, and Dionysius remitted the punish-
ment of the condemned man, urging the two men to include himself as a
third in their friendship" (Diodorus Siculus, X, 4).

Lying at the northwest corner of the Gulf of Taranto, Sybaris had
sprouted several other colonies of its own. It even founded one as far as

north as the Gulf of Salerno, Poseidonia (Paestum), c. 600, whose majestic ruins still astonish us. The only mural of a symposium is at Paestum, in a tomb near the temple dated to the early fifth century B.C. It represents two male couples, in both cases one bearded and the other not, though fully grown. Each reclines alongside the other on a couch. One *erastes* has his arm around his beloved.

Sicily

Many of the *poleis* in Sicily institutionalized pederasty during the sixth century if not before, but the bucolic love of Sicilian shepherds that Theocritus and Virgil idealized had nothing to do with it. Partly colonized by Ionians and partly by Dorians, the Sicilian *poleis* outshone the Greek settlements in Italy. Rhodians and Cretans founded Gela on the southern shore which in turn founded Agrigentum farther west. Having become allied in the eighth century during the earlier phase of the Lelantine War, Chalcis and Corinth divided up eastern Sicily, purportedly establishing Naxos in 734 and Syracuse in 733 respectively.[4] Under its greatest tyrants, Syracuse came to dominate the island, perhaps diminishing the Ionic influence there. Whatever transpired, in Sicily the various ethnic groups commingled.

Stesichorus of Himera, the first known Sicilian poet of pederastic love, may have flourished at the time of the early tyrant Phalaris (c. 570-c. 540) although the corpus ascribed to him contains earlier and perhaps later compositions. Certainly Aristotle associated him with Phalaris (*Rhetoric*, 1393b). According to the *Suda*, the Alexandrians collected his poems in twenty-six books, far more than for Pindar (17), Alcaeus (10), Sappho (9), Ibycus (7), and Anacreon (5). Thus, they thought him to be the most prolific of all the Archaic poets except for Homer himself. Stesichorus's *Geryoneis* may have had 1300 or more lines. If it did, with that single poem Stesichorus would have nearly equaled the total surviving corpus assigned to Theognis.

Papyrus fragments have confirmed the judgment of ancient critics that Stesichorus was the most Homeric of the Archaic poets. The epic themes that he used (Helen, the Trojan horse, the sack of Troy, etc.) as well as his meters and noble style strongly resemble Homer's. His name means "one who establishes a chorus," but M. L. West maintained that the poet accompanied his works with a cithara (*Greek Lyric*, 3:5). Chamaeleon, a Peripatetic, devoted a treatise to him c. 300 B.C., and in the age of Augustus Tryphon used him to analyze the dialect of Homer. The disagreements as to his dates as well as to the various places he is supposed to have visited argue, I think, that his corpus, like the one attributed to Theognis, probably evolved through recomposition over a long period and in more than one locale.

Although most of the ancient testimonies and the surviving fragments associate the Stesichoran corpus with Homeric themes and style, Athenaeus insisted, quoting Timaeus, that "Stesichorus [as well as Alcman] was immoderately erotic and has composed that type of songs [namely love songs]; these, as is well known, were of old called *paideia* and *paidika* [that is, songs of boy-love]" (XIII, 601a).[5] Athenaeus continued, mentioning that the poet's songs were popular at symposia: "After dinner they got some of the sailors and sang pieces from the paeans of Phrynichus and Stesichorus and Pindar too." I readily believe that through just such performances the amorous poems in question were inserted after the institutionalization of pederasty into what was mainly an older corpus of verses and that all was recomposed in subsequent recitations.

Simonides and Bacchylides

In 478 Hiero succeeded his brother Gelon as tyrant of Syracuse. Whereas Gelon and his immediate predecessor Hippocrates were primarily warriors, Hiero was interested in attracting pederastic intellectuals to his court at Syracuse. (Hiero himself was enthusiastically pederastic, and we even have the name of one of his boyfriends, Daelochus, recorded by Xenophon [*Hiero*, I, 32–38].) Once Ionia fell to the Persians and Sparta succumbed to anti-intellectualism, and the south Italian *poleis* to civil war, Syracuse became the second center of Hellenic culture. Like Athens this metropolis attracted refugees from Ionia. Through the lavish patronage of its tyrants Syracuse also succeeded in drawing to it Pindar, Aeschylus, Plato, Simonides, Bacchylides, and perhaps Xenophanes.

The oldest of these intellectuals was Simonides. Born at Iulis on the Ionian island of Ceos c. 556, he apparently taught music and poetry there as a young man and produced paeans for the local festivals of Apollo. Drawn to Athens first by Hipparchus, the patron par excellence of the Pisistratid tyrants, and again later after a stay in Thessaly, he finally settled down with his nephew Bacchylides at Hiero's court.

Simonides, an outstanding scholar, was said to have been the first to distinguish long from short vowels and to have invented a mnemonic system (Quintilian, XI, 2, 11). Reputedly he negotiated the end to a quarrel between Hiero and Theron, the tyrant of Agrigentum. Intimate also of both the Athenian Themistocles and his rival the Spartan Pausanias, Simonides received enormous prices for his compositions and was criticized for his greed. We have only two or three brief elegies of his. His epigrams, written in Ionic elegiac with epic influences, celebrated the heroes of Marathon and Thermopylae; some private ones appear in the *Greek Anthology* and may not really be his. Many of his odes, like those of Bacchylides and his rival Pindar, sing of the victors in the pan-Hellenic games. He thus typified the generation of Marathon, so regretted by Aristophanes for their good old-fashioned decorous ways in the courtship of adolescents and for their proper behavior at symposia and gymnasia.

Since the standard edition by F. G. Schneidewin (1835) and the fragments collected by Bergk (at which time we had approximately ninety fragments), there have been the usual additions from papyri which increased the size of the corpus to 653 fragments. When his corpus was first assembled, how it has been altered, and what critics said about him are questions to which we hardly know the answers, although Chamaeleon included him in the list of poets that he studied, and Palaephatus (c. 200 B.C.) wrote about his work. Aristophanes (*Clouds*, 1355, 1362) had the crude Strepsiades try to teach his son "Simonides' song about how Crius [a name meaning the Ram] was shorn," perhaps a song about a youth losing his locks. But his son replied that "it was old-fashioned to play the lyre and sing while drinking" and called Simonides a bad poet. That a nouveau riche bumpkin thought it proper to sing songs by Simonides at symposia and his son sought to reject the customs and values of the previous generations, including Simonides, suggests to me to what degree this poet long remained associated with the entertainment experienced at symposia.

The *Planudean Anthology* ascribes to Simonides this homage to a victorious athlete: "Learn when you look that this is Theognetus, boy winner at Olympia, skilled driver of the chariot of wrestling, most handsome to look at and no less impressive as athlete, the boy who garlanded the city of his excellent fathers" (*Greek Lyric*, 3:549). And in the *Palatine Anthology* (7, 431) we find an epitaph by Simonides for Anacreon "who all night long struck his boy-loving lyre." In short, his praise of athletes and popularity at symposia as well as his being grouped with other pederastic artists and hired by pederastic patrons hint strongly that he wrote pederastic verses even though the fragments from the Oxyrhnchus papyrus (c. 100 A.D.) reproduced in the *Greek Lyric,* volume 3, are too brief and too unclear as to attribution to prove the point conclusively.

Despite Simonides' many qualities, Hiero's favorite poet was Bacchylides. This genial Dorian, whose mother was sister to Simonides, was referred to in the treatise *On the Sublime* as a flawless poet of the second rank, and, indeed, the extraordinary discovery of papyri with thirteen or fourteen epinicians and six dithyrambs by Bacchylides has provided evidence to buttress the ancients' praise of the technical perfection of his work.

This last of the nine lyricists canonized by the Alexandrians may also have been pederastic. Lacking verses by him that repeat any of the traditional pederastic themes, we can do no more than reflect on the facts that he received the patronage of the greatest of the Sicilian tyrants at a court renowned for its pederasts and that, like his uncle and their rival Pindar, he wrote epinicians for victors at the four great pan-Hellenic festivals.

The size and cosmopolitanism of Hiero's Syracuse probably made its love life as complex as that of Athens. Dorian and Ionian influences mingled in the port's busy streets, and aristocratic landowners as well as wealthy merchants frequented its gymnasia and symposia. Sailors on leave must have sought out male and female prostitutes much as they did in Marseilles, Corinth, and the port of Piraeus outside Athens. If we are less informed about the sex life and theories of love in the other *poleis* of Sicily and Magna Graecia than we are about those in Athens, Sparta, and Thebes, we should not presume that pederasty was never practiced there.

Persian and Carthaginian attacks ended the golden age of the overseas Greeks. After the founding of Agrigentum in 581, colonization of Sicily from Greece and Anatolia all but ceased because of the dearth of suitable sites for new colonies. The growing power of Carthage put the Greeks on the defensive, arresting their expansion. Refugees fleeing Persians, Carthaginians, or native tyrants, and other immigrants attracted by money or opportunity, came to Athens before and after its height in the fifth century. Pederasty was foreign to none of them. To Athens came the best and brightest from east and west, from Sicily, Italy, Ionia, and the Aegean islands. They brought with them knowledge of the varieties of institutionalized pederasty that had evolved in the sixth century throughout the Hellenic world. Blending these with its own special tradition, Athens became the pederastic capital and school of Hellas. There, where every type was known, every possible theory was elaborated about pederasty.

Thirteen

Archaic Athens

Happy is he who has boy-friends [paides], whole-hooved steeds,
hunting hounds, and a friend in foreign parts . . . till in the flower
of youth he love a lad with the desire of thighs and sweet lips.

—Solon, 23, 25

Solon, although the city [Athens] followed the whole Ionian
manner of life and luxury and a carefree existence had made the
inhabitants effeminate, wrought a change in them by accustoming them to practice virtue and to emulate the deeds of virile
folk. And it was because of this that [the lovers] Harmodius and
Aristogiton, their spirits equipped with the panoply of his legislation, made the attempt to destroy the rule of the Pisistratidae
[tyrants].

—Diodorus Siculus, IX, 1, 3

In all of history, Athens remains the city most renowned for pederasty.
Athens has also been praised for the education it afforded its youth. Nietzsche, Wilamowitz-Moellendorff, Jaeger, and Marrou, to name four great
Continental scholars, all attested the preeminent excellence of Greek education. Even the Freudian George Devereux, while criticizing what he
dubbed the Greeks' artificially prolonged adolescence, had to admit that
they created a vibrantly intellectual youth culture: "The Greeks knew how
to use for socially beneficial ends the adolescence of the adolescent. . . .
[T]he 'Greek Miracle' . . . was a successful socialization of the adolescent's
creative potentialities, even in adult life."[1] To be sure, given the absence of
surviving documents, it is impossible to chart the precise impact of pederastic pedagogy on Athens's accomplishments. However, Athens did rise to
grandeur only after it institutionalized pederasty.

Sources

Our literary sources for Archaic Athens consist almost exclusively of classical, Hellenistic, Roman, and Byzantine writers. No Athenian writings survive between the fragments of verse attributed to Solon and Aeschylus's *Persae* (472) save for a few fragments by Hipparchus.[2] However, each of these poets had an *eromenos*. We do have considerable fragments of the verses composed by Late Archaic pederastic visitors to Athens, to wit Anacreon, Pindar, and Simonides. Herodotus and Thucydides, both of whom give us scattered bits of information about pederasty in the Archaic Age, tell us somewhat more about early Athens than about secretive Sparta. The Attic orators, notably Lysias, Demosthenes, and Aeschines, the last of whom preserved the so-called laws of Solon relative to pederasty, were full of tidbits about Archaic Athens, but we do not know how much of their corpus was interpolated by later hands or how much of what they themselves wrote is accurate. Like the orations, Aristotle's *Politics* and his *Athenian Constitution,* which was recovered from the Egyptian desert in 1891, provide much data of general interest, though much of what they say about Athenian pederasty is contradictory. Diodorus Siculus gives us some material, notably on Solon's life. Aristotle as well as Thucydides provides detailed accounts of the assassination of the tyrant Hippias's brother Hipparchus by the lovers Harmodius and Aristogiton. Plutarch's biographies of Theseus and Solon as well as of Themistocles and Aristides, which overlap the end of the Archaic Age, all discuss pederasty. Athenaeus and Diogenes Laertius are frequently invaluable. The *Suda,* like other Byzantine compilations, provides useful, if obscure, facts and definitions of words and phrases. Thus, the literary sources that we can consult are far richer for Archaic Athens than for any other *polis.* However, we are doubly fortunate in that Greek society, even in Athens, which was the most dynamic city-state in the classical age, changed slowly by our standards. As a result, classical literature and art can be used to help us understand the preceding Archaic Age.

Regarding classical literature, the lower classes' supposed ridicule of their betters' homosexuality is first fully recorded by comedians contemporary with Socrates, but, like the fourth-century orators, they only criticized adult passives, effeminates, and those who were boy-crazy, not the decorous pederast and his well-behaved beloved. Dover recognized that these orators, like the jurors whom they were addressing, accepted certain kinds of pederasty. Likewise, the comedians, playing to a substantially similar audience of typical citizens, censured only those who behaved improperly.[3] In classical Athens the middle and lower classes probably imitated rather than censured the upper-class love of youths.[4] The protests by fourth-century orators that they themselves were virtuous pederasts would tend to confirm the theory that the ridicule of the comedians was aimed not at pederasty itself, but at its most excessive practitioners. Plato's intricate and often contradictory writings about pederasty may mirror the diversity of Athenian opinion about the practice as well as the fact that his own response evolved over his long life.

Of Athenian vase paintings we have already spoken. They usually portray a decorous form of pederasty involving dallying, gift-giving, and intercrural sex rather than anal penetration. Athenian graffiti, like those from other *poleis,* often merely tagged a youth as beautiful (*kalos*). The word *katapygon* ("broad-assed," that is, a male who had submitted to anal penetration) appeared in Attic Greek far earlier than Aristophanes' use of it. It was inscribed on a shard from Mount Hymettus that Dover called eighth-century but is assigned by archeologists to the seventh century.[5] In any case, this term that perpetuates the stigmatization of the anal (adult) passive so common in eastern Mediterranean culture does not necessarily have anything to do with Greek pederasty. One shard reads: "Pythodoruʹs is beautiful. Alcaeus is a *katapygon* says Melis" (R994); another, "Sosias is a *katapygon* says Euphronius who wrote this" (*Supplementum Epigraphicum Graecum,* xxi, 215). The isle of Tenos supplies "Thressa is a *katapygon*" (SEG, xv, 523), showing that the term could be applied to a woman also.[6]

Pre-Pederastic Athens

After Athenians became prominent, they created various legends that made their city seem to have been great in remote antiquity (when, in fact, it was not very significant). Of particular importance among these legends is a revised story of their early prince Theseus, whom the Athenians in their recomposition made pederastic. The original tale said that Theseus went with other youths, two of whom dressed as maidens, to Minos's palace at Cnossos as part of the annual Athenian tribute to that king. There the youths and maidens were to be consumed by the Minotaur. Ariadne, Minos's daughter, fell in love with Theseus and, betraying her people, gave him a thread with which he found his way out of the labyrinth after entering it to slay the Minotaur. Theseus then made his escape out of Cnossos, taking Ariadne as his bride. Stopping on the island of Naxos, the triumphant hero abandoned the bride who had given up everything for him.

Although this episode angered Minos, he gave up his quarrel with Athens "because he loved Theseus and gave him his daughter Phaedra to be his wife, according to Zenis (or Zeneus) of Chios, who flourished in the fourth century B.C." (Athenaeus, XIII, 601f). Athenaeus (XIII, 601a) agrees with other late sources that Minos became the *erastes* of Theseus and gave him Phaedra in marriage. In a further revised version Theseus became the lover of the youth Pirithous, who was actually of about the same age as he.[7] After-wards Theseus reigned for many years as king of Athens. This legend greatly exaggerated the early importance of Athens, and later Greeks anachronisti-cally transformed the relationship between Theseus and Pirithous into that of an *erastes* and his *eromenos*. In making so significant a hero as Theseus the legendary founder of Athenian pederasty, the propagandists for the *polis* revealed that it did not scorn the practice. Similarly, the fact that an appro-priate age difference was superimposed on Theseus and Pirithous points to a distinct effort to portray Theseus as a model *erastes* for the Athenians of the classical and later ages.

A clearly historical, if indistinct, personality, Cylon was the first to at-tempt to establish tyranny at Athens. His conspiracy, dated variously from 632 to 552, probably actually occurred near the earlier date since authorities agree that this story predates Solon.[8] Moreover, as we shall see, it leads to an important moment in the story of Athenian pederasty. Plagues as well as the hard times caused by overpopulation perhaps underlay Cylon's conspiracy. We are told that dissidents persisted long after the Athenians murdered Cylon's coconspirators.[9] After the conspiracy was crushed, increasing over-population caused further hardship and threatened the social and political structure. A savior came in the person of Solon. Much more has doubtless been ascribed to him than he actually did, but he was instrumental in re-forming Athens and, I believe, institutionalized pederasty there.

In the century from Solon to Themistocles, Athens rose from a typi-cal *polis* with no more than 10,000 inhabitants to the largest metropolis in Greece. By its apogee in 431 the population of the city and its port Piraeus may have increased twentyfold over two hundred years,[10] imposing on Athens the same demographic pressures that encouraged the establishment of late marriage for males and pederasty throughout Hellas in the Late Ar-chaic period and sustained their retention thereafter.

Epimenides the Cretan and "Folktale" Lovers

Cretans and perhaps also other exemplars influenced Athenians to institu-tionalize pederasty. Of the ancient accounts, the most frequently mentioned is the story of Epimenides, the shamanistic Cretan sage, who purportedly came to Athens to end the plagues and to help Solon with his reforms. The legends of his great age, his miraculous fifty-seven-year-long sleep (Diogenes Laertius), and his wanderings out of his body (cf. *Suda*) resemble those of other shamans of that age such as Aristeas and Hermotimus.[11]

Our fullest account of Epimenides appears in Diogenes Laertius's *Lives of Eminent Philosophers* (c. 200 A.D.). Diogenes asserted that Epimenides wrote a book on the Cretan constitution and conveyed what he claimed was a well-attested ancient tradition about the Cretan sage's influence upon the Athenians:

> Epimenides, according to Theopompus and many other writers, was . . . a native of Cnossos in Crete. . . . [H]e became famous throughout Greece, and was believed to be a special favorite of heaven. Hence, when the Athenians were attacked by pestilence, and the Pythian priestess bade them purify the city, they sent a ship . . . to Crete to ask the help of Epimenides. And he came in the 46th Olympiad [595–592], purified their city, and stopped the pestilence. . . . According to some writers he declared the plague to have been caused by the pollution which Cylon brought on the city and showed them how to remove it. In consequence two young men, Cratinus and Ctesibius, were put to death and the city was delivered from the scourge. (I, 109–11)

The reference to "the pollution which Cylon brought to the city" is meant to recall the treacherous act of the Athenians who killed Cylon's coconspirators after they had surrendered. The sacrifice of Cratinus and Ctesibius was intended to expiate so terrible a breach of conduct. That Cratinus was an *eromenos* seems to indicate that pederasty had been introduced into Athens before the end of Epimenides' visit. The youth's story is told by Athenaeus:

> Notorious are also the things that happened in the case of Cratinus of Athens; for he was a handsome lad at the time when Epimenides was purifying Attica by the sacrifice of human blood, because of some ancient acts of abomination, as recorded by Neanthes of Cyzicus [third century B.C.] in the second book of his work, *On the Rituals of Initiation;* and Cratinus voluntarily gave himself up on behalf of the land that had nurtured him; following him his lover Aristodemus also died, and so atonement was rendered for the terrible act. (XIII, 602c–d)

Athenaeus himself was "not ignorant that Polemon the Geographer [fl. c. 190] asserts in his *Replies to Neanthes* that the story of Cratinus and Aristodemus is a fiction" (XIII, 602c). If the details of their sacrifice are highly questionable, they may nevertheless have been one of the earliest pederastic couples in Athens, and it is pertinent that they were thought to have been self-sacrificing heroes. Because neither Herodotus nor Thucydides, both of whom began to sketch Athenian history with Cylon's conspiracy, mention them, Cratinus and his lover Aristodemus may have been another folktale like that of Timorgoras and his spurned metic lover Melas, invented after pederasty had been introduced. Whatever their origin, these stories illustrate the bravery and self-sacrificing nature that Athenian society associated with pederastic lovers.

If Diogenes Laertius was right, Epimenides came to Athens during the archonship of Solon. It is then that Epimenides and Solon may have introduced institutionalized pederasty, perhaps with its concomitants, using Cretan models. The traditions about Epimenides are too pervasive and too numerous to be rejected out of hand. Like his fellow Cretans Onomacritus and Thaletas and his friend Solon, Epimenides appears to have been one of those musicians and sages who institutionalized pederasty and its concomitant features to stop the demographic explosion among the propertied classes, quell plagues, and bring "good order to the Hellenic world."[12]

Solon the Lawgiver

Solon, of whom Plutarch said that his early poems showed that he did not have the "courage to stand up to passion and meet it" ("Solon," I), came to power during an economic crisis related to overpopulation. Acutely aware of hardships resulting from that crisis, Solon apparently wished to limit the begetting of children, but each citizen who could afford them needed some, if only to carry on the honoring of the family ancestors and to provide for the difficulties of old age. If both contraception and abortion during early pregnancy failed, those with excessive progeny would often resort to exposure, which in Athens was voluntary and at the will of the father, not at the order of the ephors as in Sparta. Like Lycurgus, Solon is purported to have outlawed abortion, then as later a horrendous method of birth control dangerous to women (pseudo-Galen, *An animal sit id, quod in utero est*).[13]

Apparently to diminish the frustrations of the poor, whom he also counseled not to marry before twenty-eight, Solon allegedly instituted state-run, price-controlled brothels, for which he purchased slave girls.[14] Solon, it is said, also made the law that a father could sell a daughter who lost her virginity and stated that "the woman who leaves her house should be of such an age that those who encounter her do not ask whose wife but whose

mother she is" (Hyperides, fr. 204). Indeed, the strict seclusion of upper-
class Athenian females may have begun with Solon. In any case, no evidence
exists for the presence in Athens of schools for upper-class girls like those
of Lesbos or Sparta.

How many of those regulations and others ascribed to him actually came
into force after Solon's death remains a puzzle. In addition to the dispute
about the authenticity of his laws and sayings, there is the question of his
chronology. An article published more than a hundred years ago proposed
the most likely chronology of his career. In the year 594, as archon, Solon
passed the *seisachtheia* or remission of debts. In 586 Damasius was archon, at
which time a revolutionary movement occurred to extend the magistracies
beyond the ranks of the Eupatridae (the hereditary aristocrats). Between 570
and 560 Solon may have carried out his reforms in the direction of a democratic or mixed constitution (Herodotus II, 177). About 560 he may have
visited Croesus, the king of Lydia, in his capital at Sardis (Herodotus I, 29).[15]

Solon the Pederast

Some of Solon's sayings deemed most authentic are his poem on love of
youths and his law forbidding slaves to practice pederasty with free adolescents.[16] While the extensive regulations about who can enter gymnasia
and how the latter are to be run have been analyzed as interpolations into
Aeschines' oration *Contra Timarchum*,[17] no one denies that Solon dealt with
pederasty and with gymnasia. The overwhelming likelihood is therefore
that he introduced the practice and its concomitant institutions, given that
they are not referred to before his time. This argument *ex silentio* has not, as
far as I know, been put forth before, perhaps because Solon is not credited
in any surviving ancient source with the introduction of institutionalized
pederasty to Athens. He is, however, said to have established and ordained
the basic laws and customs of that *polis*. Moreover, Solon himself praised
pederasty, something which no Athenian before him had done.

When Solon institutionalized pederasty and its associated practices, he
changed them substantially. He neither made pederasty obligatory nor imported the kidnapping or the herding of boys. An advocate of freedom, he
encouraged rather than compelled his fellow citizens to adopt the new system. This could explain why we do not hear of some of the most famous
early Athenians—Miltiades, Pericles, or Xenophon, about whose lives we
are unusually well informed, or of Thucydides himself—as either *erastes* or
eromenos.

In Athens, messes for men, so central for Crete and Sparta, also existed in a radically different and much less austere form. Unlike their counterparts in those *poleis,* compelled to attend the *syssitia* daily, most Athenian upper-class males normally dined *en famille.* However, some dined with companions in symposia a few times a month, in what often amounted to exclusive clubs. Dinner in these clubs might be followed by intellectual discussion; other symposia turned into riotous orgies, lasting till dawn with comasts spilling out into the street to serenade boys or hassle passersby.

Solon may have founded the first Athenian gymnasia to keep the hoplites in shape and to train their *eromenoi* to become good citizens and warriors. Whether a few of those privileged enough to attend the Olympic Games or to visit Sparta may have viewed Spartan nudity and perhaps even participated nude in the games themselves, it was probably Solon (or an aristocratic clique some of whose achievements were ascribed to him) who introduced public gymnasia with nude athletic training to Athens itself.[18] As is the case elsewhere, the first Athenian gymnasia were presumably only crude outdoor running tracks. Nevertheless, as the vase paintings from this period and classical literature so carefully marshaled by Dover show, Athenian gymnasia were homoerotic cruising grounds.[19]

Solon may have been the one who promulgated the law, first attested in 424 in Aristophanes' *Knights* (876–80), that a male who had sold his body as a boy was not fit to serve in a public office. (As far as our sources indicate, Greek tastes created no market for adult male prostitutes although it is difficult to believe that there was absolutely no demand for them.) In any case, by the fourth century, boys or youths who prostituted their bodies lost their right to address the assembly when they became adults. For that offense Aeschines prosecuted a fellow orator, Timarchus. The "Legislator" may have merely feared to see ex-prostitutes (whom he considered to be too venal) become politicians or he may have intended to limit prostitution by male youths to foreigners and slaves.[20]

Solon was not said to have subsidized houses for youths as he allegedly did for females, but they too became numerous by classical times.[21] By the fourth century the Athenians levied a tax on the earnings of both male and female prostitutes.[22] Male and female brothels flourished, especially around the port of Piraeus. Disputed legal texts included in the manuscripts of Aeschines' *Contra Timarchum* make Solon specify which boys of what age could attend schools, regulate the functions of pedagogues, and set school holidays dedicated to the Muses and palaestra celebrations in honor of Hermes. The choreographer of a boys' choir had to be at least forty years of age "in order that he may have reached the most temperate time of life" before having such close contact with the youths.[23]

By Aeschines' time a great many other innovations were attributed to the great sage. Aeschines stressed the protection that Solon supposedly gave to the virtue and chastity of boys, assigning the following law to him:

No person who is older than the boys shall be permitted to enter the room while they are there, unless he be a son of the teacher, a brother, or a daughter's husband. If any one enter in violation of this prohibition, he shall be punished with death. The superintendents of the gymnasia shall under no conditions allow any one who has reached the age of manhood to enter the contests of Hermes together with the boys. A gymnasiarch who does permit this and fails to keep such a person out of the gymnasium, shall be liable to the penalties prescribed for the seduction of free-born youth. (*Against Timarchus,* 12)

One never hears of the death penalty being imposed for such a crime, however.

A scholiast explained why masters could not open schools or pedotribes (teachers of wrestling) the palaestras before sunrise or close them after sunset: "In the inner part of the house at schools and palaestras there were columns and chapels, with altars to the Muses, Hermes, and Heracles. There was also drinking water there, but many boys under pretence of drinking, came in and practiced immorality."[24] Barred from even rubbing oil on boys or men in the palaestras, slaves found courting or loving free boys received fifty lashes (Aeschines, *Against Timarchus,* 138–39).

Plutarch referred to "one of [Solon's] laws, in which there are practices forbidden to slaves, which he would appear, therefore, to recommend to freemen" ("Solon," I), a convoluted statement that suggests Plutarch saw the law as promoting pederasty among freemen while limiting it among slaves. In another work he expressed what may have been the common opinion after pederasty was institutionalized: "[Solon] forbade slaves to make love to boys or to have a rubdown, but he did not restrict their intercourse with women. For friendship is a beautiful and courteous relationship, but mere pleasure is base and unworthy of a free man. For this reason also it is not gentlemanly or urbane to make love to slave boys: such a love is mere copulation, like the love of women" (*Eroticos,* 751b). If some Athenians did make love to their young slaves, we never hear of it, but that Solon, their greatest lawgiver, loved free youths no Athenian doubted.

The Pisistratids

The economically and culturally beneficial tyranny of the Pisistratids (c. 561–510) greatly strengthened Athens. Pisistratus, the founder, was driven out of Athens about 560, only to return five years later after a victorious battle. He followed the pederastic tradition endorsed by his maternal cousin Solon, whose *eromenos* he was reputed to have been.[25] Pisistratus and his sons patronized native as well as immigrant geniuses. In the festival that he was said to have inaugurated for Dionysus, he offered a prize for tragedy.[26] Under his elder son Hippias, who ruled from 527 to 510, his younger son Hipparchus acted as a sort of minister of culture. It is allegedly thanks to the Pisistratids that Homer's works were put in writing and much edited in the process. Similarly, Orphic and perhaps other early texts with pederastic overtones were all committed to writing perhaps after recompositions for a pederastic audience. The dynasty, it should be added, was equally known for its pederastic passions. While Charmus was said to have loved Hippias (Athenaeus, XIII, 609d), Hipparchus tried to force himself on Harmodius, the *eromenos* of a simple but upright middle-class citizen, Aristogiton.

At the same time that the Pisistratids used their power to further the artistic life of their city, events beyond their *polis* conspired to produce an even greater outpouring of culture there. The Persians had curbed the Ionians' intellectual advances and lessened their supremacy over Aegean and Black Sea trade by overtaxing them and by favoring their Phoenician rivals. Ionia's decline became irreversible after Darius leveled Miletus in 494 during the great Ionian revolt. Fleeing from these crises or seeking patronage in a supportive environment, Ionian émigrés flocked to Athens. The influx accelerated during the fifth century. As Jaeger notes, "In Plato the rhetors and sophists who argue with Socrates are always at a disadvantage, simply because they are foreigners, and do not understand the real problems of Athens and the Athenians."[27]

Though lasting longer than the production of the erotic painted vases, which were replaced by silver vessels after 470, erotic poetry may have declined during the grim Peloponnesian War. Shortly before that war broke out the last of the great lyricists, Pindar, and his rival Bacchylides died. Maybe the deprivations of the war discouraged attention to such lighthearted poetry. Perhaps it came to be considered old-fashioned. Be that as it may, younger contemporaries such as Critias and his nephew Plato clearly failed to match the talent of the nine grand lyricists canonized by the Alexandrians. Indeed, no poet of that generation figured among the nine.

Of particular note here is the fact that the writing of classical drama flourished only at Athens, although the plays were performed in many other cities. Some believe that drama outshone, subsumed, or rendered outmoded lyric poetry, just as the lyric had supposedly replaced epics at an earlier time. Tragedy may have been imported to Athens by an Ionian. Arion of Lesbos (fl. c. 625) is said to have originated tragedy at Corinth or at least developed the dithyramb and taught choruses there to perform it. The history of tragedy remains murky before Aeschylus. A steady development from Thespis, who won the first prize at the Great Dionysia in Athens in 535 (so says the *Suda*) must be deduced before Phrynichus, Aeschylus's slightly older contemporary, also achieved renown there. The relationship of tragedy to pederasty is discussed in my epilogue. Suffice it to note here that, according to Athenaeus, when tales of pederastic love were presented, "[T]he audience gladly accepted such stories" (XIII, 601a).

In addition to (indeed as a component of) their patronage of the arts, the Pisistratids probably introduced intellectual instruction to the gymnasia. We know that the Pisistratids began and Cleisthenes rearranged the Panathenaic festival, which was held every fourth year, in the third year of each Olympiad, to harmonize with the other great pan-Hellenic festivals organized or reorganized in the first half of the sixth century. Its prizes were bestowed upon three groups: boys, beardless youths (*ageneioi*), and men, age-classes that Plato later employed in the *Laws*.[28] The Panathenaia eventually lasted nine days and included, as Aristotle stated (*Athenian Constitution,* LX, 4), prizes for male beauty (*evandria*). But equally significant is the fact that at this festival the *Iliad* and the *Odyssey* were recited annually; for that performance Homer's text was emended to exalt Athens and perhaps, as I have argued in chapter 3, to allude to pederasty.

The Tyrannicides

In 514 the most famous historical heroes of Athens, Harmodius and his *erastes* Aristogiton, achieved fame by slaying Hipparchus, the brother of the tyrant Hippias. Hipparchus, "fond of amusements, and interested in love affairs and the arts," had humiliated them after Harmodius rejected his sexual advance (Thucydides, VI, 54–56). According to another version Hipparchus lusted after Harmodius's sister. The would-be lover,

far from restraining his anger, gave vent to it viciously; finally, when Harmodius's sister was to carry a basket in the procession at the

Panathenaia, he stopped her, and insulted Harmodius as effeminate. Hence Harmodius and Aristogiton were provoked to their plot, in which many took part. At the time of the Panathenaia, when they were watching for Hippias on the Acropolis (for it so happened that he was receiving the procession while Hipparchus dispatched it), they saw one of the conspirators greet Hippias in a friendly way. They thought that they were betrayed. Wishing to achieve something before they were arrested, they went down into the city, and, not waiting for their fellow conspirators, killed Hipparchus as he was organizing the procession by the Leocoreion; thus they spoiled the whole attempt. (Aristotle, *Athenian Constitution,* XVIII, 2–4)

Hipparchus's bodyguard slew Harmodius at once. For an insult uttered by Aristogiton, who was being tortured to make him reveal the names of the other conspirators, Hippias personally killed him (Thucydides, VI, 54–59).

In spite of the patronage that he had once received from Hipparchus, the poet Simonides praised the tyrannicides: "A marvellous great light shone upon Athens when Aristogiton and Harmodius slew Hipparchus" (Hephaestion, *Handbook on Meters,* 4, 6), and for centuries after the overthrow of the tyrants, symposists regularly saluted Harmodius and Aristogiton with *scolia.* The lovers were also idealized as models for the city's youth. The first statue of the pair, a bronze by Antenor, commissioned by Cleisthenes, the founder of Athenian democracy, and put in place in 506, was carted off to Susa by the Persians in 480. Three years later a replacement was cast, of which a marble copy exists in the National Museum at Naples.

After the assassination, Hippias became fearful of pederasty. His reaction was to ally with Hippoclus, tyrant of Lampsacus, himself a staunch ally of the antipederastic Persians.[29] When he was overthrown four years later, he fled to Persian territory where he and his relatives denounced pederasty. The Athenians credited their deliverance from tyranny to Eros, whereas "the Pisistratidae, after they were ejected, were the first to enter upon the practice of defaming the acts which pertain to this god" (Athenaeus, XIII, 562a). However, Harmodius and Aristogiton were neither the first nor the last example of pederastic tyrannicides. Aristotle cited numerous cases of vengeance on tyrants who outraged youths (*Politics,* V, 11, 22, 28).

Pederastic Democracy in the Age
of Themistocles and Aristides

Almost all of the great democratic leaders of Archaic Athens were, like
Solon and the tyrants, pederastic. Even her most famous orators, Aeschines
and Demosthenes, when addressing the *demos* proclaimed that they were
themselves pederasts, as Dover noticed. In this new, more democratic environment, the old-style aristocratic pederasty seems to have changed somewhat. Pederastic vase paintings became more demure and less frequent. This
was not, however, because the upper classes wanted to be less obvious about
an institution which the masses did not share and, according to some interpretations of the later evidence, may not have relished. At the end of the
Archaic Age, after nearly three decades of democracy, pederasty remained
firmly ensconced in Athens, unshaken even by Plato's critique. There pederasty had taken on its peculiar Athenian stamp. In fact it may have reached its
apogee between the reforms of Cleisthenes and the battle of Salamis, but it
endured without significant abatement until Alexander's time and beyond.
Democracy did not, therefore, diminish pederasty. It still flourished even
after the production of red-figure homoerotic vases and the lyric poetry of
Pindar and Bacchylides ceased.

In 512 the King of Kings Darius the Great suffered a defeat at the hands
of the Scythians when he crossed the Danube. The loss of prestige that
this defeat occasioned encouraged the Ionians to revolt against their Persian overlords (499). From the mainland, only Athens and Plataea aided the
rebels in 499. The Spartans, Corinthians, and their Peloponnesian allies refused to join forces with the Ionians out of a (well-grounded) fear that their
intervention might provoke Persian reprisals. Too small to ensure success,
the expedition to aid the Ionians did indeed call forth Persian vengeance.
However, with 10,000 Athenian hoplites, the Philaid Miltiades, "the most
distinguished man of his day," according to his biographer Cornelius Nepos,
repulsed the Persian punitive expedition in 490 at Marathon after they had
burned Eretria, already in the last stage of its decline. Darius, distracted by
a revolt in Egypt, died before he could punish Athens in order to regain his
prestige and overawe his recently resubjugated Ionian subjects.

Darius's unbalanced son Xerxes launched the great expedition in 480.
Fleets of his Phoenician and Ionian subjects resupplied his troops, grossly
exaggerated by Herodotus as numbering 1,700,000 men. As they marched
south along the unbounteous coasts, the Thracians, Macedonians, Thessali-

ans, and Boeotians, feeling overwhelmed by the odds, went over to the
Persians. The Athenians roused the other Greeks to resist. The immortal
hippeis, the Spartan king's bodyguard, whom even Xerxes praised, fell to a
man at Thermopylae. But in the decisive battle in the bay of Salamis, the
Athenian fleet, built on the advice of Themistocles with profits from the
recently discovered silver mines at Laurium, sank fifty Persian ships before
Xerxes' own eyes. The following year at Plataea a combined Hellenic army
under the pederastic Spartan king Pausanias, with help from the Athenian
Aristides, routed Xerxes' rearguard under his nephew Mardonius.

A commoner, Themistocles, the hero of the hour, dominated Athenian
politics for a decade after Salamis, until his ungrateful countrymen ostracized him in 471. Born of a metic mother, he had the Cynosarges, the
gymnasium for bastards and metics (foreign residents), upgraded. Aristides,
Themistocles' political rival on the stage of Athenian democracy, nevertheless shared his enemy's tastes. According to Plutarch, the "great enmity"
between Themistocles and Aristides, the leaders of the triumphant democracy, "arose, it appears, purely on account of a youth, both being attached to
the beautiful Stesilaus of Ceos, as Ariston [of Ceos] the philosopher tells us;
ever after which they took opposite sides, and were rivals in politics" ("Themistocles," III). The Archaic Age in Athens thus apparently closed with two
of its greatest statesmen jealously vying for the love of an adolescent.

With this rivalry, our voyage from the most mysterious reaches of the
Indo-European tribes to fifth-century Athens comes to a close. The evidence for the institutionalization of pederasty in Greece c. 650 has been laid
before the reader to examine and judge. Much in that story is admittedly
unknown and will no doubt forever remain so, but among the materials left
to us nothing is more compelling than the fact that the best informed and
most analytical of the Greeks themselves, who possessed countless documents now irretrievably lost and who lived far closer to the event than we,
believed in the Cretan origins of pederasty.

Those same materials also reveal the impressive upsurge in literary, artistic, philosophical, and scientific activity that occurred at the time when
institutionalized pederasty was spreading through the *poleis* of the peninsula and beyond. Whether we are reading Pindar's verses to a beautiful
Olympian victor or examining various scenes from the erotic vases, we
cannot escape the presence of a pederastic sensibility. Poetry and art demonstrate no less the importance of the symposium to Archaic society. The
possibility of a relationship between the poetry and art of Archaic Greeks
and institutionalized pederasty is inconceivable, I have suggested, only to
those who choose to make it so.

Epilogue

The mightiest kings have had their minions;
Great Alexander lov'd Hephaestion,
The conquering Hercules for Hylas wept,
And for Patroclus stern Achilles droop'd.
And not kings only, but the wisest men;
The Roman Tully lov'd Octavius,
Grave Socrates wild Alcibiades.
—Marlowe, *Edward the Second,* I, iv

Although this book focuses on Archaic Greece, I have added an epilogue about the subsequent fortunes of pederasty in Greek history for two reasons. First, whereas source material for Archaic Greece is scanty or nonexistent, in later eras documents abound to attest to the importance of pederasts and pederasty to Greek civilization. There we discover from unimpeachable authorities the degree to which Greek society not only once accepted pederasty but also deemed it a worthy path to intellectual and military distinction. Secondly, although Philip of Macedon's defeat of the Greeks at Chaeronea in 338 marked the close of the classical age, pederasty did not cease to play a positive role in Greek life, even though the tendency to convey the opposite impression has been almost unanimous among scholars.[1] The story of pederastic pedagogy long outlives the Greeks' loss of freedom, and its impressive chronicle provides a fitting end to those indistinct yet crucial beginnings I have attempted to trace in the preceding chapters.

The Classical Age (490–338 B.C.)

The period between the defeat of the Persians at Marathon in 490 and Philip's triumph over the Greeks in 338 encompasses those achievements in Hellenic architecture, oratory, sculpture, philosophy, and drama of which every schoolchild has heard. It is also the Golden Age of Greek love. "So active was the pursuit of love-affairs, since no one regarded erotic persons as vulgar, that even a great poet like Aeschylus, and Sophocles, introduced

in the theatre love themes in their tragedies," wrote Athenaeus c. 200 A.D.
(XIII, 600a–b). Thus, although none of the plays by Aeschylus, Sophocles,
and Euripides we read today treat of pederasty, that theme was once part
of the genre that became the most impressive literary development of the
classical age.[2]

Athenaeus further informs us that the drama by Aeschylus he is referring
to dealt with the story of Achilles and Patroclus. The extant fragments of
this tragedy (called *Myrmidions*) suggest that the play ended with the death
of Patroclus and a lament by Achilles over their "many kisses" and the "holy
union of [their] thighs." Sophocles for his part wrote about pederastic love
in the lost *Niobe*, "and," adds Athenaeus, "the audience gladly accepted such
stories" (XIII, 600b).

Indeed, we observe acceptance of pederasty in many different contexts.
Not only did Euripides, too, write a play on a pederastic theme (the rape of
Chrysippus by Laius) but he himself loved Agathon, who in 416 won the
prestigious prize for tragedy. In Aristophanes' comedy the *Thesmophoriazusae* Agathon appears in less flattering terms. There he is mocked for wearing women's clothes in order to understand better a female character in a
play he was writing. Because of this and other portraits of male passives,
Aristophanes has often been considered as critical of pederasty. Yet nothing could be less true. His ridicule targeted only men who took the "female
role" in sex or became obsessed with pursuing boys; indeed his plays as a
whole give evidence of the pleasures Athenians took in their relations with
youths. At the conclusion of *Knights*, for example, the hero is awarded both
a woman and a youth as prizes. To be sure, Aristophanes appears to have
believed that the youth of his day lacked the decorum of an earlier time;
nevertheless, he is depicted (perhaps ironically) in Plato's *Symposium* as a
defender of male same-sex love, calling men who prefer other males "the
finest boys and young men for they have the most manly nature" (192a).
Aristophanes recognizes that some criticize the love of these individuals but
adds, "they are wrong, for their behavior is due not to shamelessness but to
daring, manliness, and virility, since they are quick to welcome their like.
Sure evidence of this is the fact that on reaching maturity these alone prove
in a public career to be men" (192a).

Whether Aristophanes here expresses a view that is consonant with
Plato's own feelings, we cannot say. In fact, given the number of speakers
in Plato's dialogues and the variety of attitudes outlined within and among
the dialogues, it is no easier to identify Plato's voice than to espy one single
perspective on pederasty to associate with the great philosopher. As we

read the dialogues that bear his name we encounter both a call for the total prohibition against the practice as "unnatural" (the "Athenian Visitor" in the *Laws*) and the belief that a spiritual pederastic friendship transcending physical love and fixed on bettering the *eromenos* is superior to heterosexual love (Pausanias in the *Symposium*). On the potential force of that peder-astic bond for instilling courage another speaker in the *Symposium* waxes eloquent as Phaedrus imagines a city or army composed exclusively of ped-erastic couples:

> Then if any device could be found how a state or an army could be made up only of lovers and beloveds, they could not possibly find a better way of living, since they would abstain from all ugly things and be ambitious in beautiful things towards each other; and in battle side by side, such troops although few would conquer pretty well all the world. For the lover would be less willing to be seen by his be-loved than by all the rest of the world, leaving the ranks or throwing away his arms, and he would choose to die many times rather than that; yes, and as to deserting the beloved, or not helping in danger, no one is so base that Love himself would not inspire him to valour, and make him equal to the born hero. (179a)

Although the importance of Plato for modern thought and letters makes debate inevitable over which perspective—the Athenian Visitor's prohibi-tion or Pausanias's and Phaedrus's praise—the author intended to advance, evidence from classical Greece suggests that within Plato's own society ac-ceptance, not proscription, dominated. The orators Aeschines and Demos-thenes, arguing before the people of Athens, spoke openly of their love of youths. Aristophanes' comedies mock certain excesses of pederasty but not the practice itself. In the *Symposium* of Xenophon (c. 430–after 355), the guests converse easily and without censure about pederastic infatuations of the day, as easily in fact as Xenophon speaks about pederasty in his other writings. In the *Anabasis,* his most famous work, he observes that Cle-archus, the most prominent of Cyrus the Younger's generals, was as willing to spend money on war as on a *paidika* or some other pleasure (II, 6, 6). Later he records that when an order was given to release captives, "the sol-diers obeyed, except for individual misappropriations through desire for a boy or a woman among the beautiful" (IV, 1, 14).[3]

The surviving works of Aristotle (c. 375–334), Plato's best student and his rival as the most influential philosopher of antiquity, express none of the glowing positive views on pederasty to be found in the Platonic dialogues.

Aristotle did not, however, call homosexuality unnatural. Rather, considering homosexuality from many points of view throughout his works, he pitied more than he condemned those adults who by nature preferred to be penetrated by other males. Such individuals he considered to be incompletely developed, not depraved. In modern parlance he was an "essentialist," believing that some males were born with an exclusive preference for their own sex. Others, he felt, acquired the taste through early practice (*Nicomachean Ethics*, VII, 3). To prevent the type of homosexuality caused by practice instead of nature, Aristotle prescribed a puritanical education that prohibited obscene paintings and sculptures as well as the kisses authorized even by Plato in his *Republic* (468b). He further recommended that boys and youths should be protected from the advances of slaves and segregated from their elders in the gymnasia (*Politics*, 1331a, 1336a).

Such a combination of praise, criticism, and concern surrounding pederasty should suffice to assure us of its importance in the classical era. Although we have every reason to believe that the Athenian of Plato's *Laws* expresses an extreme view, the tendency of Pausanias and Phaedrus to exalt the pedagogical potential of pederasty and to distance it from a simple physical bond suggests that while the educational role for pederasty remained too significant to permit a majority of philosophers to demand its end, it proved prudent to distance the *erastes*'s desire to inspire from mere physical attraction.[4] Thus, Xenophon's Socrates affirms the chasteness of some of the most famous pederastic couples, including Zeus and Ganymede and Achilles and Patroclus, and a noted Athenian author is quoted in Plato's *Phaedrus* as advising that the boy take a lover who is not in love with him. Such an *erastes* will help him more than a lover who is. In the latter the love is irrational because of jealousy and selfish because of lust. The *Phaedrus* also contains a speech by Socrates, who insists that if the couple rises above their physical feelings "they live a life of happiness and harmony here on earth, self controlled and orderly, holding in subjection that which causes evil in the soul and giving freedom to that which makes for virtue" (256a–b). In this way a constellation of attitudes is formed that will last until the advent of the Christian Empire: against the background of an accepting society, pederasty continues to be practiced, sung about, extolled, and debated.

The Hellenistic Era (322–31 B.C.)

The amount of verse surviving from the Hellenistic period that sings of pederastic relations is truly considerable. Not all of the 258 poems on the

love of youths contained in Book 12 of the *Greek Anthology* come from this
time, but the poems by Callimachus (305–240 B.C.) and Meleager of Gadara
(fl. c. 100 B.C.), some of the best, belong entirely to the Hellenistic era. The
reader will recognize many of the themes shared by this corpus with the Archaic poets (love's ardent madness and its playfulness, the fleeting splendor
of the beloved as adulthood steals in to efface boyish charms, unresponsive
or capricious boys), but in the idylls of Theocritus (c. 301–c. 260) we see
that the ideals of a pederastic relationship, too, have remained constant.

In idyll 13 the poet describes Heracles' attempt to make his *eromenos* brave
and famous and to rear him as a father would his son: "For Amphitryon's
brazen-heart son that braved the roaring lion, he too once loved a lad, to
wit the beauteous Hylas of the curly locks, and, even as father and son, had
taught him all the lore that made himself a good man and brought him
fame. . . . This did he that he might have the lad fashioned to his mind,
and that pulling a straight furrow from the outset the same might come to
be a true man." Elsewhere he reminds the *eromenos* of the passing of tran-
sient youth. Love should be steady and true so that it can develop into a
lifelong friendship, still defined in terms of the famous heroes of the *Iliad:*
"O by those soft lips I beseech you remember that you were younger a year
agone, and as we men wax old and wrinkled sooner than one may spit,
so there's no re-taking of Youth once she be fled. . . . Come then, think
on these things and be the kinder for't, and give love for love where true
loving is; and so when Time shall bring thee a beard we'll be Achilles and
his friend" (XXIX). Thus, pederasty continues not only as a practice but
also as an inspiration. Its heroes remain models to be emulated; its experience, a complex amalgam of emotions worthy to be transcribed into verse
by the finest poetic talents of the day.

Greeks under the Pagan Emperors (31 B.C.–312 A.D.)

The decades surrounding the reign of Hadrian (117–38 A.D.) witnessed a
distinct revival of Greek letters, and prominent among the authors of that
revival is Plutarch (c. 46/47–c. 120 A.D.). His impressive production includes
the *Parallel Lives* of famous Greek and Romans and the *Moralia,* ethical essays
on a wide variety of subjects. As the *Lives* afford us indispensable information about the pederastic lives of many Greeks, so revealing words on
pederasty surface in two of the *Moralia: On the Education of Children* and the
Eroticos.[5]

The lines in *On the Education of Children* that speak about pederasty are few but highly pertinent to our review. The speaker recognizes that harsh fathers may view "the society of admirers [of youths]" as "an intolerable outrage to their sons." Nevertheless,

> when I think of Socrates, Plato, Xenophon, Aeschines, Cebes, and that whole band of men who sanctioned affection between males, and thus guided the youth onward to learning, leadership, and virtuous conduct, I am of a different mind again, and am inclined to emulate their example. Euripides gives testimony in their favour when he says:
>
> > Among mankind another love exists,
> > That of an upright, chaste, and noble soul. [fr. 388]
>
> Nor may we omit the remark of Plato wherein jest and seriousness are combined. For he says that those who have acquitted themselves nobly ought to have the right to kiss any fair one they please [*Republic,* 468b]. Now we ought indeed to drive away those whose desire is for mere outward beauty, but to admit without reserve those who are lovers of the soul. And while the sort of love prevailing at Thebes and in Elis is to be avoided, as well as the so-called kidnapping in Crete, that which is found at Athens and in Lacedaemon is to be emulated. (11e–12a)

Again the pederastic ideal appears undiminished in its ability to inspire the finest qualities, and again its defense is interestingly interwoven with a reference to chastity and the observation that "lovers of the soul" are the only proper *erastai* to be welcomed. Plutarch's *Eroticos* offers a similar network of ideas.

Discussion in the *Eroticos* is generated by the desire of a wealthy widow to marry a younger youth. A group of men debates the advisability of the marriage, some upholding a belief in the superiority of pederastic relations, others, an appreciation of the qualities of marriage. The second position is given the last word. There, Plutarch espouses a practical and conciliatory attitude: beauty may be found in both males and females, love involves the body as well as the soul, and "physical union [with lawful wives] is the beginning of friendship, a sharing, as it were, in the great mysteries" (769a). "[W]hat is there dreadful about a sensible older woman piloting the life of a young man? She will be useful because of her superior intelligence; she will be sweet and affectionate because she loves him," Plutarch says, as if to underscore that the woman can quite adequately play the same role as an *erastes* (754d). However, the arguments ascribed by Plutarch to the defender

of pederasty are not lacking in eloquence. Protogenes insists from the outset that the pederastic bond must be distinguished from the mere physical
copulation that takes place between men and women or between slaves and
youths. The pederastic bond is "beautiful and courteous" and stirs young
men "to the pursuit of virtue" (751a–b). "Every *eromenos* becomes generous, single hearted, high-minded, even though he was miserly before. His
meanness and avarice are melted away like iron in the fire, so that he is made
happier giving to those he loves than he is made by receiving gifts from
others himself" (762b–c). Loyalty, like that of Aristogiton to his insulted
lover, and bravery in battle are further qualities pederasty instills in youth.
Such a vigorous rehearsal at this late date in Greek history of the virtues of
pederastic pedagogy certainly has to make us marvel at the longevity of that
tradition. But there is one more point that should be made. The response
that Protogenes receives in the *Eroticos* is a defense of marriage far more
than an attack against or a call for the proscription of pederasty.[6] Taken in
its totality, the *Eroticos* challenges the pederastic ethos for its denigration of
marriage, women, and sex, not for any crime against the laws of nature.

A comparable debate on pederasty and heterosexual love by pseudo-
Lucian survives also.[7] The *Erotes* (Loves) is less sophisticated than the essay
by Plutarch and reviews many of the same arguments on both sides. Callicratidas affirms that pederasty is "the only activity combining both pleasure
and virtue" (31), whereas his opponent Charicles insists that pederasts "call
themselves lovers of virtue" only to hide their actual love of the body (23).
Charicles maintains that in the beginning men obeyed the laws of nature
and coupled with women. Pederasty must be seen as a falling away from
those laws (20). Callicratidas admits that the practice came late but denies
that such a chronology signals inferiority and degeneracy: "we must consider the pursuits that are old to be necessary, but assess as superior the later
additions invented by human life when it had leisure for thought" (35). Pederasty belongs with the arts as the product of the growing sophistication
of society. "[M]arriage is a remedy invented to ensure man's necessary per-
petuity, but only love for males is a noble duty enjoined by a philosophic
spirit" (33).[8]

Thus, although history has often recorded the demise of an ideal which
over time lost its ability to appeal to the imagination, pederastic pedagogy does not, in pagan times, figure among such concepts. No matter how
often criticism of pederasty appeared after the Archaic period, vigorous de-
fenses of the ideal were equally present to counter the attack. Indeed, as

late as the *Dionysiaca* of Nonnus, which has been variously dated from 390 to 500 A.D., the pederastic love of a god-hero and a youth was celebrated unapologetically. Only with the triumph of Christianity, which produced the animadversions of St. Paul and repromulgated the prohibitions of the Mosaic law against homosexuality, did the tradition of a thousand years finally give way.[9]

Notes

Introduction

1. I have used most often the Loeb translations, except where they have put the "obscene" Greek passages into Latin, and other older standard versions such as Jowett's Plato, Clough's Plutarch, Finley's Thucydides, and Rawlinson's Herodotus when they seemed accurate and reliable. Occasionally I have preferred a more modern or, for our purposes, accurate version, perhaps from some commentator or recent article, or even made my own. Accuracy rather than style or taste has been my criterion. For the fragments I have used whatever came to hand, often German translations that I have rendered into English. Warren Johansson, who commanded a score of ancient, medieval, and modern languages, made a number of these translations.

2. "The Greek culture of the classic age is a male culture. . . . The erotic relation of men to youths was the necessary and sole preparation, to a degree unattainable to our comprehension, of all manly education. . . . All idealism of the strength of the Greek nature threw itself into that relation, and it is probable that never since have young men been treated so attentively, so lovingly, so entirely with a view to their welfare (virtus) as in the fifth and sixth centuries B.C.—according to the beautiful saying of Hölderlin: 'For it is when loving that mortal man gives of his best' " (Nietzsche [1909–13] VI, 1, 259).

3. Hartmann (1932) 2:197–98. (Throughout, references to modern works will be cited in the endnotes in this abbreviated form, with complete bibliographical information given in the Bibliography.) The Dutch writer L. S. A. M. von Römer coined the terms *didascalophile* for those attracted to sexual partners from whom they could learn and *manthanophile* for those attracted to partners whom they could educate (Hirschfeld [1914] 285).

4. Dover (1978) 202.

5. For example, I draw upon Licht's pre-1914 detailed, technical articles. They are far more thorough than any before or since in that he tried in them to analyze every fragment then known relating to homosexuality. His articles have essentially been ignored by classical scholars; none has ever been translated into English.

6. *Oxford Classical Dictionary* (1970) 961.

7. Clarke (1978) argued that Homer did; Price (1989) and Halperin (1990) that he did not.

8. Cantarella ([1992] 22–27) argued forcefully that pedication prevailed. Kinsey's

studies indicate that once an adolescent male found enjoyment in a particular sexual practice he rarely gave it up entirely. Accordingly, there should have been some adults seeking the passive role. Compare: "The data which we have already published on social levels show that by fourteen years of age perhaps as many as eighty-five percent of all boys have acquired the patterns of sexual behavior which will characterize them as adults, and something like nine out of ten of them do not materially modify their basic patterns after sixteen years of age" (Kinsey [1949] 21). For this reference I am indebted to Dr. C. A. Tripp.

9. Jocelyn (1980) 16.

10. Dover (1978) 98, partially disavowed by him in a new essay (1988).

11. Dover (1978) 104 and 140–42.

12. In Plato's *Gorgias* the context indicates an individual with an insatiable itching in his posteriors. He therefore craves penetration by another male; this theory is also expounded in the pseudo-Aristotelian *Problems*. Chantraine could give no satisfactory etymon for the word. (Warren Johansson suggested to me that it derived from a Semitic *khunaitha*, cognate with Classical Arabic *khanith* and *mukhannath* in the same meaning, sometimes with other aspects of gender inversion.) From the Greek word is derived Latin *cinaedus* and from that Italian *cinedo*.

13. Dover (1978), 20. The words *pornos* and *porne* Chantraine derived ([1968–80] 3:888) from the verb *pérnemi* 'to sell'. The feminine form is first attested in Archilochus, fr. 302 W = Lasserre 91, while the masculine first appears in the inscriptions of Thera, then in Aristophanes. The *pornos/porne* is most commonly the slave whose body was sold to the brothel keeper or to the client. Still earlier, Homer alluded to "an extensive trade in boys, who were chiefly bought by Phoenician ship-masters, or more frequently carried off, to fill the harems of wealthy pashas." The passages cited are *Odyssey* XIV, 297, and XV, 449, with a further reference to Movers, *Phönizien*, ii, 3, 80. (See Licht [1932] 437, 452.) The word has numerous compounds in later writers, notably the hapax legomenon (a word occurring only once) *pornographoi* in Athenaeus, where it means "portraitists of courtesans."

14. On the contrary, note among others Pausanias's words in the *Symposium* 181d to the effect that a lover of boys will await the first signs of intelligence (and beard) before choosing his lover.

15. Parker Rossman's 1985 study deserves to be included with these titles, refining as it does in even greater detail the various forms of pederasty that have been observed.

16. Hirschfeld (1914), 308–24, Weinrich (1987), LeVay (1993), and Hamer and Copeland (1994) argue for biological causes of homosexuality which would transcend the chronological limitations conceived by the social constructionists and operate in all periods and societies. However, this is not the place to discuss the controversy between "essentialists" and social constructionists. For a provocative assessment of both positions with regard to ancient Greece, see Lambert and Szesnat (1994).

17. As committed as I am to stressing the mentoring role of Greek pederasty, I do not hesitate to recognize that indifferent and lustful *erastai* must have existed. In-

deed, scholars from Edward Perry Warren to Parker Rossman have made this point and recognized that pederasty has often fallen short of the educational goals established in Greece. Still, so have human institutions of all kinds and eras.

Chapter 1: Indo-European Pederasty

1. Renfrew's approach overlooks the crucial difference between the earlier (Paleo-eurasian) and later (Indo-European) settlers of Europe. Whatever the achievements of prehistoric Europeans were in agriculture or metallurgy, the fact remains that they did not develop a high civilization on their own. The Greeks and Romans borrowed heavily from and copied the material culture of the Hamites and the Semites, who were indebted to the Sumerians, as Bernal's *Black Athena* emphasizes. However, the end result of cultural evolution in the Mediterranean region and the Near East was that Indo-European and Semitic triumphed over the previous linguistic families. Even Sumerian and Etruscan had become dead languages by the onset of late antiquity, and Coptic survived solely as the liturgical language of the Christian church in Egypt. The "classical" languages that shaped medieval and modern civilization throughout the region were Greek, Latin, and Arabic.

2. The best summaries of information indicating the existence of such practices among primitive peoples are Karsch-Haack (1911), Ford and Beach (1951), and Greenberg (1988).

3. Plentiful, if later, evidence for Celtic pederasty is also provided by Welsh and Irish penitentials. See Payer (1984).

4. Strabo, writing under Roman ascendancy, asserted that "it is notorious that the Celts are quarrelsome and also that they do not believe that it is shameful that youths (*neoi*) are very generous with the charms of their adolescence" (IV, 4, 6 = 198). He and perhaps some of the others, including Diodorus, were presumably using Poseidonius, a true authority, who took down a great deal of information about the people of Gaul when he visited there (*Fragmenta Historicorum graecorum,* ed. T. Müller [1841–70], 87 F116).

5. Summarized by Bleibtreu-Ehrenberg (1978) 19.

6. See C. Williams (1992).

7. Dynes (1990) "Scandinavia, Medieval." I should add that there is no pertinent evidence for Slavic or Baltic pederasty.

8. Everson (1989) 170–71.

9. Bernal (1987).

10. Bernal has told me that he did not find the subject of homosexuality too repugnant to discuss. He did not mention it in his first volume, or in his second, which deals primarily with archeology. He did tell me that he plans to discuss it in his third volume, which is primarily on philology. Like me, he is totally convinced that however much else the Greeks borrowed from the Egyptians and the Semites, they did not borrow pederasty. He feels that the Egyptians were very hostile to homosexuality.

11. See my articles, "Indo-European Pederasty" in Dynes (1990) and "The Ori-

gins of Institutionalized Pederasty" (1992), where I show that Sergent failed to disprove Dover's (1978) maxim that no evidence for Greek pederasty predates 630.

12. Burkert (1985) 125–26.
13. Renfrew (1987) chap. 3.
14. Burkert (1985) 34, 45.
15. Graham (1962) 87–88.
16. *The Cambridge Ancient History* (1973) 2, part 1:572–73.
17. *The Cambridge Ancient History* (1973) 2, part 1:161.
18. Athenaeus, who repeated all sorts of opinions without necessarily endorsing them, said that Minos seized Ganymede from the Harpagion on Crete and that Minos loved the Athenian hero Theseus (XIII, 601). Thus, Athenaeus may also have presumed that Greek pederasty had its origin in Minoan Crete.
19. Jeanmaire (1939) 453–54 n. 26.
20. Willetts (1965) 116–17 n. 27.
21. Koehl (1986) 106.
22. Boardman (1978) fig. 47.
23. Koehl (1986) 108.
24. Vermeule (1964) 90, 91, 92, 93, 96–97, 101, 102.
25. Greenberg (1988) 141.
26. Chadwick (1976).

Chapter 2: Dorian Knabenliebe

1. Stiebing (1980) 8–9.
2. True, Plutarch speaks in his *Eroticos* of the Thessalian warrior Cleomachus (who had a lover) aiding the Chalcidians. Aristotle said the hero was from the Chalcidian peninsula in northeast Greece, but I will argue below that these regions imported institutionalized pederasty from Crete and/or Sparta.
3. A believer in pure, asexual pederasty, Karl Müller further rhapsodized: "This passionate inclination of men for boys, this intimate attachment that makes the former second fathers, must have deeper roots than an individual institution. . . . So we come to the conclusion that this peculiar relationship had formed among the pre-Hellenic peoples in a completely uncompromised and noble fashion, before the physical abuse of boys, probably from Lydia, had become known in Greece. . . . The brotherhood-in-arms of older and younger heroes in faraway adventures may have offered the points of departure for it [citing Ramdohr, *Venus Urania*, 3, 1, p. 138]" ([1844] 290, 292, 293).
4. K. Müller (1830) 2:310.
5. Meier (1837) 160–61.
6. See, for example, Plutarch, *On the Education of Children,* 11F–12A; and Vettius Valens, 122, 1.
7. Hiller von Gaertringen (1898) 536, 537, 538b (1411), 540 (I, II, III), 541, 543, 545 (1415), 546, 547, 581 (1437). The same publication includes illustrations of the graffiti.
8. Sergent (1987a) 41.

9. Huxley (1962) 24.

10. Boardman (1964b) 170.

11. Hiller von Gaertringen (1899–1909) 1:152–53.

12. Dover placed them at the end of the seventh century ([1978] 195). R. Carpenter dated them to the middle of the sixth century ([1933] 26).

13. Dover (1978) 123 and Buffière (1980) 59. For an argument that recognizes the sexual reality of the pederastic activity at Thera, yet posits that the inscriptions contained a religious dimension, see Brongersma (1990).

14. Bethe (1907) 464 nn. 57–58. See also above, p. 17.

15. Bethe (1907) 460.

16. Semenov (1911) 150.

17. For his full reaction, see Ruppersberg (1911) 151–54.

18. Patzer (1982) 14–15, 73–74.

19. Jaeger (1943–45) 1:194–95.

20. Pogey-Castries (1930) chap. 5.

21. Licht (1932) 418.

22. Patzer (1982) 75.

Chapter 3: Pre-Pederastic Immortals

1. Meier (1837).

2. G. Murray (1960) 124.

3. Lachmann (1841) argued that the *Iliad* consisted of sixteen independent lays that were reworked.

4. Still, it has even been claimed unconvincingly that Homer rarely if ever referred to pederasty because it was a Dorian importation and he was either ignorant of it or too embarrassed by the custom to speak of it.

5. Dover (1978) 197 and Sichtermann (1988) 154.

6. "The *Iliad* therefore has for its whole subject the passion of Achilles—that ardent energy . . . of the hero which displayed itself first as anger against Agamemnon, and afterwards as love for the lost Patroclus" (Symonds [1873–76] 2:44–45). Benecke echoed Symonds, calling the story of Achilles and Patroclus "the main motive of the epic" (1896) 76.

7. Symonds (1883) 1–2, 4.

8. See, for example, Boswell (1980) 47.

9. Sergent (1986) 13.

10. Halperin (1990) 75–87.

11. According to Warren Johansson, *therapon* should be derived from a cognate of classical Arabic *tarafawu* 'they formed an alliance'.

12. Halperin (1990) 85. See also Nagy (1979a) 292–93 and MacCary (1982) 127–36.

13. Clarke (1978) has added yet another possibility, to wit that Achilles and Patroclus were adolescent same-age lovers.

Chapter 4: Situational Homosexuality and Demography

1. Marrou (1956) 26–31.

2. Dover (1978) 195.

3. Although soldiering, education, seafaring, travel, colonies, and politics have rarely been considered from a homosocial angle, some studies have appeared. R. R. Burg's (1983) on seventeenth-century English pirates; J. R. de Symons Honey's (1977) and J. Chandos's (1984) on English public schools; and P. Fussell's (1975) on the military are also pertinent and show how in these particular environments males have often had their most intimate relationships.

4. Dover (1978) 201.

5. Rougé (1970) passim.

6. In 1796, eight years after the first convicts landed in Australia, Francis Wilkinson was accused of buggery.

7. Dynes (1990) "Australia." See also Lindner (1951).

8. For studies of such activity in modern history see Burg (1983) and Gilbert (1974, 1977).

9. See Bérubé (1990) for modern examples.

10. I use Dover's translation of Eubulus ([1978] 135).

11. Perhaps also the population had been so thinned by the original onslaught and the periodic return of epidemics and war that it was no longer dense enough for certain diseases to transmit themselves effectively from one human host to another.

12. For a discussion of climate changes in this part of the Mediterranean, see the theory of Rhys Carpenter (1966), according to which a shift north in the trade winds c. 1200 led to drought in Palestine, Syria, central Anatolia, Crete, and much of the Peloponnesus.

13. Die-offs and system collapses may be easier to envisage as the result of microbes and their evolutions than of human actions. Sallares ([1991] 221–93) did not accept this theory. He argued that the breakdown of the age-class system (see below, "Cretan Knights") and of compulsory pederasty, which he thought had been instituted to curb births and continued only in Crete and Sparta, caused the population explosion everywhere else.

14. From Snodgrass's arguments one can extrapolate a population of about 150,000 at the nadir between 1000 and 800 (approximately one-fourth of the 800,000 attained by Myceneans). Seven times that figure yields about 1,000,000 people around the year 700. By 600 the total Greek-speaking population, including all the overseas extensions, may have doubled again to 2,000,000.

15. Sallares (1991) 84.

16. "Bring home a wife to your house when you are of the right age, while you are not far short of thirty years nor much above; this is the right age for marriage. Let your wife have been grown up four years, and marry her in the fifth. Marry a maiden, so that you can teach her careful ways, and especially marry one who lives near you, but look well about you and see that your marriage will not be a joke to your neighbors" (Hesiod, *Works and Days*, 695–702).

17. Prominent supporters of this theory are Welcker (1816), Meier (1837), and Patzer (1982).

18. Dynes (1990) "Kadesh."

19. Isocrates, whose *Bousiris* portrayed Egypt as the most blessed of lands, added that "in former times any barbarians who were in misfortune presumed to be rulers over the Greek cities [for example] Danaos, an exile from Egypt, occupied Argos; Kadmos from Sidon became king of Thebes" (*Praise of Helen*, X, 68). This has given occasion to those ancients who supported a Theban origin of pederasty through Laius, king of Thebes, to connect the introduction of pederasty to the Near East, but no moderns have argued this line of thought.

20. On the other hand, he noted that the Greeks adopted the phallic procession and Dionysiac ritual, along with, he thought "all the gods" from Egypt: "Now I have an idea that Melampous . . . introduced the name of Dionysus into Greece, together with the sacrifice in his honour and the phallic procession. . . . Probably Melampous got his knowledge about Dionysos through Kadmos of Tyre and the people who came with him from Phoenicia to the country now called Boiotia. The names of nearly all the gods came to Greece from Egypt. I know from the enquiries I have made that they came from abroad, and it seems most likely that it was from Egypt, for the names of all the gods have been known in Egypt from the beginning of time. . . . These practices, then, and others which I shall speak of later, were borrowed by the Greeks from Egypt" (Herodotus, II, 49–51). Bernal in essence agrees ([1987] 67).

21. See in particular Harrison (1965) and Robertson (1975).

22. Bowra ([1957] 40) gives no evidence to support his claim. Sergent ([1986] 103ff.) bases his remarks on homosexual elements that were in fact added later to the myths that he cites.

Chapter 5: The Immortals Become Pederasts

1. Meier (1837) 156.

2. "This vice, which never appears in the writings of Homer and Hesiod, doubtless arose under the influence of the public games, which accustoming men to the contemplation of absolutely nude figures, awoke an unnatural passion, totally remote from all modern feelings, but which in Greece it was regarded as heroic to resist. The popular religion in this, as in other cases, was made to bend to the new vice. Hebe, the cup-bearer of the gods, was replaced by Ganymede, and the worst vices of earth were transported to Olympus" (Lecky [1911] 2:294).

3. Beyer (1910) 7–8.

4. Burkert (1985) 128.

5. Beyer (1910) 75–76. *Philtatos* is an epic word, the superlative of *philos* 'beloved', which is used, however, in Homer in a nonsexual sense. The passage in question is discussed by Löffler ([1963] 32 n. 13 and 35 n. 30), who does not mention an erotic implication.

6. Sergent (1986) 262–65.

7. Bremmer (1990) 141.

8. When Greek ceremony featured the abduction of youths (as in Crete) and of females (as in Sparta), the act was apparently merely ritualistic, accomplished by consent, not by brute force. Public opinion, custom, and law all censured and in fact forbade actual force.

9. Pogey-Castries ([1930] 25) said the thirty-third, which he wrongly calculated as c. 635. The *Oxford Classical Dictionary* ([1970] 794) assigned Peisander to the seventh or sixth century, as does the *Kleine Pauly*.

10. Bowra (1961) 91.

11. Licht (1932) 463.

12. According to Theocritus, *Epigrams,* XX, and Pausanias, II, 47, 4.

13. For Sergent's general views, see pp. 16–17.

14. Sergent considered as definitely old the founding myths of the pairs Poseidon/Pelops (for the *polis* of Pisatis), Laius/Chrysippus (Thebes) Apollo/Hyacinthus (Sparta), Apollo/Cyparissus (Chios and Orchomenus), Ameinias/Narcissus (Thespiai), Apollo/Admetus (Delphi), Apollo/Carmos or Carneus (Sicyon), Apollo/Branchus (Didyma), Apollo/Hippolytus (Thebes, Thespiai, Agyrion), Heracles/Elacatas (Sparta), Diocles/Philolaus (Thebes), Cleomachus/? (Chalcis), Polymnus or Prosymnus/Dionysus (Lerna, Argos), Zeus or Minos or Tantalus/Ganymedes (Crete, Chalcis), Archias/Actaeon (Corinth), Eurybatus/Alcyoneus (Delphi), Phylius/Cycnus (Aetolia), Hermes or Paris or Deiphobus/Antheus (Assessos), Poseidon/Kainis or Kaineus (northern Thessaly) (Sergent [1986] 262–65).

Chapter 6: Cretan Knights and "Renowned Ones"

1. See, for example, Wilamowitz-Moellendorff and Niese (1910). Of all of the nineteenth-century German scholars, Meier came closest to the truth about the origins of Greek pederasty, but he avoided making any definitive analysis: "It is therefore most convenient to begin with the states of the Doric tribe, namely those of Crete, all the more as the Cretans are named by some writers [e.g., Servius on the *Aeneid,* X, 328] as exactly those who first knew boy love and transmitted it to the other Greeks; also not a few myths refer to Crete where the institution exercised the most significant influence. Data are lacking to determine whence it came to Crete and whether the Greeks obtained it from Lydia, as Welcker thinks [(1824–26) 356], or only the physical abuse of boys [Meier's term for pederasty that involved sexual relations]. If we find boy-love in the most specific and indeed pedagogical form everywhere in the Dorian tribe, then one could designate not so much Crete as the northern districts of Greece, which were the cradle of this tribe, as the areas in which it first developed in this form. The most extensive account of Cretan boy-love we owe to Ephorus. The relationship was here not, as in the other Greek locales, begun by a proposition on the part of the older man, but by abduction (as in Sparta the brides were abducted). . . . That boy-love in Crete was not free of filthiness and vice is proven by the reproach that Plato [*Laws* I, 636; VIII, 836] and Plutarch [*De puerorum educatione* c. 14] express in regard to it and by the saying 'Cretan way' for boy-love. The legislator cannot escape the reproach of having favored an institution

that could so easily lead to vileness; but so publicly favored an establishment that bore such fair fruit of courage [Aelian, *Animalium Historia,* IV, 1] cannot be ascribed to this filthiness. The intention is attributed to the legislator, probably falsely, by Aristotle [*Politics,* II, 7, 5] as though he had meant to restrict thereby the increase of the population. [Such an assumption] should probably be perceived for the honor of the human race as untrue. Nevertheless, it did lie in the spirit of the Dorian constitution to maintain the equilibrium between population and property, between the number of households (*oikoi*) and the lots (*kleroi*) for each, even in a compulsory manner. If lastly in the sagas Harpagias is named as the port from which Ganymede was abducted, we should probably conclude that it was from there that the abduction of the boys in Crete customarily occurred" (Meier [1837] 160–61).

2. Morrow (1960).

3. Effenterre (1948) 35–36, 40–44.

4. Morrow (1960) 20–21.

5. Best summarized and documented by Beyer (1910) 72 and by Sergent (1986) 29 and 262–65.

6. I am indebted to Warren Johansson for this information.

7. For discussions of the vocabulary of pederasty, see Pogey-Castries (1930), Vorberg (1932), Licht (1932), and Greenberg (1988).

8. Snodgrass (1980) chap. 1.

9. Willetts (1967) 8–10.

10. The reader may be surprised by Aristotle's phrase "between males," which to the twentieth century would include a much wider range of activity than is understood by the term pederasty. Such activity may well have existed in Archaic Greece; it was not, however, "instituted" by the state. For that reason I feel confident that Aristotle's phrase refers to pederasty, despite his use of the broader description.

11. Hirschfeld (1914).

12. It should be pointed out that whereas Diels ([1891] 395ff.) affirmed the reality of Epimenides, Wilamowitz-Moellendorff ([1891] 243ff.) denied it.

13. "In Crete all those who are selected out of the 'Troop' of boys at the same time are forced to marry at the same time, although they do not take the girls whom they have married to their own homes immediately, but as soon as the girls are qualified to manage the affairs of the house. A girl's dower, if she has brothers, is half of the brother's portion. The children must learn, not only their letters, but also the songs prescribed in the laws and certain forms of music" (Strabo, X, 4, 20). Willetts believed on the basis of the *Ekdysia,* a festival at the Cretan city of Phaistos to celebrate the final step in the process of the "honeymoon" with his older male lover and return to acceptance into society as an adult, that "At the conclusion of the *Ekdysia,* the newly enfranchised young men also participated in mass marriage ceremonies" ([1955] 121, n. 27). This may have occurred, but as the youths were still quite young, they did not live with their still younger "wives" for a number of years.

14. In the mountains, the adult *philetor* (lover) taught the *parastates* (literally, comrade and bystander in the ranks of battle and life, but practically shield bearer) to hunt. According to Hirschfeld, "*Parastates* was probably a designation of the later

relationship and referred to the position in the chorus and army. Cf. *parastates* in Aristotle, *Politics* III, I, 4" (Hirschfeld [1914] 764 n. 90). The boy's killing of a large animal proved his prowess, as later among some German tribes.

15. The claim that "In Crete it is thought praiseworthy for young men [*adulescentuli*] to have had the greatest possible number of lovers" (Cornelius Nepos, preface) is late. Nepos died c. 24 B.C. Therefore, his statement may not be accurate or may not describe the customs of the Archaic or classical period. Moreover, the word "Crete" (Creta) in the sentence is a scholar's emendation of the manuscript reading "Greece" (Graecia).

16. The fullest treatment is in Willetts (1955) 10–14.

17. *Alcestis* 989: "theon skotioi. Kretes de tous anebous skotious legousi" ("Obscure [children] of the gods. The Cretans call minors obscure"). Ruijgh ([1957] 108) comments on this use of *skotios* without realizing the contrast to *kleinos*.

18. Jeanmaire ([1939] 326) maintained that *skotios* and *kryptos* both refer exclusively to the boy while "secluded" on his honeymoon, but this is improbable.

19. Eustathius on *Iliad,* VIII, 518 says: "Kretes de apodromous, ou dia to pepauthai ton dromon" ("The Cretans call [ephebi] pre-racers, from not frequenting the *dromoi*").

20. Kretschmer (1911) 269f. See also Meister (1963) 241, part 5:9–15.

21. Willetts ([1955] 13 n. 2) added: "Guarducci reads *pentekaidekadromos* (fifteen-racer) in the Code, XI, 34. Cf. X. *HG* 3.4.23: *Ton deka aph' hebes* (of those forty from adolescence), and also the meaning 'finito ephebiae tempore ex agela exire' which it seems necessary to attach to the word *egdramein*" (IC I.XVI.5.21 and Guarducci ibid.), which verb would thus mean 'to graduate from the *agele*'.

22. The belief that a boy remained in the *agele* for ten years, seen for example in Daremberg and Saglio (1873–1919), rests solely upon the gratuitous emendation of a corrupt gloss in the manuscript and editio princeps of Hesychius by Valckenaer (1739) 54: "*dekadromoi:* hoi deka ete en tois andrasi eskekotes" ("ten-racers: those who have for ten years trained among the men"). But a comparison of the remark of Aristophanes of Byzantium (c. 257–180) in Eustathius's commentary on *Odyssey,* VIII, 247: "en Krete, apodromous, dia to medepo ton koinon dromon metechein" ("in Crete, [the *ephebi* are called] pre-racers, from not yet taking part in the common races [gymnastic training]") indicates that the correct reading of the lemma is rather: "*dekadromoi:* hoi deka en tois andrasi dromon meteschekotes, hypo Kreton" ("ten-racers: those who have taken part among the [adult] men in ten races [athletic contests], in the dialect of the Cretans"), so that *pentekaidekadromos* would mean "one who taken part in fifteen races."

23. Hansen explained the origins of his model: "Now, there has never been a reliable and detailed population census in a society which had a life expectancy at birth of less than 30 years. So we lack empirical data; but for about two decades we have had at our disposal computerized models of all possible (stable) populations at 24 different mortality levels (ranging from 20 to 75.5 years for females), and for each mortality level the age distribution is recorded for various growth rates (ranging from an annual decrease of 1% to an annual increase of 5%). Four different

demographic system (called Model West, North, East and South) have been computed at all 24 mortality levels. The authors suggest utilizing Model West where there is no reliable guide to the age pattern of mortality actually prevailing. I have followed their advice but one should note that, for my purposes, the variations between the four model populations are so small that the other models might have served equally well. Thus, for this study, I suggest, as a proper analogy: Model West, males, mortality level 4 (life expectancy at birth: 25.26 years) and growth rate 5.00 (an annual increase of ½%)" (Hansen [1985] 11). Hansen believed that Model West (the European experience between 1500 and 1750) was most analogous to classical Greece because after 1750 the lower mortality rates distorted what happened in history. I transfer this model from classical to Archaic Greece with many reservations.

24. "Soon after the middle of the seventh century the Theran party sailed for North Africa, and were guided by a Cretan to the offshore island of Platea. . . . Crete joined Rhodes in founding Gela, but Cretan (?) flasks are found in earlier Euboean colonies, and it may be that the island shared with Corinth some of the trade in perfume to the west. . . . The last of the major Dorian foundations in Sicily was a joint effort by the Rhodians and Cretans. Thucydides dates it to 688. . . . Acragas (Agrigento) was founded in 580 by Gela, and by the Rhodian settlers there, with reinforcements from home, rather than by the Cretans" (Boardman [1964b] 170, 179, 190, 198).

25. Schulten (1922); Hennig (1934) 57. Warren Johansson has given me this information from a letter written by Professor Schulten.

26. Bury (1975) 99.

27. "The Cretan constitution is similar to the Lacedaemonian; in some few particulars it is certainly no worse, but in general it is less finished. It is said, and it appears to be true, that to a very great extent the Cretan constitution was taken as a model by the Lacedaemonian. (Generally, later forms of constitution are more fully developed than earlier.) They say that Lycurgus, after laying down his guardianship of King Charillus, went abroad and on that occasion spent most of his time in Crete. He chose Crete because the two peoples were akin, the Lyctians being colonists from Sparta; and when the colonists came, they found the inhabitants at that time living under a legal system which they then adopted. Hence to this day the peripheral populations use those laws unchanged, believing Minos to have established the legal system in the first place" (Aristotle, *Politics,* 1271b).

28. Buffière (1980) 62.

29. Another case of borrowing, according to Ephorus, was the class of knights (*hippeis*), who in Crete seem actually to have ridden horses in battle long after the hoplite displaced them in Sparta (X, 4, 18), but knights may at one time have been common to Dorians. Cretans like early Spartans divided themselves into the three traditional tribes found among other Dorian peoples. The phratry seems to have been of Indo-European origin. The Cretan *agora,* so similar to the Spartan *apellas,* may have descended from a common Dorian institution. Thus Cretans and Spartans brought the class of knights, the phratries, and the three tribes with them to the peninsula and instituted serfdom in situ.

30. Scholiast on Apollonius of Rhodes, IV, 1212; Diodorus Siculus, VIII, 10; Plutarch, *Eroticos,* 772e–f, Maximus of Tyre, 24, cf. Alexander Aetolus v. 7 in Parthenenius, 14.

Chapter 7: Spartan Hoplite "Inspirers" and Their "Listeners"

1. Michell (1952) 195.

2. Forrest (1968) 19–20.

3. "It now appears that the several items of hoplite equipment were adopted piecemeal; none of them is attested before 750, but all of them appeared by 700. However, at first they were used separately, not combined into a complete set of equipment; the full hoplite panoply is first shown in a vase ca. 675. Further, the adoption of hoplite equipment did not at once bring a change in tactics; men using some or all the items of hoplite equipment continued to fight in the less organized fashion of the eighth century. The hoplite phalanx does not appear on vases before ca. 650" (Sealey [1976] 29–30).

4. Lorimer, who argued that the new equipment came into use simultaneously with the phalanx, presumed that Sparta adopted the porpax shield, the long rectangular shield used by hoplites in the phalanx, within the first quarter of the seventh century. See Lorimer (1947) 128.

5. Cartledge (1987) 25.

6. Wade-Gery in *Cambridge Ancient History* (1965) 3, chap. 22.

7. Andrewes (1956) 70–71.

8. "Some report besides, that the priestess [of Apollo at Delphi] delivered to him the entire system of laws which are still observed by the Spartans. The Lacedaemonians, however, themselves assert that Lycurgus, when he was guardian of his nephew, Labotas, king of Sparta, and regent in his room, introduced them from Crete; for as soon as he became regent, he altered the whole of the existing customs, substituting new ones, which he took care should be observed by all. After this he arranged whatever appertained to war, establishing the companies of thirty, messmates, and sworn brotherhoods, besides which he instituted the senate, and the ephoralty. Such was the way in which the Lacedaemonians became a well-governed people" (Herodotus, I, 65).

9. Eusebius, *Chronologia,* VII, p. 198 b, 12 Helm.

10. Licht (1906) 627. For a different reading, see Dover (1978) 195.

11. The fact that such an early credible source as the contemporary poet Pratinas, who actually resided at Sparta, recorded that Thaletas stayed the plague at Sparta lends credence to the story. See Plutarch "On Music," 42, 1146b–c.

12. Jaeger (1943–45) 1:85.

13. *Oxford Classical Dictionary* (1970) 922.

14. Andrewes (1956) 76–77.

15. Boardman (1964b).

16. Meister (1963).

17. See Crowther (1989).

18. Gardiner (1930). Girls and boys ran and wrestled together on Chios (Athenaeus, XIII, 566) as well as at Sparta, but so far as we know not in other *poleis,* though, according to one tradition, there were originally competitions for women at Olympia.

19. Chrimes (1949) chap. 3.

20. See also Plutarch, "Lycurgus," XII.

21. Dover (1978) 188–89.

22. Hodkinson (1988).

23. See Plutarch, "Lycurgus," XVI.

24. See Dover (1978), 184–203, Tarán (1985). On the other hand, for some, the beard enhanced the youth's beauty. Compare *Iliad,* XXIV, 347–48; Plato, *Protagoras,* 309a–b; Xenophon, *Symposium,* IV, 23.

25. Bremmer (1980) 283.

26. Xenophon, *Constitution,* II, 13, *Symposium,* VIII, 35; Plutarch, "Lycurgus," XVIIf; "Agesilaus," XX; "Cleomenes III"; *Institutions of the Lacedemonians,* VII.

27. We know that after victory in the Peloponnesian War Spartan harmosts "abused" boys, by which buggery is clearly meant (Plutarch, *Moralia,* 773f–774a; Xenophon, *Hellenica,* III, 5, 12–13). Their hero King Agesilaus (399–360), however, fought his passion for Megabates (Plutarch, "Agesilaus," XI, 2 and 5).

28. Jaeger (1943–45) 1:195.

29. See also West (1965) 188 and Dover (1978) 179 n. 26.

30. Filippo (1977) 17–22.

31. See Gentili (1976) 60–61, 65–66.

32. Statius with Pindar and Ibycus (*Silvae,* 5, 3, 146), Plutarch with Pindar, Simonides, and Bacchylides ("On Music" 17, 1136f), and Athenaeus with Stesichorus and Simonides (XIV, 638e).

33. Easterling (1974) 40–41.

Chapter 8: Gymnasia, Symposia, and Pederastic Art

1. The variation in the lists of these sages is as great as the number of lists we possess. No one except Ephorus excluded the pederastic physicist Thales of Miletus. In place of the obscure Cleobulus of Lindus on Rhodes and Myson of Chen, Meandrius included the son of Gorgiadas, Leophantus of Lebidus (or Ephesus), and Epimenides the Cretan, who, I believe, helped Solon introduce pederasty to Athens. Plato included Myson but left out Periander of Corinth. Some added Pythagoras. Dicaearchus gave Thales, Solon, Bias, and Pittacus, tyrant of Mytilene in the lifetime of Sappho and Alcaeus. He then added six others: Aristodemus, tyrant of Cumae, dubbed "the Effeminate" in spite of his brilliant military achievements, the obscure Pamphylus, Chilon (the Spartan ephor), Cleobulus, Anacharsis, and Periander, son of Cypselus of Corinth. Other lists survive from Hermippus of Smyrna (third century B.C.), Hippobotus (late third century B.C.), Plutarch (in his *Dinner of the Seven Wise Men*), and Diogenes Laertius.

2. Just as socialism had its voluntary efforts like Brook Farm and, in France,

Fournier's *phalanges* before Marxist state imposition, the spread of institutionalized pederasty may have been helped in part at least by the voluntary actions of aristocratic adolescents and young adults, the groups always most open to trends and eager for change and experimentation. Witness our recent sexual revolution. I can imagine youths in various *poleis* rapidly adapting Cretan and Spartan innovations such as nude athletics on improvised clearings at the city's edge and all-male dinners. Early on, especially as in Alcaeus's Mytilene, these dinners may have been lifelong clubs, composed of those related by blood or other ties and having common agendas (a trace of which we see in the later aristocratic groups that made the oligarchic revolution in Athens in 411, establishing the so-called 400), rather than the later elegant meals to which anyone might be invited such as we see in Aristophanes, where an elderly bumpkin was invited, or in the symposia described by Plato and Xenophon. These undertakings by young aristocrats could have preceded any state intervention such as I think Solon effected in Athens to support or regulate gymnasia. In short, it is not inconceivable that the sages or lawgivers countenanced and regulated a spontaneously evolved new style rather than imposing it by fiat on a "willing" society.

3. Dover (1978) 200.

4. Lefkowitz (1981) viii–ix.

5. Poliakoff (1987).

6. Robertson (1975) 1:96.

7. Sergent (1986) 98 and Dover (1978) 204.

8. Sergent (1986) 73.

9. "Consider also how Love (Eros) excels in warlike feats, and is by no means idle, as Euripides called him, nor a carpet knight, nor 'sleeping on soft maidens' cheeks.' For a man inspired by love needs not Ares to help him when he goes out as a warrior against the enemy" (Plutarch, *Eroticos,* 760d). See also Aelian, *Varia Historia,* III, 9.

10. Flacelière (1962) 51.

11. *Oxford Classical Dictionary* (1970) 498–99; Licht (1932) 230–31.

12. Surviving evidence shows no sharp dividing line in the Greek mind between *gymnasion* and *palaestra. Gymnasion* seems the more general term; *palaestra,* the word for a place dedicated to wrestling. See Krause (1841), 1, 107ff.

13. Poliakoff (1987) 97.

14. See Dover (1978) 54–55.

15. Chantraine (1968) 1:241–42.

16. Eustathius (commentary on *Iliad,* XXIII, 1, 683) placed the event in the fourteenth Olympiad, as did Eusebius (*Chronicle,* ed. Schoene, I, 195). In contradiction, Dionysius of Halicarnassus (VII, 72, 3–4) set it in the fifteenth, claiming that it was not Orsippus who innovated nudity by accident or design, but Acanthus the Lacedaemonian. Didymus and the *Etymologicum Magnum* dated Orsippus to the thirty-second Olympiad. The sundry Olympic datings for Orsippus are all far too early for the taste of Plato and Thucydides, who claimed that athletic nudity was an innovation closer to their own time. The authors cited seem to have indulged in loose chronological speculation, and the evidence for Orsippus himself as for other

supposed early victors in the games is probably not to be taken more seriously than other Just-So stories with which the Greeks embellished and explained their early history. Never again, the stories went, would a male Greek athlete be clothed; henceforth he would compete in a nudity disdained by the barbarians but gloried in by the Hellenes themselves. Gardiner suggested, on the basis of a vase from the late sixth century in which the athletes wore a white loincloth, that an attempt may have been made to reintroduce the loincloth at that time ([1930], 191). Gardiner was himself very uncertain on this point, raising it simply as a question, and there is no real evidence for the reintroduction of the loincloth. Rather, McDonnell has recently determined that all such athletes with loincloths from the late sixth century were depicted on vases marked for export to Etruria ([1991], 186–88).

17. Licht (1932) 88–89.
18. Furtwängler (1905) 4.
19. Richter (1970).
20. Rösler (1990) 233.
21. The analysis of symposia has proceeded irregularly. Perhaps the most important early contributions were Casaubon's in 1600 and Burckhardt's in volume 4 of his *Greek Culture*. In 1902 Schurtz produced an important analysis of male bonding, including the importance of hetairai to it. Then study languished until recently. The *Sympotica* (ed. Murray, 1990), to which twenty-three authors from a number of countries contributed, is a tour de force, summing up scholarship on the subject and also breaking new ground. Together the authors cited approximately one thousand secondary works. Articles average thirty bibliographical references and at the end there is an eighteen-page selective general bibliography. The erudition is formidable, covering archeology, art history, literary criticism, philology, and economic history. The work tends to support the theory that symposia took on their classical form in late seventh-century or early sixth-century Ionia. However, it downplayed the role of pederasty. Only one of its twenty-three articles treats the subject. Bremmer (1990) imagined that symposia deteriorated with the old aristocracy as democracy took over Athens in the fifth century.
22. Bremmer (1990).
23. "It is perhaps more likely that Eastern habits of reclining at feasts, as well as any funerary connotations, were transmitted via Anatolia and East Greece rather than directly to mainland Greece, despite the fact that our earliest Greek representations are Corinthian and Attic" (Boardman [1990] 129). I must add that the addition of couches occurred only outside Crete, which retained the use of chairs or benches.
24. Tecusan (1990) 247.
25. Vanhouette (1954) 26.
26. See Rossi (1983) 44.
27. West (1990) 272.
28. Dover (1978) passim.
29. Jeffery ([1990] 74), citing Roebuck ([1940] 225, fig. 43), tells of a vase dated c. 550 bearing the signature "Paideros," a word attested more than a century later in

Teleclides, fragment 49, with the meaning of "pederast." The signature "Paidikos" (perhaps another nickname with the same connotation) is also attested. See Haspels (1936) 102.

30. See Carpenter, Mannack, and Mendonca (1989).

31. In addition to such mislabeling of erotic scenes, curators and art historians have made a number of other errors. Some believed that the Anacreontic vases produced from c. 520 to c. 500 portray bearded transvestites. In reality they portray an elaborate new style of dress in which men wore long chitons and carried parasols. The style was imported to Athens from Ionia and remained popular there for about a generation.

32. Frel (1963) 61–62. It is a puzzle why the erotic vases decreased noticeably c. 470, whereas pederasty continued unabated (see my epilogue). In their 1994 study Michael Vickers and David Gill contend that the upper class always dined on plate of precious metal. For the symposia given by hoplites, they believe, ceramic pots were used and constituted cheap copies of the elegant silver vessels owned by the Athenian elite. This highly original notion requires that we accept as well that large numbers of hoplites possessed sufficient wealth to afford the cost of giving symposia, including the luxury of the special men's dining room where these gatherings took place. I say "large numbers" because judging by the considerable remnants of Greek vases that have survived to the present day, the original output by potters for the hoplite symposia must have been considerable indeed. However, despite the unorthodox nature of their theory, Vickers and Gill provide no evidence that such wealth existed among the hoplite population. They do insist that the pottery was inexpensive, but ceramic tableware represented only a small portion of the cost of a proper symposium. Even more important is the absence in their text of any explanation as to why after 470 production of erotic ceramic pots became significantly rarer.

I believe that when the Athenians' wealth grew as a result of their new predominance in trade, the discovery of silver at Laurium, and the booty taken from the Persians, aristocrats substituted silverware for the pottery that had previously appeared on their tables. (In so doing, they may also have been influenced by the Persians, who used metal tableware.) This reading of the known facts raises no difficult questions about the financial resources of the hoplite class and its purported interest in giving symposia. It also explains why ceramic pots disappeared after 470: they were simply no longer the tableware of choice among the upper class, the only group rich enough to give symposia.

Sir Kenneth Dover has brought to my attention in a personal letter that by *symposion* could be understood any gathering of men for drink and song and that dividing a house into quarters for men and women was a normal practice, not one signifying particular wealth. I accept both observations, although the passages used by Dover to illustrate these points—Theocritus 14, 12 and Lysias 1, 9 respectively—belong to periods much later than the Archaic age, and Lysias's comment about his two-floor dwelling refers to a time when Athens was far richer and more populous than it had been during the Archaic period. I use *symposium* to refer to the kind of elegant gatherings described by Plato and Xenophon, that is, dinners on a scale mentioned in Aristophanes' *Acharnians* (vv. 1086–90), where a herald speaks of the "couches, tables, cushions, chaplets, perfumes, dainties, . . . biscuits, cakes, sesame bread, tarts, lovely dancing women" that have been readied for the feast. At such events, where *scolia* were sung and boys courted, ceramic ware with pederastic scenes was hardly out of place, as it most assuredly would have been in just any gathering of men. Similarly, it is worth noting a passage from Aristophanes' *Wasps* (vv. 1122ff.), where we are treated to the portrait of a common man who does not understand how to behave at the kind of symposium I am concerned with. No doubt he attended many dinners in his life, but that was not sufficient to prepare him to know the ways of a proper, elegant symposium. He may even have been prosperous enough to possess his own cup, as apparently was sometimes the custom. (Aristophanes' herald also says, "Come quickly to the feast and bring your basket and your cup.") Still, this is no assurance that he could afford to host an event at which only metal tableware was used. (I might add that in our correspondence Jasper Griffin has expressed doubt as to whether the ability to give such symposia was widespread. Griffin has further written me of his agreement with my position that prior to 480 ceramic tableware prevailed. Before that time, he adds, "it is hard to imagine so much plate on Athenian tables as Vickers and Gill believe in.")

The aristocrats' preference after 470 for metal plate at symposia is pertinent to this study in that some have previously hypothesized that ceramic vases rapidly declined because Greek aristocrats did not dare flaunt their pederastic tradition in an increasingly democratic Athens. Since, as I argue here, the arrival of democracy in Athens did not spell the end of institutionalized pederasty, it is interesting to realize that the fate of ceramic pots can be understood in terms quite unrelated to the later history of Greek pederasty.

33. Friis Johansen (1942) 131.

34. Jocelyn (1980).

Chapter 9: The Mainland

1. Grote (1888) 2:223 and Jeffery (1976) 133–78.

2. Snell (1953) chap. 13.

3. Tomlinson (1972) has written the most recent survey of the region.

4. Ibid., 237.

5. Licht (1906) 652. Praxilla is praised in Eusebius's *Chronicle,* Olympiad 82.2 and in Athenaeus, XV, 694a: "Praxilla of Sicyon also was admired for her composition of drinking-songs."

6. The only other verse we have by Cydias is a line reproduced by a scholiast on Aristophanes' phrase "A far-traveling shout" in his *Clouds.*

7. Licht (1932) 460.

8. Scheliha (1968) 124–25.

9. *Oxford Classical Dictionary* (1970) 1056.

10. Symonds (1873–76) 1:238.

11. Kyle (1987) 65.

12. Figueira and Nagy (1985) 197.

13. Jaeger (1943–45) 1:194–95.

14. Grote (1888) 2:200–213.

15. Dover (1978) 172.

16. Licht (1932) 444–45.

17. Dynes (1990) "Thebes"; Demand (1982) 64–65.

18. It is true that remarks by Diodorus Siculus on Carthage's Sacred Band (XVI, 80, 4) make no reference to pederasty; however, any Greek would have understood that a Sacred Band was bound together by pederastic affection.

19. Wilamowitz-Moellendorff and Niese (1910) 93.

20. Wilamowitz-Moellendorff (1922) 52–53.

21. Jaeger (1943–45) 1:205–12.

22. Buffière (1980) 261–62.

23. Ibid., 263–66; Pogey-Castries (1930) 244.

24. Hirschfeld (1914) 655.

25. Unlike his predecessors, Pindar wrote verses whose complexity excludes the possibility that they evolved at symposia or through choral recitals. However, certain glosses and lacunae common to all surviving manuscripts almost certainly indicate that they derived from a prototype that did not evolve before the late second century. They fall into two groups. The older one from late antiquity, though often corrupt, is comparatively free of interpolation. The younger, deriving from a Byzantine recension, is full of unrestrained conjectures dating as late as the fourteenth and fifteenth centuries. Renaissance editions are for the most part based on late and unreliable manuscripts, the only ones accessible to sixteenth-century printers. Quite different from them is August Böckh's edition of 1811–21, regarded as the foundation of the modern critical text. Twentieth-century editions have taken advantage of a much fuller corpus of contemporary papyri texts and inscriptions that exhibit the dialectal forms blurred and distorted by copyists and earlier editors. See the *Encyclopedia Britannica*, 14th edition, endnote, and Nisetich (1980 and 1989), who summarized the textual history outlined by Irigoin (1952).

26. Jaeger (1943–45) 1:214–22.

27. Because none of the general books on Pindar go into any detail about his pederasty, a complete list of his pederastic citations and allusions has not heretofore been compiled. Perhaps this is one reason why this aspect of his writings has been so neglected in spite of Wilamowitz-Moellendorff's belated and reluctant recognition of its importance. We arrive at the following list: *Olympian I, II, III, VI, VII, VIII, X, and XIII; Pythian II and XIV; Nemean III, V, VIII, X,* and *XI; Isthmian II,* and fragments 122, 123, and 128, for a total of sixteen complete odes and three fragments. Ten of the forty-five mostly complete odes were addressed to boy victors: *Olympian VIII, IX, X, XIV, Pythian X, XI,* and *Nemean IV, V, VI.* No surviving Isthmians were. Of these, only *Olympia VIII* and *X* and *Nemean V* are cited by modern authorities as pederastic.

28. West (1988) 170–72.

29. Hirschfeld (1914) 20.

30. Ibid.

31. Licht (1906) 639.

32. Boardman (1964b) 66: "It may not be by chance that we hear first of hoplite battles, with armies of bronze-clad warriors, in Euboea, whose merchants had first sought out the new sources of metals for the Greek world. Chalcis in particular held a reputation in antiquity for being the home of various innovations in bronze armour."

Chapter 10: Amorous Aeolia

1. Cook (1962) 15.

2. The following figures show the degree to which the various corpora have grown: Sappho, 159 fragments, plus testimonies, on 76 pages in the 1928 Loeb edition, to 214 on 101 pages in the 1982 edition; Alcaeus, 180 fragments on 56 pages in the 1928 edition, to 450 fragments on 102 pages in the 1982 edition; Alcman, 165 fragments on 42 pages in the 1928 edition, to 177 fragments on 73 pages in the 1988 edition.

3. While the nineteenth-century theory of an Aeolian epic preceding the Ionic one is no longer advocated by many, no one can deny the Aeolicisms in Homer and Hesiod. Nagy (1990), using complex analyses of meters, has recently argued, in direct contradiction to received wisdom, that the lyric (in the broad sense of verses set to music) developed before the epic and like it long remained oral. I believe that the pederastic poems appeared first only after 630, however ancient that oral tradition may have been.

4. Burnett (1983) 110.

5. Cook (1962) 97.

6. Vetta (1982a) 7.

7. Rösler (1980); Vetta (1982a); and Burnett (1983).

8. Burnett (1983) 121–23, 240–41.

9. Ibid., 121–30.

10. Perrotta and Gentili (1965) 219–20.

11. Burnett (1983), 137–40.

12. Not one of the classical Athenian comedies entitled "Sappho" portrayed her as lustfully homosexual. With Horace and the Latin poets of the Augustan age and the *Oxyrhynchus papyrus* (c. 200 A.D.) come references to her love for girls. In the *Heroides* XV Ovid has her renounce that love late in life out of a passion for the beautiful young boatman Phaon. For details, see DeJean (1989). Wilamowitz-Moellendorff depicted her as a chaste headmistress of a boarding school for girls. Page did not mince words about this view: "[T]he theory finds no support whatsoever in anything worthy of the name of fact" ([1955] 111).

Chapter 11: Insouciant Ionia

1. The elegies they composed were short poems sung to the accompaniment of a woodwind resembling an oboe or a flute. The first elegists wrote before the insti-

tutionalization of pederasty. Exhorting citizens to bravery and glory when facing death at the hands of Cimmerian invaders who sacked Sardis, Callinus of Ephesus supposedly invented the elegy in the first half of the seventh century.

2. Cook (1962) 17.

3. Hermesionax in Athenaeus, XIII, 597f and Strabo 643.

4. Bowra (1961) 241. The visit is reported by the fourth-century A.D. Bithynian rhetorician Himerius (*Oration* 66, 5 Colonna).

5. Note also this tribute by Dioscorides (fl. c. 230 B.C.): "O Anacreon, delight of the Muses, lord of all revels of the night, thou who wast melted to the marrow of thy bones for Thracian Smerdies, O thou who often bending o'er the cup didst shed warm tears for Bathyllus, may founts of wine bubble up for thee unbidden, and streams of ambrosial nectar from the gods; unbidden may the gardens bring thee violets, the flowers that love the evening, and myrtles grow for thee nourished by tender dew, so that even in the house of Demeter thou mayest dance delicately in thy cups, holding golden Eurypyle in thy arms" (VII, 31).

6. See Athenaeus X, 429b.

7. Garzón Diaz (1979) 88–91.

8. Licht (1906) 647.

Chapter 12: Outré Tyrants and Eccentric Philosophers in the Archaic West

1. For extended discussion of the laws of both individuals, see Aristotle, *Politics*, 1274a, and Diodorus Siculus, *The Library*, XII, 11–21.

2. Sjöqvist (1973) 64.

3. Dunbabin (1948) v–vii.

4. According to latest scholarship, the Lelantine War lasted almost two centuries, extending from the early eighth century to nearly 600 B.C. See Brelich (1961).

5. This view was supported by the tragedian Eupolis c. 425 (fr. 139 K).

Chapter 13: Archaic Athens

1. Devereux (1967) 90–92.

2. See *Elegy and Iambus*, I, 407–9 for these meager survivals.

3. For further discussion of this point, see my epilogue.

4. In stating that this "probably" occurred, I am being perhaps too cautious. The data for fifteenth-century Florence gathered by Rocke on the prosecution and conviction of men for sodomy show that far more lower-class males were punished than their noble contemporaries (and that the overwhelming proportion of cases involved pederastic activity). This imbalance stems no doubt from the ability of the wealthy to avoid such difficulties, but there is no escaping his proof for the extent to which the lower classes practiced pederasty. Rocke's study is so much more detailed than any work previous or subsequent on societies before the eighteenth century that I am tempted to dub his book the "Kinsey Report of the late Middle Ages."

5. Blegen (1934) 10–12; R. Young (1939) 227 n. 5; Milne and von Bothmer (1953) 218.

6. Dover (1978) 113–14.

7. See in particular Xenophon's *Symposium,* VIII, 31, where the author argues against the veracity of this version.

8. Gomme (1959) 1:428–30.

9. Athenaeus, XIII, 602c–d; Diogenes Laertius, I, 220 "Epimenides"; Herodotus V, 71; Thucydides I, 126; Aristotle, *Athenian Constitution,* 1; Plutarch, "Solon," XII.

10. See *Oxford Classical Dictionary* (1970) on "Population" and Ehrenberg (1960) 32–35.

11. Diels (1934) 1:28–30; *Oxford Classical Dictionary* (1970) 399.

12. See Sergent (1986) and Jeanmaire (1939) 444–47 for alternate views.

13. Kühn (1821–33) 19:179, cited in Eyben (1980–81) 21.

14. "Now [the Middle Comic] Philemon [368/60–267/63] . . . in *Brothers* [fr.4] records incidentally that Solon, impelled by the crisis which comes in young men's lives, purchased and established wenches in houses of resort; just so Nicander of Colophon [fl. c. 250] records the same in the third book of his *History of Colophon* [no longer extant = *Fragmenta Historicorum graecorum,* ed. Karl Müller and Theodor Müller, 271–72, fr. 9]; Nicander alleges that Solon was the first to found a temple of Aphrodite Pandemus from the profits taken in by the women in charge of the houses" (Athenaeus, XIII, 569d).

15. Case (1888) 242.

16. Ruschenbusch (1966) 97–98: the law forbidding slaves to practice pederasty is cited as authentic from Hermias of Alexandria on Plato's *Phaedrus* 231e and Plutarch, *Life of Solon* 1, 6. See also Cantarella (1992). It is commonly recognized today that Athenian orators attributed laws to Solon in order to give such regulations more weight and validity.

17. Ruschenbusch ([1966] 110–11, 115) dismisses all laws interpolated into the text of Aeschines' *Contra Timarchum* 6, 19, 25, 27, 28, 29, 30, 32, 33, 183 as "False, dubious, unusable." As noted above, orators routinely ascribed laws to Solon when they wanted to emphasize their hoary antiquity or otherwise enhance their legitimacy. Drerup ([1897] 305–6) adds on this subject: "To the evidence of the oration *Against Timarchus,* which betrays a considerably more unskilled hand than the forged interpolations of the oration *On the Crown* and of the Midiana, correspond the legal formulae among which not a single one is to be found that could with even slight probability be regarded as a product of the Attic spirit. Already the law on the instruction of boys interpolated in §12 is in contrast with the statements of the orator in §§9–10 so incomplete that it cannot be thought of as an excerpt from the original law: thus despite the express reference provisions are lacking on the time when school begins and ends as well as on the number of boys to be instructed together; the paedotribes and the palaestras are not mentioned; we do not learn what youths and of what age should attend the school or palaestra, hear nothing of the official who is to be charged with this, nothing of the supervision of the pedagogues, of the festival of the Muses in the schools and of the *symphoitesis ton paidon* [the boys' going to school together] (§10). Only the two notices on the opening and closing of the *didaskaleia* and on the age of the choregoi now confirmed by Aristotle *Athenian Constitution* c. 56 are utilized by the forger; but alongside these stand suspicious

regulations, which partly contradict other data from antiquity: since if the gymna-siarch is assigned the duty of admitting no one of adult age into the palaestra on the festival of the Hermaea, Plato *Lysis* 206D attests the contrary, as Franke has already noted, and the situation of this same dialogue proves that entry was in no way forbidden to older people (cf. L. Grasberger, *Erziehung und Unterricht im klassischen Altertum* I, 251). The exceptions specified in the law (son, brother, son-in-law of the teacher; where for example is the father?) are quite strange, while the inescapable death penalty for the violator of the law appears monstrous. There was no statute on the corruption of free persons in Attic law, which for the case indicated knows only the *graph proagogeias* [indictment for procuring]; the choregoi are likewise according to Aristotle *Athenian Constitution* c. 56 set over the phylai, not over the people."

18. Perhaps indicating that they realized that gymnasia had come to Athens from Sparta, Spartans when they were ravaging the rest of Attica in the Peloponnesian War spared the Academy (the oldest gymnasium in Athens) in honor of its anony-mous founder (Plutarch, "Theseus," XXXII, 3–4; cf. Herodotus, IX, 73). See Sergent (1987a) 119.

19. Dover (1978) 54–55.

20. Demosthenes argued that Solon had not legislated to stop citizens from pros-tituting themselves because if he had so intended he could have imposed harsh penalties, but merely to keep them from entering politics because of their venality and disreputability (*Against Androtion,* 22, 25).

21. Keuls (1985) 5, 88; Halperin ([1989] chap. 5) has the best description of male prostitution in Athens.

22. See the sources in *Paulys Realencyclopädie* (1953) under "Pornikon telos" in entry "Porne."

23. "Although the very livelihood of [teachers], to whom we necessarily entrust our own children, depends on their good character, while the opposite conduct on their part would mean poverty, yet it is plain that the lawgiver [Solon] distrusts them; for he expressly prescribes, first, at what time of day the free-born boy is to go to the schoolroom; next, how many other boys may go there with him, and when he is to go home. He forbids the teacher to open the schoolroom, or the gymnastic trainer the wrestling school, before sunrise, and he commands them to close the doors before sunset; for he is exceeding suspicious of their being alone with a boy, or in the dark with him. He prescribes what children are to be ad-mitted as pupils, and their age at admission. He provides for a public official who shall superintend them, and for the oversight of slave-attendants of school-boys. He regulates the festivals of the Muses in the school-rooms, and of Hermes in the wrestling schools. Finally, he regulates the companionships that the boys may form at school, and their cyclic dances. He prescribes, namely, that the choregus, a man who is going to spend his own money for your entertainment, shall be a man of more than forty years of age when he performs this service, in order that he may have reached the most temperate time of life before he comes into contact with your children" (Aeschines, *Against Timarchus,* 9–11).

24. Quoted in Licht (1932) 453.

25. "[Solon's] mother, as Heraclides Ponticus affirms, was cousin to Pisistratus'

mother, and the two at first were great friends, partly because they were akin, and partly because of Pisistratus' noble qualities and beauty. And they say Solon loved him; and that is the reason, I suppose, that when afterwards they differed about the government, their enmity never produced any hot and violent passion, they remembered their old kindnesses, and retained 'Still in its embers living the strong fire' of their love and dear affection. . . . Pisistratus, it is stated, was similarly attached to one Charmus; [Charmus] it was who dedicated the figure of Love in the Academy, where the runners in the sacred torch race light their torches" (Plutarch, "Solon," I). Rhodes, following Aristotle, attempted to disprove the story that Solon and Pisistratus were lovers on chronological grounds ([1981] 202).

26. W. R. Connor (1990) has argued that the Great Dionysia was started only after Cleisthenes established democracy, but according to tradition Pisistratus founded it.

27. Jaeger (1943–45) 3:50.

28. Kyle (1987) 37.

29. Sealey (1976) 146.

Epilogue

1. In *A Problem in Greek Ethics* (1883) J. A. Symonds proposed that Greek pederasty degenerated after the Greeks lost their independence at the battle of Chaeronea. In particular he believed that thereafter the heroism that had characterized the race and the pederastic ethos declined. Dover's groundbreaking volume on Greek homosexuality, too, slights the Hellenistic era, albeit for a quite different reason. Declaring that "the distinctive features of Greek civilization were fully developed before the end of the classical period," he omits the Hellenistic period from his investigation ([1978] 4).

2. See Crompton (1995).

3. Hindley (1994) has argued convincingly that Xenophon is one of the most informative ancient authors about eros and pederasty. He had carefully honed and discriminating opinions which tend to be neglected by modern writers on Greek homosexuality. For example, he recognized the military value of erotic bonding but also cited cases where excesses of male-male lust caused commanders to become negligent and to lose both battles and lives.

4. However, Socrates does acknowledge that an occasional slip into physicality may occur: "If however they live a life less noble and without philosophy, but yet ruled by the love of honour, probably, when they have been drinking, or in some other moment of carelessness, the two unruly horses, taking the souls off their guard, will bring them together and seize upon and accomplish that which is by the many accounted blissful; and when this has once been done, they continue the practice, but infrequently, since what they are doing is not approved by the whole mind" (*Phaedrus,* 256c).

5. Many scholars have doubted that Plutarch wrote *On the Education of Children* although the tradition to include it among the *Moralia* is of long duration. Marrou (1956), however, believes that it is authentic.

6. It is significant, however, that Protogenes' attempt to distinguish between the

"friendship" (*philia*) that characterizes pederasty and the crude passion that rules in heterosexual love is roundly challenged. Such friendship is declared to be "a philosopher and disciplined on the outside. . . . But when night comes and all is quiet, 'Sweet is the harvest when the guard's away' " (752a).

7. These works are part of a long line of such treatises and dialogues, some of which John Dillon (1994) recently arranged according to philosophical school. Dillon assumes, as I do, that most of these works by the Academicians, early Stoics, and Neo-Platonists discussed pederasty. They contrast markedly with Ovid's exclusively heterosexual *Ars Amatoria* and offer further testimony to the endurance of institutionalized pederasty in Greek regions until the triumph of Christianity.

8. I must mention here another source of information on the continuity and acceptance of male same-sex love: the little-known astrological manuals. The manuals produced in late Hellenistic times are lost, but they exerted such a direct influence on those composed under the pagan emperors that through the latter we learn much about their predecessors. The *Tetrabiblos* of Claudius Ptolemy, for example, who lived in Alexandria under Antonius Pius and Marcus Aurelius (121–80 A.D.), specified not just whether the subject of the horoscope would be attracted to his own sex but also what sorts of partners he would seek, what roles he would assume, what acts he would perform, and whether he would engage in such conduct openly and scandalously or furtively and in secret: "If the luminaries are attended in masculine signs, males exceed in the natural, females in the unnatural, so as merely to accent the virility and activeness of the soul. . . . But on the other hand, when the luminaries in the aforesaid configuration are unattended in feminine signs, then the females exceed in the natural, the males in the unnatural, so that their souls become soft and effeminate. If Venus too is made feminine, the women become depraved, adulterous, and lustful. . . . The men, on the other hand, become effeminate and submissive with regard to unnatural unions and women's roles and are used as pathics, albeit privily and secretly" (*Tetrabiblos*, IV, 13).

9. I have with Warren Johansson documented the implacable Christian opposition to and ultimate destruction of Greek pederastic pedagogy in our forthcoming article, "Homosexuality."

Bibliography

Adcock, F. E. 1957. *The Greek and Macedonian Art of War.* Berkeley.

Aeschines. 1978. *Orationes post Fr. Frankium curavit Fridericus Blass.* Ed. Ulrich Schindel. Stuttgart.

Africa, Thomas W. 1982. "Homosexuals in Greek History." *Journal of Psychohistory* 9: 401–19.

———. 1983. "Psychohistorians Discuss Psychohistory." *Journal of Psychohistory* 11: 129–32.

Allen, Thomas William, ed. 1924. *Homer: The Origins and the Transmission.* Oxford.

Aloni, Antonio. 1980–81. "Lotta politica e pratica religiosa nella Lesbo di Saffo e Alceo." *Centro ricerche e documentazione sull'antichità classica. Atti* 11:213–32.

———. 1982. "Osservazioni sul rapporto tra schiavitú, commercio e prostituzione sacra nel mondo arcaico." *Index* 11:257–63.

———. 1983. "Eteria e tiaso: I gruppi aristocratici di Lesbo tra economia e ideologia." *Dialoghi di archeologia.* 3d series. 1:21–35.

Amundsen, Darrel W., and Carol Jean Diers. 1969. "The Age of Menarche in Classical Greece." *Human Biology* 41:125–32.

———. 1970. "The Age of Menopause in Classical Greece and Rome." *Human Biology* 42:79–86.

Amyx, Darrell Arlynn, and Patricia Lawrence. 1975. *Archaic Corinthian Pottery and the Anaploga Well.* Princeton, N.J.

Andrewes, Antony. 1956. *The Greek Tyrants.* London.

———. 1967. *The Greeks.* New York.

Angel, J. Lawrence. 1972. "Ecology and Population in the Eastern Mediterranean." *World Archaeology* 4, no. 1:88–105.

Anthes, Rudolf. 1963. "Affinity and Difference between Egyptian and Greek Sculpture and Thought in the Seventh and Sixth Centuries B.C." *Proceedings of the American Philosophical Society* 107:60–81.

Arafat, K. W. 1990. "Fact and Artefact: Texts and Archaeology." *Hermathena* 148:45–67.

Arbeitman, Yoël L. 1988. "Minos, the *Oaristes* of Great Zeus: *ha-, a-,* and *o-* Copulative, the Knossan Royal Titulary and the Hellenization of Crete." In *A Linguistic Happening in Memory of Ben Schwartz: Studies in Anatolian, Italic, and Other Indo-European Languages.* Louvain-la-Neuve. 411–62.

Arbois de Jubainville, Henri d'. 1905. *La famille celtique.* Paris.

Arieti, James A. 1975. "Nudity in Greek Athletics." *Classical World* 68:431–36.

Arnheim, M. T. W. 1981–82. "Homeric Social Values." *Scripta Classica Israelica* 6:1–13.

Astour, Michael C. 1967. *Hellenosemitica: An Ethnic and Cultural Study in West Semitic Impact on Mycenean Greece.* Leiden.

Atnally, Richard F. 1992. "The Line and the Labyrinth: Symbolic Keys to Cultural History." *Mankind Quarterly* 32:337–58.

Austin, M. M. 1990. "Greek Tyrants and the Persians, 546–479 B.C." *Classical Quarterly* n.s. 40:289–306.

Austin, M. M., and P. Vidal-Naquet. 1977. *Economic and Social History of Ancient Greece.* Trans. and rev. M. M. Austin. Berkeley.

Bachofen, Johann Jacob. 1967. *Myth, Religion, and Mother Right: Selected Writings.* Princeton.

Bain, David. 1991. "Six Greek Verbs of Sexual Congress." *Classical Quarterly* 41:51–77.

Barkan, Leonard. 1991. *Transuming Passion: Ganymede and the Erotics of Humanism.* Stanford.

Barkhuizen, J. H. 1977. "Helena in Alkaios en Sappho — Aspekte van die Mite in die Vroeë Griekse Digkuns." *Acta Classica* 20:1–21.

Bartol, Krystyna. 1992. "Where Was Iambic Poetry Performed? Some Evidence from the Fourth Century B.C." *Classical Quarterly* 42:65–71.

Battisti, Daniela. 1990. "*Synetós* as Aristocratic Self-Description." *Greek, Roman and Byzantine Studies* 31:5–25.

Baumann, Hermann. 1955. *Das doppelte Geschlecht: Studien zur Bisexualität in Ritus und Mythos.* Berlin.

Bazant, Jan. 1983. "Homosexuals on Athenian Vases." In *Concilium Eirene XVI. Proceedings of the 16th International Eirene Conference, Prague 31.8–4.9. 1982,* ed. Pavel Oliva and Alona Pavlíková. Prague. 2:31–34.

Beazley, J. D. 1925. *Attische Vasenmaler des rotfigurigen Stils.* Tübingen.

———. 1947. "Some Attic Vases in the Cyprus Museum." *Proceedings of the British Academy* 33:197–244.

———. 1951. *The Development of Attic Black-Figure.* Berkeley.

Beccaria, Cesare, Marchese de. 1764. *Dei Delitti e delle Pene.*

Becker, Howard. 1963. *Outsiders: Studies in the Sociology of Deviance.* New York.

Becker, Wilhelm Adolph (ed. Hermann Göll). 1877. *Charikles. Bilder altgriechischer Sitte, zur genaueren Kentniss des griechischen Privatlebens.* Berlin.

Bekker, August Immanuel. 1814. *Anecdota Graeca I.* Berlin.

Beloch, K. J. 1886. *Bevölkerung der griechisch-römischen Welt.* Leipzig.

Benecke, Edward F. M. 1896. *Antimachus of Colophon and the Position of Women in Greek Poetry.* London.

Bentham, Jeremy. (1785, unpubl.). "Offences against One's Self: Paederasty." Cited in *Journal of Homosexuality* 3 (1978): 392.

Benveniste, Emile. 1973. *Indo-European Language and Society.* Trans. Elizabeth Palmer. London.

Bérard, J. 1941. *La colonisation grecque de l'Italie méridionale et de la Sicile.* Paris.

Bernal, Martin. 1987. *Black Athena.* London.

Bernheim, Frederick, and Ann Adams Zener. 1978. "The Sminthian Apollo and the Epidemic among the Achaeans at Troy." *Transactions of the American Philological Association* 108:11–14.

Bersani, Leo. 1985. "Pederasty and Pedagogy." *Raritan* 5, no. 1:14–21.

Bérubé, Allan. 1990. *Coming Out under Fire: The History of Gay Men and Women in World War Two.* New York.

Bethe, Erich. 1907. "Die dorische Knabenliebe: Ihre Ethik und ihre Idee." *Rheinisches Museum für Philologie* 62:438–75.

———. 1922. *Homer, Dichtung und Sage.* Vol. 2: *Odyssee. Kyklos. Zeitbestimmung, nebst den Resten des troischen Kyklos.* Leipzig.

Beye, Charles Rowan. 1987. *Ancient Greek Literature and Society.* 2d ed. Ithaca, N.Y.

Beyer, Rudolf. 1910. *Fabulae Graecae quatenus quave Aetate Puerorum Amore Commutatae Sint.* Weida, Germany.

Blegen, Carl W. 1934. "Inscriptions on Geometric Pottery from Hymettos." *American Journal of Archaeology* 38:10–28.

Bleibtreu-Ehrenberg, Gisela. 1978. *Tabu Homosexualität.* Frankfurt am Main.

———. 1980. *Mannbarkeitsriten, zur institutionellen Päderastie bei Papuas und Melanesiern.* Frankfurt am Main.

———. 1987. "New Research into the Greek Institution of Pederasty." *Homosexuality, Which Homosexuality? International Scientific Conference on Gay and Lesbian Studies. History* 2:50–58. Amsterdam.

Bloch, Iwan. 1907. *Das Sexualleben unserer Zeit in seinen Beziehungen zur modernen Kultur.* Berlin.

Bloch, Marc. 1961. *Feudal Society.* Trans. L. A. Manyon. London.

Blüher, Hans. 1917–19. *Die Rolle der Erotik in der männlichen Gesellschaft.* 2 vols. Jena.

Boardman, John. 1964a. *Greek Art.* New York.

———. 1964b. *The Greeks Overseas.* Baltimore.

———. 1978. *Greek Sculpture: The Archaic Period.* New York.

———. 1990. "*Symposion* Furniture." In *Sympotica: A Symposium on the Symposion,* ed. Oswyn Murray. Oxford. 122–31.

Boardman, John, and Eugenio La Rocca. 1979. *Eros in Greece.* New York.

Bon, Michel, and Antoine D'Arc. 1974. *Rapport sur l'homosexualité de l'homme.* Paris.

Bonanno, Maria Grazia. 1973. "Osservazioni sul tema della 'giusta' reciprocità amorosa da Saffo ai comici." *Quaderni Urbinati di cultura classica* 16:110–20.

Bonner, R. J., and G. Smith. 1930–38. *The Administration of Justice from Homer to Aristotle.* Chicago.

Bornmann, Fritz. 1992. "Kleine Gemeinsamkeiten bei Nietzsche und Wilamowitz." *Zeitschrift für Papyrologie und Epigraphik* 91:18–19.

Bosch-Gimpera, Pedro. 1961. *Les Indo-Européens: Problèmes archéologiques.* Paris.

Boswell, John. 1980. *Christianity, Social Tolerance and Homosexuality: Gay People in Western Europe from the Beginning of the Christian Era to the Fourteenth Century.* Chicago.

———. 1982–83. "Towards the Long View: Revolutions, Universals and Sexual Categories." *Salmagundi* 58/59:89–113.

———. 1988a. *The Kindness of Strangers.* New York.

———. 1988b. Review of Sergent, *Homosexuality in Greek Myth*. *Journal of Religion* 68:485–87.

———. 1994. *Same-Sex Unions in Premodern Europe*. New York.

Botsford, George Willis, and Charles Alexander Robinson. 1956. *Hellenic History*. 4th ed. New York.

Bowra, C. M. 1957. *The Greek Experience*. Bergenfield, N.J.

———. 1961. *Greek Lyric Poetry*. Oxford.

Boyd, Robert, and Peter J. Richerson. 1985. *Culture and the Evolutionary Process*. Chicago.

Brandt, Paul (see Licht, Hans).

Brashear, William M. 1979. "Ein Berliner Zauberpapyrus." *Zeitschrift für Papyrologie und Epigraphik* 33:261–78.

Brelich, A. 1961. *Guerre, Agoni e Culti nella Grecia arcaica*. Bonn.

———. 1969. *Paides e parthenoi*. Rome.

Bremer, J. M. 1982. "A Reaction to Tsagarakis' Discussion of Sappho Fr. 31." *Rheinisches Museum für Philologie* n.s. 125:113–16.

Bremmer, Jan. 1980. "An Enigmatic Indo-European Rite: Paederasty." *Arethusa* 13, no. 2:279–98.

———. 1989. "Greek Pederasty and Modern Homosexuality." In *From Sappho to De Sade: Moments in the History of Sexuality*, ed. Jan Bremmer. London. 1–14.

———. 1990. "Adolescents, Symposion, and Pederasty." In *Sympotica*, ed. Oswyn Murray. Oxford. 135–48.

Brendel, Otto J. 1970. "The Scope and Temperament of Erotic Art in the Greco-Roman World." In *Studies in Erotic Art*, ed. Theodore Bowie. New York. 3–107.

Broadbent, Molly. 1968. *Studies in Greek Genealogy*. Leiden.

Brongersma, Edward. 1986–90. *Loving Boys: A Multidisciplinary Study of Sexual Relations between Adult and Minor Males*. Introduction by Vern Bullough. Elmhurst, N.Y.

———. 1990. "The Thera Inscriptions—Ritual or Slander?" *Journal of Homosexuality* 20, nos. 1–2:31–40.

Brouwer, Petrus van Limburg. 1833–42. *Histoire de la civilisation morale et religieuse des Grecs*. Groningen.

Brown, Edwin L. 1991. "Sappho the 'Numinous.'" *Illinois Classical Studies* 16:59–63.

Brown, Peter. 1988. *The Body and Society*. New York.

Budge, E. A. Wallis. 1926. *The Dwellers on the Nile*. New York.

Buffière, Félix. 1980. *Eros adolescent: la pédérastie dans la Grèce antique*. Paris.

Bullough, Vern L. (with W. Dorr Legg, Barrett W. Elcano, and James Kepner, eds.) 1976a. *An Annotated Bibliography of Homosexuality*. New York.

Bullough, Vern L. 1976b. *Sexual Variance in Society and History*. Chicago.

———. 1979. *Homosexuality: A History*. Bergenfield, N.J.

Burckhardt, Jacob. [1898–1902] 1963. *History of Greek Culture*. Trans. Palmer Hilty. New York.

Burette, Pierre-Jean. 1735. *Dialogue de Plutarque sur la Musique, traduit en françois avec des remarques*. Paris.

Burg, R. R. 1983. *Sodomy and the Perception of Evil: English Sea Rovers in the Seventeenth Century Caribbean.* New York.

Burkert, Walter. 1985. *Greek Religion.* Trans. John Raffan. Cambridge, Mass.

Burn, A. R. 1960. *The Lyric Age of Greece.* London.

Burnett, Anne Pippin. 1983. *Three Archaic Poets.* Cambridge, Mass.

Bury, J. B. [1900] 1975. *A History of Greece to the Death of Alexander the Great.* Rev. ed., ed. Russell Meiggs. New York.

———. 1908. *The Ancient Greek Historians.* New York.

Butler, Eliza Marian. 1935. *The Tyranny of Greece over Germany.* Cambridge.

Butler, Samuel. 1897. *The Authoress of the Odyssey.* London.

Calame, Claude. 1977. *Les choeurs de jeunes filles en Grèce archaïque.* Rome.

———. 1984. "Eros inventore e organizzatore della società greca antica." In *L'amore in Grecia.* Rome. ix–xl.

———. 1986. *Le récit en Grèce ancienne: Enonciations et représentations de poètes.* Paris.

Calder, William M. 1986. "F. G. Welcker's *Sapphobild* and Its Reception in Wilamo-witz." In *Friedrich Gottlieb Welcker: Werk und Wirkung,* ed. William M. Calder, Adolf Köhnken, Wolfgang Kullmann, and Günther Pflug. Stuttgart. 131–56.

Cambridge Ancient History. 1939–92. 12 vols. 2d ed.

Cambridge History of Classical Literature. Vol. 1: *Greek Literature.* New York, 1985. Vol. 2: *Latin Literature.* New York, 1982.

Cameron, A. 1932. "The Exposure of Children and Greek Ethics." *Classical Review* 46:105–14.

Camp, John McK. 1979. "A Drought in the Late Eighth Century B.C." *Hesperia* 48, no. 4:397–411.

Campbell, David A. 1967. *Greek Lyric Poetry: A Selection of Early Greek Lyric, Elegiac and Iambic Poetry.* London.

———. 1983. *The Golden Lyre: The Themes of the Greek Lyric Poets.* London.

Cantarella, Eva. 1980. "Aítios. Archeologia di un concetto." In *Studi in onore di Cesare Grassetti.* Milan. 1:209–40.

———. 1987. *Pandora's Daughters: The Role and Status of Women in Greek and Roman Antiquity.* Baltimore.

———. 1988b. *Secondo natura: La bisessualità nel mondo antico.* Rome.

———. 1992. *Bisexuality in the Ancient World.* New Haven.

Cantor, Norman F. 1963. *Medieval History: The Life and Death of a Civilization.* New York.

Carcopino, Jérôme. 1956. *De Pythagore aux apôtres. Études sur la conversion du Monde Romain.* Paris.

Carpenter, Edward. 1911. *Intermediate Types among Primitive Folk.* London.

———. [1917] 1982. *Ioläus.* New York.

Carpenter, Rhys. 1933. "The Antiquity of the Greek Alphabet." *American Journal of Archaeology* 37:8–29.

———. 1966. *Discontinuity in Greek Civilization.* Cambridge.

Carpenter, Thomas H., Thomas Mannack, and Melanie Mendonca (eds.). 1989.

Beazley Addenda: Additional References to ARV, ARV2 & Paralipomena. 2d ed. London.

Carter, Charles. 1988. "Athletic Contests in Hittite Religious Festivals." *Journal of Near Eastern Studies* 47:185–87.

Cartledge, P. A. 1981a. "The Politics of Spartan Pederasty." *Proceedings of the Cambridge Philological Society* 207:17–36.

———. 1981b. "Spartan Wives: Liberation or License?" *Classical Quarterly* 31:84–105.

———. 1987. *Agesilaos and the Crisis of Sparta.* Baltimore.

Case, Thomas. 1888. "Chronology of the Solonian Legislation." *Classical Review* 2: 241–42.

Cassio, Albio Cesare. 1983. "Post-Classical Lesbiai." *Classical Quarterly* 33:296–97.

Cavin, Susan. 1985. *Lesbian Origins.* San Francisco.

Chadwick, John. 1976. *The Mycenean World.* Cambridge.

Chalmers, James. 1903. "Notes on the Natives of Kiwai Island, Fly River, British New Guinea." *Journal of the Anthropological Institute of Great Britain and Ireland* 33:108–10.

Chamay, Jacques, and Jean-Louis Maier. 1984. *Céramiques corinthiennes: Collection du docteur Jean Lauffenburger.* Geneva.

Chandos, John. 1984. *Boys Together: English Public Schools, 1800–1864.* New Haven.

Chantraine, Pierre. 1968–80. *Dictionnaire étymologique de la langue grecque: Histoire des mots.* 4 vols. Paris.

Childe, Vere Gordon. 1925. *The Dawn of European Civilization.* London.

———. [1942] 1954. *What Happened in History.* Rev. ed. New York.

———. 1951. *Man Makes Himself.* New York.

Chirassi Colombo, I. 1979. "Paides e gynaikes. Note per una tassonomia del comportamento rituale nella cultura attica." *Quaderni Urbinati di cultura classica* 30 (n.s. 1): 25–58.

Chrimes, K. M. T. 1949. *Ancient Sparta.* Manchester.

Christopoulos, George A., et al. 1975. *History of the Hellenic World.* Trans. Philip Sherrard et al. Vol. 2: *The Archaic Period.* Athens.

Ciaceri, E. 1927–32. *Culti e Miti nella Storia dell'antica Sicilia.* 3 vols. Milan.

Clarke, W. M. 1978. "Achilles and Patroclus in Love." *Hermes* 106:381–96.

Clerc, Michel. 1927–29. *Massalia. Histoire de Marseille dans l'antiquité des origines à la fin de l'Empire Romain d'Occident (476 ap. J.-C.).* 2 vols. Marseille.

Cohen, David. 1992. "Sex, Gender, and Sexuality in Ancient Greece." *Classical Philology* 87:145–60.

Cohen, Gerald Leonard, and Joseph Wallfield. 1985. "Etymology of Greek *agape* 'love'." *Indogermanische Forschungen* 90:99–103.

Cohn, Norman. 1957. *The Pursuit of the Millennium.* New York.

———. 1975. *Europe's Inner Demons: An Enquiry Inspired by the Great Witch-Hunt.* New York.

Collinge, Anna. 1989. "The Case of Satyrs." In *Images of Authority: Papers Presented to Joyce Reynolds on the Occasion of Her Seventieth Birthday,* ed. Mary Margaret MacKenzie and Charlotte Roueché. Cambridge. 82–103.

Connor, W. R. 1990. "City Dionysia and the Athenian Democracy." In *Aspects of Athenian Democracy.* Classica et Mediaevalia Dissertations 11. Copenhagen.

Cook, J. M. 1962. *The Greeks in the East.* London.

Cordiano, Giuseppe. 1982. "Ibico fu solo un poeta erotico?" *Calabria sconosciuta* 18/19:17–20.

Courouve, Claude. 1986. *Tableau synoptique de références à l'amour masculin: Auteurs grecs et latins.* Paris.

Crew, Louie, ed. 1978. *The Gay Academic.* Palm Springs, Calif.

Crompton, Louis. 1985. *Byron and Greek Love: Homophobia in 19th-Century England.* Berkeley.

———. 1995. "Ancient Greek Literature." In *The Gay and Lesbian Literary Heritage,* ed. Claude Summers. New York. 342–48.

Crotty, Kevin. 1982. *Song and Action: The Victory Odes of Pindar.* Baltimore.

Crowther, Nigel B. 1985. "Male 'Beauty' Contests in Greece: The Euandria and Euexia." *L'Antiquité Classique* 54:285–91.

———. 1988. "Elis and the Games." *L'Antiquité Classique* 57:301–10.

———. 1989. "Boy Victors at Olympia." *L'Antiquité Classique* 58:206–10.

———. 1990. "Recent Trends in the Study of Greek Athletics (1982–1989)." *L'Antiquité Classique* 59:246–55.

Daim, Wilfried. 1958. *Der Mann, der Hitler die Ideen gab.* Munich.

Daremberg, Charles Hector, and Edmond Saglio. 1873–1919. "Agelai." "Stuprum." *Dictionnaire des Antiquités Grecques et Romaines d'après les textes et les monuments.* Paris.

Davies, J. K. 1971. *Athenian Propertied Families 600–300 B.C.* Oxford.

Davies, Malcolm. 1980. "The Eyes of Love and the Hunting-Net in Ibycus 287 P." *Maia* 32:255–57.

———. 1981. "Artemon Transvestitus? A Query." *Mnemosyne* 34:288–99.

Davies Morpurgo, Anna. 1986. "The Linguistic Evidence." In *The End of the Early Bronze Age in the Aegean,* ed. G. Cadogan. Leiden.

Davison, John Armstrong. 1955. "Peisistratus und Homer." *Transactions of the American Philological Association* 86:1–21.

Degani, Enzo. 1976. "Note archilochee." *Quaderni Urbinati di cultura classica* 21:23–25.

Deissman-Merten, Marieluise. 1986. "Zur Sozialgeschichte des Kindes im antiken Griechenland." In *Zur Sozialgeschichte der Kindheit.* Munich. 267–316.

DeJean, Joan. 1989. *Fictions of Sappho, 1546–1937.* Chicago.

Delcourt, Marie, and Karl Hoheisel. 1988. "Hermaphrodit." *Reallexikon für Antike und Christentum* 14:649–82.

Delepierre, Joseph Octave. 1879. *Dissertation sur les idées morales des Grecs et sur le danger de lire Platon.* Rouen.

Delorme, Jean. 1960. *Gymnasion: Étude sur les monuments consacrés à l'éducation en Grèce.* Paris.

Delorme, Jean, and Wolfgang Speyer. 1984. "Gymnasium." *Reallexikon für Antike und Christentum* 13:155–76.

Demand, Nancy H. 1982. *Thebes in the Fifth Century.* London.

Demoulin, Hubert. 1901. *Epiménide de Crète.* Brussels.

Dentzer, Jean-Marie. 1982. *Le Motif du Banquet Couché dans le proche-orient et le monde grec du VIIe au IVe siècle avant J.C.* Rome.

De Sanctis, G. 1939. *Storia del Greci.* Florence.

Desborough, V. R. d'A. 1964. *The Last Myceneans and Their Successors.* Oxford.

———. 1972. *The Greek Dark Ages.* London.

Devereux, George. 1967. "Greek Pseudo-Homosexuality and the 'Greek Miracle.'" *Symbolae Osloenses* 47:69–92.

———. 1970. "The Nature of Sappho's Seizure in Fr. 31 LP as Evidence of Her Inversion." *Classical Quarterly* n.s. 20:17–31.

Devoto, Giacomo. 1962. *Origini Indoeuropee.* Florence.

Diano, Carlo. 1953. "L'Eros greco." *Ulisse* 18:698–708.

———. 1968. *Saggezza e poetiche degli antichi.* Vicenza.

Diels, Hermann. 1891. "Über Epimenides von Kreta." *Sitzungsberichte der Preussischen Akademie der Wissenschaften zu Berlin.* 1:387–403.

———. 1934. *Die Fragmente der Vorsokratiker.* 6 vols. 5th ed. Berlin.

Dietel, Käthe. 1939. *Das Gleichnis in der frühen griechischen Lyrik.* Ph.D. dissertation, Munich.

Dillon, John. 1994. "A Platonist *Ars Amatoria.*" *Classical Quarterly* 44:387–92.

Diner, Helen. 1965. *Mothers and Amazons: The First Feminine History of Culture.* New York.

Dodds, E. R. 1951. *The Greeks and the Irrational.* Berkeley.

Döllinger, John J. I. 1862. *The Gentile and the Jew in the Courts of the Temple of Christ: An Introduction to the History of Christianity.* 2 vols. London.

Donlan, Walter. 1973. "The Origin of *Kalòs kagathós.*" *American Journal of Philology* 94:65–74.

Dornseiff, Franz. 1956. *Antike und alter Orient: Interpretationen.* Leipzig.

Dover, Kenneth J. 1964. "Eros and Nomos." *Bulletin of the University of London Institute of Classical Studies* 11:31–42.

———. 1973. "Classical Greek Attitudes to Sexual Behaviour." *Arethusa* 6:59–73.

———. 1978. *Greek Homosexuality.* New York.

———. 1987. *Greek and the Greeks.* Oxford.

———. 1988. *The Greeks and Their Legacy: Collected Papers.* Oxford.

Drerup, Engelbert. 1897. "Über die bei den attischen Rednern eingelegten Urkunden." Ph.D. dissertation, Munich.

Drews, Robert. 1988. *The Coming of the Greeks: Indo-European Conquests in the Aegean and the Near East.* Princeton.

Ducat, Jean. 1976. "Fonctions de la statue dans la Grèce archaïque: *kouros* et *kolossos.*" *Bulletin de correspondance hellénique* 100:239–51.

Dugas, Ludovic. 1894. *L'amitié antique d'après les moeurs populaires et les théories des philosophes.* Paris.

Dumézil, Georges. 1956. *Aspects de la fonction guerrière chez les Indo-Européens.* Paris.

Dunbabin, T. J. 1948. *The Western Greeks.* Oxford.

Durup-Carré, Sylvie. 1986. "L'Homosexualité en Grèce antique: tendance ou institution?" *L'Homme* 26:371–77.

Dynes, Wayne R. 1978. "Orpheus without Eurydice." *Gai Saber* 1, nos. 3/4: 267–73.

———. 1985. *Homolexis*. New York.

———. 1987. *Homosexuality: A Research Guide*. New York.

———. 1990. *Encyclopedia of Homosexuality*. 2 vols. New York.

Easterling, P. E. 1974. "Alcman 58 and Simonides 37." *Proceedings of the Cambridge Philological Society* 200 (n.s. 20):37–43.

Easterling, P. E., and J. V. Muir. 1985. *Greek Religion and Society*. Cambridge.

Edmunds, Lowell. 1988. "Foucault and Theognis." *Classical and Modern Literature* 8: 79–91.

Effenterre, Henri van. 1948. *La Crète et le monde grec de Platon à Polybe*. Paris.

———. 1988. "La Crète serait-elle une terre de colonisation?" *Cretan Studies* 1:73–82.

Eglinton, J. Z. 1964. *Greek Love*. New York.

Ehrenberg, Victor. 1960. *The Greek State*. London.

———. 1973. *From Solon to Socrates*. 2d ed. London.

Ehret, Christopher. 1988. "Language Change and the Material Correlates of Language and Ethnic Shift." *Antiquity* 62:564–74.

Ellis, Havelock. [1897] 1975. *Sexual Inversion*. New York.

Else, Gerald F. 1965. *The Origin and Early Form of Greek Tragedy*. Cambridge, Mass.

Encyclopaedia Judaica. 1971. "Homosexuality."

Encyclopedia of Religion and Ethics. "Sodomy."

Engels, Donald. 1980. "The Problem of Female Infanticide in the Greco-Roman World." *Classical Philology* 75, no. 2: 112–20.

Erasmus, Desiderius. 1599. *Des. Erasmi Roterodami Adagiorum chiliades iuxta locos communes digestae*. Ed. Johann Jakob Grynaeus. Frankfurt am Main.

Everson, Michael. 1989. "Picture out of Focus: Colin Renfrew's *Archaeology and Language*—The Puzzle of Indo-European Origins." *Mankind Quarterly* 30, nos. 1–2: 159–73.

Eyben, E. 1980–81. "Family Planning in Graeco-Roman Antiquity." *Ancient Society* 11–12:5–82.

Fagan, Brian. 1990. "Rethinking Prehistory." *Archaeology* 43, no. 4:32–39.

Faraone, Christopher A. 1992a. "Aristophanes, *Amphiaraus* fr. 29 (Kassel-Austin): Oracular Response or Erotic Incantation?" *Classical Quarterly* 42:320–27.

———. 1992b. *Talismans and Trojan Horses: Guardian Statues in Ancient Greek Myth and Ritual*. Oxford.

Fehling, Detlev. 1985. Review of Patzer, *Die griechische Knabenliebe*. *Gnomon* 57:116–20.

Ferguson, John. 1973. *The Heritage of Hellenism*. London.

Ferguson, W. S. 1918. "The Zulus and the Spartans: A Comparison of Their Military Systems." *Harvard African Studies* 1:197–234.

Fernández-Galiano, M. 1984. "Le poète dans le monde archaïque, sa personnalité et son rôle: Sappho." *Actes du VIIe Congrès de la Fédération Internationale des Associations d'Études Classiques* (Budapest). 1:131–48.

Fernbach, David. 1976. "Toward a Marxist Theory of Gay Liberation." *Socialist Review* 28:29–41.

Ferri, Silvio. 1938. "Sui vasi greci con epigrafi 'acclamatorie.'" *Rendiconti della R. Accademia nazionale dei Lincei; classe di scienze morali storiche e filologiche* 14:93–179.

———. 1968. *Fifty Years (and Twelve) of Classical Scholarship.* London.

Figueira, Thomas J., and Gregory Nagy. 1985. *Theognis of Megara: Poetry and Polis.* Baltimore.

Filippo, Adele. 1977. "'Eros, di nuovo, dolce versando . . .': Alcmane fr. 59a P." *Quaderni Urbinati di cultura classica* 25:17–22.

Fink, Josef. 1952. "Zur Bärtigkeit der griechischen Götter und Helden in archaischer Zeit." *Hermes* 80:110–14.

Finley, Moses I. 1954 (1965). *The World of Odysseus.* New York.

———. 1980. *Ancient Slavery and Modern Ideology.* New York.

———. 1981. *Early Greece: The Bronze and Archaic Ages.* London.

———, ed. 1984. *The Legacy of Greece.* New York.

Flacelière, Robert. 1962. *Love in Ancient Greece.* Trans. James Cleugh. New York.

Flandrin, Jean-Louis. 1975. *Les Amours paysannes (xvie–xixe siècle).* Paris.

———. 1981. *Le Sexe et l'Occident.* Paris.

Ford, Clellan S., and Frank A. Beach. 1951. *Patterns of Sexual Behavior.* New York.

Fornara, Charles W. 1970. "The Cult of Harmodius and Aristogeiton." *Philologus* 114:155–80.

———. 1977. *Archaic Times to the End of the Peloponnesian War.* Baltimore.

Forrest, W. G. 1968. *A History of Sparta, 950–192 B.C.* New York.

Foucault, Michel. 1980–86. *The History of Sexuality.* Vol. 1: *An Introduction.* New York, 1980 (Paris, 1976). Vol. 2: *The Use of Pleasure.* New York, 1985 (Paris, 1984). Vol. 3: *The Care of the Self.* New York, 1986 (Paris, 1984).

Francis, E. D., and Michael Vickers. 1981. "Leagros Kalos." *Proceedings of the Cambridge Philological Society* 207:97–136.

Fränkel, Herman. 1973. *Early Greek Poetry and Philosophy.* London.

Franz, Marie-Luise von. 1964. "Über religiöse Hintergründe des Puer-Aeternus-Problems." In *Der Archetyp: Verhandlungen des 2. Internationalen Kongresses für analytische Psychologie, Zürich 1962,* ed. Adolf Guggenbühl-Craig. Basel. 141–56.

Freeman, Kathleen. 1926. *The Work and Life of Solon, with a Translation of His Poems.* Cardiff.

Frel, Jiří. 1963. "Griechischer Eros." *Listy filologické* 86:60–64.

Friis Johansen, Knud. 1942. "Attic Motives on Clazomenian Sarcophagi." *From the Collections of the Ny Carlsberg Glyptothek* 3:123–43.

Furtwängler, Adolf. 1874. *Eros in der Vasenmalerei.* Munich.

———. 1905. *Die Bedeutung der Gymnastik in der griechischen Kunst.* Leipzig.

Fussell, Paul. 1975. *The Great War and Modern Memory.* New York.

Gagarin, Michael. 1986. *Early Greek Law.* Berkeley.

Gallo, Luigi. 1984. *Alimentazione e demografia della Grecia antica.* Salerno.

Gamberini, Leopoldo. 1979. *Plutarco «Della Musica»*. Florence.

Gamkrelidze, T., and V. Ivanov. 1985. "The Ancient Near East and the Indo-European Question [and] The Migration of Tribes Speaking Indo-European Dialects." *Journal of Indo-European Studies* 13:3–91.

Gangutia Elícegui, Elvira. 1971. "Poesia griega «de amigo» y poesia arabigo-española." *Emerita* 40:329–96.

Gardiner, E. Norman. [1930] 1978. *Athletics of the Ancient World*. Oxford.

Garland, Yvon, and O. Masson. 1982. "Les acclamations pédérastiques de Kalami (Thasos)." *Bulletin de Correspondance Hellénique* 106:3–22.

Garyza, Antonio. 1971. "Per la fortuna di Saffo a Bisanzio." *Jahrbuch der Österreichischen Byzantinistik* 20:1–5.

Garzón Diaz, Julian. 1979. "Vino y banquete desde Homero a Anacreonte." *Helmantica* 30:63–96.

Gengoux, J. 1965. "Psychanalyse littéraire: de Platon à Gide." In *Le psychiatre devant l'homosexuel*. Montreal. 53–84.

Gentili, Bruno. 1972. "Il 'letto insaziato' di Medea e il tema dell'*adikia* a livello amoroso nei lirici (Saffo, Teognide) e nella *Medea* di Euripide." *Studi classici e orientali* 21:60–72.

———. 1973. "La ragazza di Lesbo." *Quaderni Urbinati di cultura classica* 16:124–28.

———. 1976. "Il *Partenio* di Alcmane e l'amore omoerotica femminile nei tiasi spartani." *Quaderni Urbinati di cultura classica* 22:59–67.

———. 1985. "Nel tiaso saffico." In *Le Donne in Grecia*, ed. Giampiera Arrigoni. Bari. 3–13.

———. 1988. *Poetry and Its Public in Ancient Greece: From Homer to the Fifth Century.* Baltimore.

Georgiev, Vladimir. 1961. "Das Problem der homerischen Sprache im Lichte der kretisch-mykenischen Texte." In *Minoica und Homer*, ed. Vladimir Georgiev and Johannes Irmscher. Berlin. 10–19.

Gerber, Douglas E. 1976. "Archilochus, Fr. 42 West." *Quaderni Urbinati di cultura classica* 22:7–14.

Gernet, Louis. 1968. *Anthropologie de la Grèce ancienne*. Paris.

Gesner, Johann Matthias. 1769. *Socrates sanctus paederasta*. Utrecht.

Giacomelli, Anne. 1980. "The Justice of Aphrodite in Sappho Fr. 1." *Transactions of the American Philological Association* 110:135–43.

Giangrande, Giuseppe. 1973. "Anacreon and the Lesbian Girl." *Quaderni Urbinati di cultura classica* 16:129–33.

———. 1976. "On Anacreon's Poetry." *Quaderni Urbinati di cultura classica* 21:43–46.

———. 1980. "Sappho and the *ólisbos*. " *Emerita* 48:249–50.

———. 1981. "Anacreon and the *fellatrix* from Lesbos." *Museum Philologum Londiniense* 4:15–18.

———. 1983. "A che serviva l'olisbos di Saffo?" *Labeo* 29:154–155.

Gilbert, Arthur N. 1974. "The 'Africaine' Courts Martial: A History of Buggery in the Royal Navy." *Journal of Homosexuality* 1:111–12.

——. 1977. "Buggery and the British Navy: 1700–1861." *Journal of Social History* 10:72–98.

Gillis, John R. 1974. *Youth and History: Tradition and Change in European Age Relations, 1770–Present.* New York.

Gimbutas, Marija. 1973. "The Beginning of the Bronze Age in Europe and the Indo-Europeans: 3500–2500 B.C." *Journal of Indo-European Studies* 1:163–214.

Glass, D. V., and D. E. C. Eversley, eds. 1965. *Population in History.* London.

Gobry, I. 1979. "Les origines orientales de la doctrine pythagoricienne de l'âme." *Diotima* 7:81–85.

Golden, Mark. 1981. "Demography and the Exposure of Girls at Athens." *Phoenix* 35:316–31.

——. 1984. "Slavery and Homosexuality at Athens." *Phoenix* 38:308–24.

Goldstein, Melvin. 1982. "Some Tolerant Attitudes toward Female Homosexuality throughout History." *Journal of Psychohistory* 9:437–60.

Gomme, A. W. 1913. "The Legend of Cadmus and the Logographi." *Journal of Hellenic Studies* 33:53–72, 223–45.

——. 1959. *A Historical Commentary on Thucydides.* 5 vols. Oxford.

González-Reigosa, Fernández, and Angel Velez-Diaz. 1983. "Psychohistorians Discuss Psychohistory." *Journal of Psychohistory* 10:511–19.

González-Reigosa, Fernández, and Howard Kaminsky. 1989. "Greek Homosexuality, Greek Narcissism, Greek Culture: The Invention of Apollo." *Psychohistory Review* 17, no. 2: 149–81.

Goody, Jack. 1983. *The Development of the Family and Marriage in Europe.* Cambridge.

Gordon, Cyrus H. 1965. *The Ancient Near East.* New York.

——. 1965. *Greek and Hebrew Civilizations.* New York.

Graham, James Walter. 1962. *The Palaces of Crete.* Princeton.

Graves, Robert. 1955. *The Greek Myths.* 2 vols. London.

——. 1966. *The White Goddess: A Historical Grammar of Poetic Myth.* Rev. ed. New York.

Greenberg, David F. 1988. *The Construction of Homosexuality.* Chicago.

Greifenhagen, A. 1957. *Griechische Eroten.* Berlin.

Griffin, Jasper. 1980. *Homer on Life and Death.* Oxford.

Griffith, R. Drew. 1989. "Pelops and Sicily: The Myth of Pindar *Ol.* 1." *Journal of Hellenic Studies* 109:171–73.

Grmek, Mirko Drazen. 1989. *Diseases of the Ancient Greek World.* Trans. Mireille Muellner and Leonard Muellner. Baltimore.

Groningen, Bernhard Abraham van. 1966. *Théognis, le premier livre.* Paris.

Grote, George. 1888. *A History of Greece.* 10 vols. London.

Guarino, Antonio. 1981. "Professorenerotismus." *Labeo* 27:439–40.

Hadas, Moses. 1936. "Observations on Athenian Women." *Classical Weekly* 29, no. 13: 97–100.

Hallett, Judith P. 1982. "Beloved Cleïs." *Quaderni Urbinati di cultura classica* 39 (n.s. 10):21–31.

Halperin, David M. 1989. "Is There a History of Sexuality?" *History and Theory* 28, no. 3.

————. 1990. *One Hundred Years of Homosexuality and Other Essays on Greek Love.* New York.

Hamer, Dean, and Peter Copeland. 1994. *The Science of Desire: The Search for the Gay Gene and the Biology of Behavior.* New York.

Hammond, N. G. L. [1959] 1986. *A History of Greece to 322 B.C.* 3d ed. Oxford.

————. 1975. *The Classical Age of Greece.* New York.

Hansen, Mogens Herman. 1985. *Demography and Democracy.* Copenhagen.

Hanson, Victor Davis. 1989. *The Western Way of War: Infantry Battle in Classical Greece.* New York.

Hardy, E. G., and J. S. Mann. 1880. *The Antiquities of Greece.* London.

Harnack, Adolf. 1957. *Outlines of the History of Dogma.* Boston.

Harrison, E. L. 1991. "Homeric Wonder-Horses." *Hermes* 119:252–54.

Harrison, Evelyn B. 1965. *The Athenian Agora. 11. Archaic and Archaistic Sculpture.* Princeton.

Hartmann, Nicolai. 1932. *Ethics.* 3 vols. London.

Haspels, C. H. Emilie. 1936. *Attic Black-Figured Lekythoi.* Paris.

Hatfield, Henry Caraway. 1964. *Aesthetic Paganism in German Literature: From Winckelmann to the Death of Goethe.* Cambridge, Mass.

Havelock, Eric A. 1982. *The Literate Revolution in Greece and Its Cultural Consequences.* Princeton.

Hefner, Philip. 1991. "Myth and Morality: The Love Command." *Zygon* 26:115–36.

Heitsch, Ernst. 1965. *Aphroditehymnos, Aeneas und Homer: Sprachliche Untersuchungen zum Homerproblem.* Göttingen.

Hennig, Richard. 1925. *Von rätselhaften Ländern.* Munich.

————. 1934. *Die Geographie des Homerischen Epos.* Leipzig.

Herdt, Gilbert H. 1981. *Guardians of the Flutes: Idioms of Masculinity.* New York.

————. 1982. *Rituals of Manhood.* Berkeley.

————. 1984. *Ritualized Homosexuality in Melanesia.* Berkeley.

Herlihy, David, and Christiane Klapisch-Zuber. 1978. *Les Toscans et leurs familles. Une étude du catasto florentin de 1427.* Paris.

Herlihy, David. 1985. *Medieval Households.* Cambridge, Mass.

Herter, Hans. 1959. "Effeminatus." *Reallexikon für Antike und Christentum* 4:620–50.

Hiller von Gaertringen, F., ed. 1898. *Inscriptiones graecae.* Vol. 12, fasc. 3: *Inscriptiones graecae insularum maris Aegaei.* Berlin.

————. 1899–1909. *Thera. Untersuchungen, Vermessungen und Ausgrabungen in den Jahren 1895–1898.* 4 vols. Berlin.

Hillman, James, Henry A. Murray, Tom Moore, James Baird, Thomas Cowan, and Randolph Severson. 1979. *Puer Papers.* Irving, Tex.

Hindley, Clifford. 1994. "*Eros* and Military Command in Xenophon." *Classical Quarterly* 44:347–66.

Hirschfeld, Magnus. 1914. *Die Homosexualität des Mannes und des Weibes.* Berlin.

Hodkinson, Stephen. 1988. "Inheritance, Marriage and Demography: Perspectives upon the Success and Decline of Classical Sparta." In *Classical Sparta: Techniques behind Her Success,* ed. Anton Powell. London. 79–121.

Hoeck, Karl. 1829. *Kreta.* Leipzig.

Hoessli, Heinrich. 1836–38. *Eros: die Männerliebe der Griechen: ihre Beziehungen zur Geschichte, Erziehung, Literatur und Gesetzgebung aller Zeiten.* 2 vols. Glarus.

Hoffman, Richard J. 1980. "Some Cultural Aspects of Greek Male Homosexuality." *Journal of Homosexuality* 5, no. 3:217–25.

———. 1984. "Vices, Gods, and Virtues: Cosmology as a Mediating Factor in Attitudes toward Male Homosexuality." *Journal of Homosexuality* 9, nos. 2–3:27–44.

Hoffmann, Herbert. 1988. "Why Did the Greeks Need Imagery? An Anthropological Approach to the Study of Greek Vase Painting." *Hephaistos* 9:143–62.

Hoheisel, Karl. 1992. "Homosexualität." *Reallexikon für Antike und Christentum* 16: 289–364.

Holm, Adolf. 1899–1902. *The History of Greece from Its Commencement to the Close of the Independence of the Greek Nation.* 4 vols. London.

Honey, John Raymond de Symons. 1977. *Tom Brown's Universe: The Development of the English Public School in the Nineteenth Century.* New York.

Horstmanshoff, Herman Frederik Johan. 1984. "Pestilenties in de Griekse wereld." *Lampas* 17:433–52.

———. 1989. *De pÿlen van de pest. Pestilenties in de Griekse wereld, 800–400 v.C.* Amsterdam.

Humphreys, S. C. 1978. *Anthropology and the Greeks.* London.

Huxley, G. L. 1962. *Early Sparta.* London.

Immerwahr, Henry R. 1982. "A Lekythos in Toronto and the Golden Youth of Athens." *Studies in Attic Epigraphy History and Topography Presented to Eugene Vanderpool. Hesperia, Supplement* 19:59–65.

Instone, Stephen. 1990. "Love and Sex in Pindar: Some Practical Thrusts." *Bulletin of the Institute of Classical Studies* 37:30–42.

Irigoin, Jean. 1952. *Histoire du texte de Pindare.* Paris.

Isler-Kerényi, Cornelia. 1990. "Identità maschili e femminili intorno a Dionysos nell'opera del pittore di Amasis (Iconografia dionisiaca III)." *Numismatica e Antichità classiche* 19:59–76.

Jaeger, Werner. 1943–45. *Paideia: The Ideals of Greek Culture.* Trans. Gilbert Highet. Vol. 1: *The Ideals of Greek Culture.* New York, 1945. Vol. 2: *In Search of the Divine Centre.* New York, 1943. Vol. 3: *The Conflict of Cultural Ideals in the Age of Plato.* New York, 1944.

Jameson, Michael. 1983. "Famine in the Greek World." In *Trade and Famine in Classical Antiquity,* ed. Peter Garnsey and C. R. Whittaker. *Cambridge Philological Society, Supplementary Volume 8.* 6–16.

Janko, Richard. 1990. "The *Iliad* and Its Editors: Dictation and Redaction." *Classical Antiquity* 9:326–34.

Jay, Peter. 1973. *The Greek Anthology.* London.

Jeanmaire, Henri. 1939. *Couroï et Courètes.* Lille.

Jeffery, Lilian Hamilton. 1961. *The Local Scripts of Archaic Greece.* Oxford.

———. 1976. *Archaic Greece.* New York.

———. 1990. *The Local Scripts of Archaic Greece,* rev. ed. with supplement by A. W. Johnston. Oxford.

Jenkyns, Richard. 1980. *The Victorians and Ancient Greece.* Cambridge, Mass.

Jocelyn, H. D. 1980. "A Greek Indecency and Its Students: laikazein." *Proceedings of the Cambridge Philological Society* 206:12–66.

Johnston, Alan. 1983. "The Extent and Use of Literacy, the Archaeological Evidence." In *The Greek Renaissance of the Eighth Century B.C.: Tradition and Innovation,* ed. Robin Hägg (Acta Instituti Atheniensis Regni Sueciae, series in quarto, vol. 30). Stockholm. 63–68.

———. 1990. "*Katápygos.*" *Parola del passato* 45:41.

Jones, J. S. 1991. "Population Genetics: Farming Is in the Blood." *Nature* 351:97–98.

Kahr, Brett. 1991. "The Sexual Molestation of Children: Historical Perspectives." *Journal of Psychohistory* 19:191–214.

Karsch-Haack, Ferdinand. 1911. *Das gleichgeschlechtliche Leben der Naturvölker.* Munich.

Kelly, Raymond C. 1974. *Etoro Social Structure: A Study in Structural Contradiction.* Ann Arbor, Mich.

———. 1976. "Witchcraft and Sexual Relations: An Exploration in the Social and Semantic Implications of the Structure of Belief." In *Man and Woman in the New Guinea Highlands,* ed. Paula Brown and Georgeda Buchbinder. Washington. 36–53.

Kelsen, Hans. 1933. "Die platonische Liebe." *Imago* 19:34–98, 225–55.

Kempter, Gerda. 1980. *Ganymed: Studien zur Typologie, Ikonographie und Ikonologie.* Cologne.

Keuls, Eva C. 1985. *The Reign of the Phallus.* New York.

Kilmer, Martin F. 1993. *Greek Erotica on Attic Red-Figure Vases.* London.

Kinsey, Alfred, et al. 1948. *Sexual Behavior in the Human Male.* Philadelphia.

———. 1949. "Concepts of Normality and Abnormality in Sexual Behavior." In *Psychosexual Development in Health and Disease,* ed. P. H. Hoch and J. Zubin. New York.

Kirk, George S. 1962. *The Songs of Homer.* Cambridge.

———. 1974. *The Nature of Greek Myths.* New York.

———. 1985. *The Iliad: A Commentary.* Vol. 1: Books 1–4. Cambridge.

———. 1990. *The Iliad: A Commentary.* Vol. 2: Books 5–8. Cambridge.

Kirsch, John A. W., and James Eric Rodman. 1977. "The Natural History of Homosexuality." *Yale Scientific Magazine* 51, no. 3:7–13.

Klare, Rudolf. 1937. *Homosexualität und Strafrecht.* Hamburg.

Klein, W. 1898. *Die griechischen Vasen mit Lieblingsinschriften.* Leipzig.

Kleine Pauly. Lexikon der Antike. 1979. 5 vols. Munich.

Koch-Harnack, Gundel. 1983. *Knabenliebe und Tiergeschenke: Ihre Bedeutung im päderastischen Erziehungssystem Athens.* Berlin.

Koehl, Robert B. 1986. "The Chieftain Cup and a Minoan Rite of Passage." *Journal of Hellenic Studies* 106:99–110.

Köhnken, Adolf. 1974. "Pindar as Innovator: Poseidon Hippios and the Relevance of the Pelops Story in Olympian 1." *Classical Quarterly* 24:199–206.

Komornicka, Anna M. 1976. "A la suite de la lecture 'La ragazza di Lesbo.'" *Quaderni Urbinati di cultura classica* 21:37–41.

Krause, J. H. 1841. *Die Gymnastik und Agonistik der Hellenen*. Leipzig.

Kretschmer, Paul. 1911. "Zu den lakonischen Knabenagoninschriften." *Glotta* 3:269–72.

Kroll, Wilhelm. 1927. *Freundschaft und Knabenliebe*. Munich.

Kunstler, Barton. 1991. "The Werewolf Figure and Its Adoption into the Greek Political Vocabulary." *Classical World* 84:189–205.

Kurke, Leslie. 1992. "The Politics of *habrosyne* in Archaic Greece." *Classical Antiquity* 11:91–120.

Kyle, Donald G. 1987. *Athletics in Ancient Athens*. Leiden.

Labarbe, Jules. 1962. "Un décalage de 40 ans dans la chronologie de Polycrate." *L'Antiquité Classique* 31:153–88.

Lachmann, K. K. F. W. 1841. *Betrachtungen über Homers Ilias*. Berlin.

Lambert, Michael, and Holger Szesnat. 1994. "Greek 'Homosexuality': Whither the Debate?" *Akroterion* 39:46–63.

Landtmann, G. 1927. *The Kiwai Papuans of British New Guinea*. London.

Lang, Mabel. 1976. "Love Names and Hate Names." *Graffiti and Dipinti: The Athenian Agora* 21:11–15.

Lardinois, André. 1989. "Lesbian Sappho and Sappho of Lesbos." In *From Sappho to De Sade: Moments in the History of Sexuality*, ed. Jan Bremmer. London. 15–35.

Larrañaga, Hortencia D. 1969. "Safo." *Revista de estudios clásicos* 13:73–102.

Lasserre, François. 1944. "*Erotikoì lógoi.*" *Museum Helveticum* 1:169–78.

———. 1954. Plutarque, *De la Musique. Texte, traduction, commentaire précédés d'une étude sur l'éducation musicale dans la Grèce antique*. Olten.

———. 1974. "Ornements érotiques dans la poésie lyrique archaïque." In *Serta Turyniana: Studies in Greek Literature and Palaeography in Honor of Alexander Turyn*, ed. John L. Heller. Urbana, Ill. 5–33.

———. 1976. "L'historiographie grecque à l'époque archaïque." *Quaderni di storia* 4:113–42.

Lecky, W. E. H. 1911. *History of European Morals*. 2 vols. London.

Leeuwen, J. van. 1917. *Odyssea, cum notis criticis, commentariis exegeticis, indicibus ad utrumque epos pertinentibus*. 2 vols. Leiden.

Lefkowitz, Mary R. 1981. *The Lives of the Greek Poets*. Baltimore.

———. 1986. *Women in Greek Myth*. Baltimore.

Lefkowitz, Mary R., and Maureen B. Fant. 1982. *Women's Life in Greece and Rome*. Baltimore.

Lehnus, Luigi. 1975. "Note stesicoree: I poemetti 'minori' (fr. 277–9 PMG)." *Studi classici e orientali* 24:191–96.

Lembesis, A. 1976. "A Sanctuary of Hermes and Aphrodite in Crete." *Expedition* 18:2–13.

LeVay, Simon. 1993. *The Sexual Brain*. Cambridge, Mass.

Levinson, Daniel J., Charlotte N. Darrow, Edward B. Klein, Maria H. Levinson, and Braxton McKee. 1978. *The Seasons of a Man's Life*. New York.

Lewes, Kenneth. 1988. *The Psychoanalytic Theory of Male Homosexuality*. New York.

Lewis, Bernard. 1990. *Race and Slavery in the Middle East: An Historical Enquiry*. New York.

Lewis, Thomas S. W. 1982–83. "The Brothers Ganymede." *Salmagundi* 58/59:147–65.

Licht, Hans (pseud. Paul Brandt). 1906. "Der *paidon eros* in der griechischen Literatur: I. Die lyrische und bukolische Dichtung." *Jahrbuch für sexuelle Zwischenstufen* 8:619–84.

———. 1908. "Der *paidon eros* in der griechischen Dichtung: II. Die Gedichte der Anthologie." *Jahrbuch für sexuelle Zwischenstufen* 9:213–312.

———. 1910. "Der *paidon eros* in der griechischen Dichtung: III. Die attische Komödie." *Anthropophyteia* 7:128–78.

———. 1912. "Homoerotik in den homerischen Gedichten." *Anthropophyteia* 9:291–300.

———. 1922. "Die Erotik in den epischen Gedichten der Griechen mit besonderer Berücksichtigung des Homoerotischen." *Zeitschrift für Sexualwissenschaft* 9:65–74.

———. 1924. *Beiträge zur antiken Erotik*. Dresden.

———. 1932. *Sexual Life in Ancient Greece*. Trans. J. H. Freese. London.

Lincoln, Bruce. 1981. *Emerging from the Chrysalis: Studies in Rituals of Women's Initiation*. Cambridge, Mass.

Lindner, Robert. 1951. "Sex in Prison." *Complex* 6:5–20.

Lissarrague, François. 1987. "De la sexualité des satyres." *Mêtis* 2, no. 1:63–79.

Löffler, Ingrid. 1963. *Die Melampodie. Versuch einer Rekonstruktion des Inhalts*. Meisenheim am Glan.

Lombardo, Mario. 1985. "Nuovi documenti su Pisticci in età arcaica. II. Il graffito." *Parola del passato* 40:294–307.

Lopez, Robert S. 1967. *The Birth of Europe*. Philadelphia.

Lord, Albert B. 1960. *The Singer of Tales*. Cambridge, Mass.

Lorimer, H. L. 1947. "The Hoplite Phalanx with Special Reference to the Poems of Archilochus and Tyrtaeus." *Annual of the British School at Athens* 42:76–188.

Lucas, F. L. 1951. *Greek Poetry for Everyman*. London.

MacCary, W. Thomas. 1982. *Childlike Achilles: Ontogeny and Phylogeny in the Iliad*. New York.

MacDowell, Douglas M. 1978. *The Law in Classical Athens*. London.

———. 1986. *Spartan Law*. Edinburgh.

MacLachlan, Bonnie. 1992. "Sacred Prostitution and Aphrodite." *Studies in Religion* 21:145–62.

Macmullen, Ramsay. 1982. "Roman Attitudes to Greek Love." *Historia* 31:484–502.

Mahaffy, J. P. 1874. *Social Life in Greece from Homer to Menander*. London.

———. 1883. *A History of Classical Greek Literature*. 2 vols. London.

Mallory, J. P. 1989. *In Search of the Indo-Europeans*. London.

Mandell, Sara. 1990. "The Story of Telemachus as Multiple Cult Myth." *Journal of Ritual Studies* 4:65–83.

Manieri, Flavio. 1972. "Saffo: appunti di metodologia generale per un approccio psichiatrico." *Quaderni Urbinati di cultura classica* 14:46–64.

Marandon de Montyel, E. 1877. "De la maladie des Scythes." *Annales médico-psychologiques,* 5th series, 17:161–74.

Marcovich, Miroslav. 1983. "Anacreon, 358 PMG." *American Journal of Philology* 104: 372–83.

Marinatos, Nanno. 1984. *Art and Religion in Thera: Reconstructing a Bronze Age Society.* Athens.

Marmor, Judd. 1980. *Homosexual Behavior: A Modern Reappraisal.* New York.

Marrou, Henri-Irénée. 1956. *A History of Education in Antiquity.* Trans. George Lamb. Madison, Wis.

Mattusch, Carol C. 1988. *Greek Bronze Statuary: From the Beginnings through the Fifth Century B.C.* Ithaca, N.Y.

Mauritsch, Peter. 1990. "Sexualität bei Homer: Untersuchungen zu Norm und Abweichung im Sexualverhalten in den Homerischen Epen." Ph.D. dissertation, University of Graz.

Mazel, Jacques. 1984. *Les métamorphoses d'Eros: l'amour dans la Grèce antique.* Paris.

Mazon, Paul. 1942. *Introduction à l'Iliade.* Paris.

McCabe, Joseph. 1930. *A History of Human Morals.* Girard, Kans.

McDonald, W. A., and R. H. Simpson. 1969. "Further Explorations in Southwestern Peloponnese, 1964–1968." *American Journal of Archaeology* 73:123–77.

McDonnell, Myles. 1991. "The Introduction of Athletic Nudity: Thucydides, Plato, and the Vases." *Journal of Hellenic Studies* 111:182–93.

Meier, M. H. Eduard. 1837. "Päderastie." *Encyclopädie der Wissenschaften und Künste.* Leipzig. 9:149–89.

Meister, Richard. 1963. "Die spartanischen Altersklassen vom Standpunkt der Entwicklungspsychologie betrachtet." *Österreichische Akademie der Wissenschaften. Sitzungsberichte* 241, no. 5:3–24.

Merkelbach, Reinhold. 1952. "Die pisistratische Redaktion der homerischen Gedichte." *Rheinisches Museum für Philologie* n.s. 95:23–47.

———. 1957. "Sappho und ihr Kreis." *Philologus* 101:2–29.

Meulengracht Sørensen, Preben. 1983. *Unmanly Men: Concepts of Sexual Defamation in Early Northern Society.* Odense.

Michell, H. 1952. *Sparta.* Cambridge.

Miller, Stella G. 1986. "Eros and the Arms of Achilles." *American Journal of Archaeology* 90:159–70.

Milman, Adam, ed. 1971. *The Making of Homeric Verse: The Collected Papers of Milman Parry.* Oxford.

Milne, Marjorie J., and Dietrich von Bothmer. 1953. "KATAPYGON, KATAPYGAINA." *Hesperia* 22:216–24.

Mitford, William. 1838. *History of Greece.* 2d ed. London.

Moretti, Luigi. 1982. "Sulla legge ginnasiarchica di Berea." *Rivista di filologia e di istruzione classica* 110:45–63.

Morris, Ian. 1986. "The Use and Abuse of Homer." *Classical Antiquity* 5, no. 1:81–138.

————. 1987. *Burial and Ancient Society.* Cambridge.

Morrow, Glenn R. 1960. *Plato's Cretan City.* Princeton.

Mossé, Claude. 1984. *La Grèce archaïque d'Homère à Eschyle. VIIIe–VIe siècles av. J.-C.* Paris.

Mosse, George L. 1985. *Nationalism and Sexuality: Respectability and Abnormal Sexuality in Modern Europe.* New York.

Müller, Friedrich von. 1959. *Unterhaltungen mit Goethe.* Ed. Renate Grumach. Munich.

Müller, Karl Otfried. 1830. *The History and Antiquities of the Doric Race.* Trans. Henry Tufnell. 2 vols. Oxford.

————. 1844. *Die Dorier.* 4 vols. 2d ed. Breslau.

Mure, William. 1850. *A Critical History of the Language and Literature of Antient Greece.* 5 vols. London.

————. 1857. "Sappho, and the Ideal Love of the Greeks." *Rheinisches Museum für Philologie* n.s. 12:564–93.

Murray, Gilbert. 1925. *Five Stages of Greek Religion.* New York.

————. 1960. *The Rise of the Greek Epic.* Oxford.

Murray, Oswyn. 1980. *Early Greece.* London.

————, ed. 1990. *Sympotica.* Oxford.

Musti, Domenico. 1986. *Le Origini dei Greci. Dori e Mondo Egeo.* Bari.

Mylonas, George E. 1946. "The Eagle of Zeus." *American Journal of Archaeology* 50:286.

Nagy, Gregory. 1973. "Phaethon, Sappho's Phaon, and the White Rock of Leukas." *Harvard Studies in Classical Philology* 77:137–77.

————. 1979a. *The Best of the Achaeans.* Baltimore.

————. 1979b. "On the Origins of the Greek Hexameter: Synchronic and Diachronic Perspectives." In *Studies in Diachronic, Synchronic, and Typological Linguistics. Festschrift for Oswald Szemerényi on the Occasion of His 65th Birthday,* ed. Bela Brogyanyi. Amsterdam. 2:611–31.

————. 1982. "Hesiod." In *Ancient Writers: Greece and Rome,* ed. T. James Luce. New York. 1:43–73.

————. 1990. *Pindar's Homer: The Lyric Possession of an Epic Past.* Baltimore.

Neumann, J., and Simo Parpola. 1987. "Climatic Change and the Eleventh-Tenth-Century Eclipse of Assyria and Babylonia." *Journal of Near Eastern Studies* 46:161–82.

Nietzsche, Friedrich. 1909–13. *The Complete Work of Friedrich Nietzsche.* 18 vols. New York.

————. 1966. *Werke in drei Bänden.* Ed. Karl Schlechta. Munich.

Nilsson, Martin P. 1912. "Die Grundlagen des spartanischen Lebens." *Klio* 12:308–40.

————. 1933. *Homer and Mycenae.* Philadelphia.

————. 1955. *Die hellenistische Schule.* Munich.

Nisetich, Frank, trans. 1980. *Pindar's Victory Songs.* Baltimore.

————. 1989. *Pindar and Homer.* Baltimore.

O'Higgins, James. 1982–83. "Sexual Choice, Sexual Act: An Interview with Michel Foucault." *Salmagundi* 58/59:10–24.

Ollier, F. 1933–43. *Le Mirage spartiate.* 2 vols. Paris.

Oxford Classical Dictionary. 1970. Oxford.

Oxford History of the Classical World. 1986. Oxford.

Page, Denys L. 1955. *Sappho and Alcaeus: An Introduction to the Study of Ancient Lesbian Poetry.* Oxford.

———. 1959. *History and the Homeric Iliad.* Berkeley.

———. 1961. *Alcman: The Partheneion.* Oxford.

———. 1962. *Poetae Melici Graeci.* Oxford.

———. 1968. *Lyrica Graeca Selecta.* Oxford.

———. 1974. *Supplementum Lyricis Graecis.* Oxford.

Paoli, U. E. 1953. *La donna greca nell'antichità.* Florence.

Parker, Robert. 1983. *Miasma: Pollution and Purification in Early Greek Religion.* Oxford.

Parsons, Edward Alexander. 1952. *The Alexandrian Library, Glory of the Hellenic World: Its Rise, Antiquities, and Destructions.* New York.

Pastre, Geneviève. 1980. *De l'amour lesbien.* Paris.

———. 1987. *Athènes et "Le Péril saphique."* Paris.

Patzer, Harald. 1982. *Die griechische Knabenliebe.* Wiesbaden.

Paulys Realencyclopädie der classischen Altertumswissenschaft.

———. 1894. "Anteros." 2356–57.

———. 1896. "Bäder." 2743–58.

———. 1905. "Dosiadas." 1596–1603.

———. 1905. "Echemenes." 1913–14.

———. 1905. "Ephebia." 2737–46.

———. 1907. "Ephoros." 1–16.

———. 1907. "Eros." 484–544.

———. 1912. "Gymnasium." 2004–26.

———. 1912. "Gymnopaidien." 2087–89.

———. 1913. "Hippias." 1703–4.

———. 1916. "Iolaos." 1843–46.

———. 1921. "Kinaidos." 459–62.

———. 1921. "Knabenliebe." 897–906.

———. 1925. "Lesbische Liebe." 2100–2102.

———. 1929. "Spintria." 1814.

———. 1930. "Matrimonium." 2259–86.

———. 1931. "Symposion." 1266–70.

———. 1932. "Minos." 1890–1927.

———. 1932. "Symposion-Literatur." 1273–82.

———. 1934. "Thaletas." 1213.

———. 1937. "Nuptiae." 1478–89.

———. 1938. "Phallophorie." 1673–81.

———. 1938. "Phallos." 1681–1748.

———. 1938. "Philippos von Opus." 2351–66.

———. 1939. "Onomakritos." 491–93.

———. 1952. "Polykrates." 1726–34.

———. 1953. "Porne." 264–65.

———. 1967. "Zaleukos." 2298–2301.

Pavese, Cesare Odo. 1972. *Tradizioni e generi poetici della Grecia arcaica.* Rome.

———. 1974. *Studi sulla tradizione epica rapsodica.* Rome.

Payer, Pierre. *Sex and the Penitentials: The Development of a Sexual Code, 550–1150.* Toronto.

Pelekides, C. 1962. *Histoire de l'éphébie attique des origines à 31 avant Jésus-Christ.* Paris.

Percy, William A. 1987. "Greek Pederasty." *Gay Community News,* Nov. 22–28.

———. 1992. "The Origins of Institutionalized Pederasty." In *Homosexuality in the Ancient World,* ed. Wayne R. Dynes and Stephen Donaldson. New York. 375–80.

Percy, William A., and Warren Johansson. N.d. (forthcoming). "Homosexuality." In *Handbook of Medieval Sexuality,* ed. James A. Brundage and Vern L. Bullough. New York.

Perrotta, Gennaro, and Bruno Gentili. 1965. *Polinnia. Poesia greca arcaica.* Messina.

Peters, F. E. 1970. *The Harvest of Hellenism.* New York.

Pfeiffer, Rudolf. 1978. *History of Classical Scholarship from the Beginnings to the End of the Hellenistic Age.* 2d ed. Oxford.

Pickard-Cambridge, Arthur. 1927. *Dithyramb, Tragedy and Comedy.* Oxford.

———. 1968. *The Dramatic Festivals of Athens.* Oxford.

Pocock, L. G. 1957. *The Sicilian Origin of the Odyssey.* Wellington.

Pogey-Castries, L. R. de. 1930. *Histoire de l'amour grec dans l'antiquité.* Paris.

Poliakoff, Michael. 1987. *Combat Sports in the Ancient World: Competition, Violence, and Culture.* New Haven.

Poliakov, Leon. 1974. *The Aryan Myth.* New York.

Pomeroy, Sarah. 1975. *Goddesses, Whores, Wives, and Slaves: Women in Classical Antiquity.* New York.

Powell, Barry B. 1989. "Why Was the Greek Alphabet Invented? The Epigraphical Evidence." *Classical Antiquity* 8:321–50.

Preller, Ludwig. 1846. "Phanokles und die Mythologie der Knabenliebe." *Rheinisches Museum für Philologie* n.s. 4:399–405.

Price, Sarah D. 1990. "Anacreontic Vases Reconsidered." *Greek, Roman and Byzantine Studies* 31:132–75.

Privitera, G. Aurelio. 1969. "Il commento del *perì hypsus* al fr. 31 L.P. di Saffo." *Quaderni Urbinati di cultura classica* 7:26–35.

Pucci, Pietro. 1987. *Odysseus Polutropos: Intertextual Readings in the Odyssey and the Iliad.* Ithaca, N.Y.

Raepsaet, G. 1971. "Étude d'un Comportement social: Les relations entre parents et enfants dans la société athénienne à l'époque classique." *L'Antiquité Classique* 20: 589–606.

Raile, Arthur Lyon (pseud. of Edward Perry Warren). 1928–30. *A Defence of Uranian Love.* Vol. 1: *The Boy Lover.* Vol. 2: *The Uranian Eros.* Vol. 3: *The Heavenly Wisdom and Conclusion.* London.

Raschke, Wendy J., ed. 1988. *The Archaeology of the Olympics: The Olympics and Other Festivals in Antiquity.* Madison, Wis.

Rawson, Elizabeth. 1969. *The Spartan Tradition in European Thought.* Oxford.

Redfield, J. M. 1975. *Nature and Culture in the Iliad.* Chicago.

Reinach, Salomon. 1905–28. *Cultes, mythes et religions.* 5 vols. Paris.

Reinhardt, Karl. 1961. *Die Ilias und ihr Dichter.* Göttingen.

Reinsberg, Carola. 1989. *Ehe, Hetärentum und Knabenliebe im antiken Griechenland.* Munich.

Renehan, R. 1984. "Anacreon Fragment 13 Page." *Classical Philology* 79:28–33.

Renfrew, Colin. 1987. *Archaeology and Language.* London.

Reynen, Hans. 1967. "Philosophie und Knabenliebe." *Hermes* 95:308–16.

Rhodes, P. J. 1981. *A Commentary on the Aristotelian Athenaion Politeia.* Oxford.

Richter, Gisela Marie Augusta. 1962. *Greek Portraits.* Vol. 4: *Iconographical Studies: A Few Suggestions.* Collection Latomus 54. Brussels-Berchem.

———. 1970. *Kouroi: Archaic Greek Youths.* 3d ed. London.

Ridgway, Brunilde Sismondo. 1966. "Greek Kouroi and Egyptian Methods." *American Journal of Archaeology* 70:68–70.

Riemschneider, Margarete. 1950. *Homer: Entwicklung und Stil.* Leipzig.

Rihll, T. E. 1989. "Lawgivers and Tyrants (Solon, frr. 9–11 West)." *Classical Quarterly* 39:277–86.

Ritoók, Zsigmond. 1983. "Zu zwei Alkman-Fragmenten (*PMG* 30 und 59 b)." *Eirene* 20:33–38.

Robbins, E. 1986. "The Broken Wall, the Burning Roof and Tower: Pindar, *Ol.* 8.31–46." *Classical Quarterly* 36:317–21.

Robertson, Martin. 1975. *History of Greek Art.* 2 vols. Cambridge.

Robinson, David M., and Edward J. Fluck. 1937. *A Study of the Greek Love-Names, including a Discussion of Paederasty and a Prosopographia.* Baltimore.

Robinson, Rachel Sargent. 1981. *Sources for the History of Greek Athletics in English Translation.* Chicago.

Rocco, Antonio. 1652. *Alcibiade fanciullo a scola.* Oranges [Venice].

Rocke, Michael J. 1989. "Male Homosexuality and Its Regulation in Late Medieval Florence." Ph.D. dissertation, SUNY at Binghamton.

Roebuck, Carl. 1940. "Pottery from the North Slope of the Acropolis, 1937–1938." *Hesperia* 9:141–260.

Rolle, Renate. 1989. *The World of the Scythians.* Trans. Gayna Walls. Berkeley.

Rose, H. J. 1934. *A Handbook of Greek Literature.* New York.

Rosenbaum, Julius. [1837] 1898. *The Plague of Lust.* Paris.

Rösler, Wolfgang. 1980. *Dichter und Gruppe. Eine Untersuchung zu den Bedingungen und zur historischen Funktion früher griechischer Lyrik am Beispiel Alkaios.* Munich.

———. 1990. "*Mnemosyne* in the Symposion. " In *Sympotica: A Symposium on the Symposion,* ed. Oswyn Murray. Oxford. 230–37.

Rossi, L. E. 1983. "Il simposio greco arcaico e classico come spettacolo a se stesso." In *Spettacoli conviviali dall'antichità classica alle corti italiane del'400: Atti del VII convègno di studio.* Viterbo. 41–50.

Rossman, Parker. 1985. *Sexual Experience between Men and Boys.* N.p.

Rougé, Jean. 1970. "La colonisation grecque et les femmes." *Cahiers d'histoire* 15:307–17.

Ruijgh, C. J. 1957. *L'Élément achéen dans la langue épique.* Assen.

Ruppersberg, Albert. 1911. "Eispnelas." *Philologus* 70:151–54.

Ruschenbusch, Eberhard. 1966. *SOLONOS NOMOI. Die Fragmente des solonischen Gesetzeswerkes mit einer Text-und Überlieferungs-geschichte* [= *Historia. Einzelschriften* 9]. Wiesbaden.

———. 1985. "Die Zahl der griechischen Staaten und Arealgrösse und Bürgerzahl der 'Normalpolis.'" *Zeitschrift für Papyrologie und Epigraphik* 59:253–63.

Russell, W. M. S. 1983. "The Palaeodemographic View." In *Disease in Ancient Man: An International Symposium,* ed. Gerald D. Hart. Toronto. 217–53.

Salac, Antonín. 1961. "Der Zeusadler und Homer." In *Minoica und Homer,* ed. Vladimir Georgiev and Johannes Irmscher. Berlin. 45–50.

Sallares, Robert. 1991. *The Ecology of the Ancient Greek World.* Ithaca, N.Y.

Salmon, J.B. 1984. *Wealthy Corinth.* Oxford.

Sandys, John Edwin. 1908. *A History of Classical Scholarship.* 3 vols. Cambridge.

Sansone, David. 1988. *Greek Athletics and the Genesis of Sport.* Berkeley.

Sartre, Maurice. 1985. "L'homosexualité dans la Grèce ancienne." *L'Histoire* 76:10–17.

Saslow, James. 1978. "Closets in the Museum: Homophobia and Art History." In *Lavender Culture,* ed. Karla Jay and Allen Young. New York. 215–27.

Schauenburg, Konrad. 1965. "Erastes und Eromenos auf einer Schale des Sokles." *Archäologischer Anzeiger* 80:850–67.

Schefold, Karl. 1981. *Die Göttersage in der klassischen und hellenistischen Kunst.* Munich.

Schein, Seth L. 1984. *The Mortal Hero.* Berkeley.

Scheliha, Renata von. 1968. *Freiheit und Freundschaft in Hellas. Sechs Basler Vorträge. Castrum Peregrini* 82–83. Amsterdam.

Schieffelin, Edward. 1976. *The Sorrow of the Lonely and the Burning of the Dancers.* New York.

———. 1982. "The Bau A Ceremonial Lodge: An Alternative to Initiation." In *Rituals of Manhood,* ed. Gilbert Herdt. Berkeley. 155–200.

Schliemann, Heinrich. 1875. *Troy and Its Remains.* London.

Schmidt, Ludwig. 1990. *Beobachtungen zu der Plagenerzählung in Exodus VII 14–XI 10.* Leiden.

Schmitz, Heinz. 1970. *Hypsos und Bios: Stilistische Untersuchungen zum Alltagsrealismus in der archaischen griechischen Chorlyrik.* Bern.

Schneider, Jean. 1985. "La chronologie d'Alcman." *Revue des études grecques* 98:1–64.

Schulten, Adolf. 1922. *Tartessos.* Hamburg.

Schurtz, Heinrich. 1902. *Altersklassen und Männerbünde.* Berlin.

Schwarz, Gerda. 1976–77. "Iris und Ganymed auf attischen Vasenbildern." *Jahreshefte des Österreichischen archäologischen Institutes in Wien* 51:1–10.

Sealey, Raphael. 1976. *A History of the Greek City States 700–338 B.C.* Berkeley.

———. 1990. *Women and Law in Classical Greece.* Chapel Hill, N.C.

Seeberg, Axel. 1971. *Corinthian Komos Vases. University of London Institute of Classical Studies. Bulletin Supplement* 27.

Segal, Lester. 1989. *Historical Consciousness and Religious Tradition in Azariah de Rossi's Me'or Einayim.* Philadelphia.

Semenov, Anatol. 1911. "Zur dorischen Knabenliebe." *Philologus* 70:146–50.

Sergent, Bernard. 1986. *Homosexuality in Greek Myth.* Trans. Arthur Goldhammer. Boston.

———. 1987a. *L'homosexualité initiatique dans l'Europe ancienne.* Paris.

———. 1987b. "To the Origins of the Expansion of Homosexuality in the Ancient Greek Society." *Homosexuality, Which Homosexuality? International Scientific Conference on Gay and Lesbian Studies. History* 2:89–93. Amsterdam.

Seyffert, Oskar. 1908. *A Dictionary of Classical Antiquities.* Rev. Henry Nettleship and J. E. Sandys. New York.

Shapiro, H. Alan. 1980. "Hippokrates Son of Anxileos." *Hesperia* 49:289–93.

———. 1981. "Courtship Scenes in Attic Vase-Painting" and "Exekias, Ajax, and Salamis: A Further Note." *American Journal of Archaeology* 85:133–43, 173–75.

———. 1982a. "Epilikos and Skythes." *American Journal of Archaeology* 86:285.

———. 1982b. "Kallias Kration Alopethen." *Hesperia* 51:69–73.

———. 1990. "Old and New Heroes: Narrative, Composition, and Subject in Attic Black-Figure." *Classical Antiquity* 9:114–48.

Shelley, Percy Bysshe. [1818] 1949. "A Discourse on the Manners of the Antient Greeks Relative to the Subject of Love." In *The Platonism of Shelley,* ed. James A. Notopoulos. Durham, N.C.

Sherwin-White, Susan M. 1978. *Ancient Cos: An Historical Study from the Dorian Settlement to the Imperial Period.* Göttingen.

Shipley, Graham. 1987. *A History of Samos 800–188 B.C.* Oxford.

Sichtermann, Hellmut. 1953. *Ganymed: Mythos und Gestalt in der antiken Kunst.* Berlin.

———. 1988. "Ganymedes." In *Lexicon Iconographicum Mythologiae Classicae.* Zurich. Vol. 4, ed. H. C. Ackermann and J.-R. Gisler. Part 1:154–70.

Sigerist, Henry E. 1961. *A History of Medicine.* Vol. 2: *Early Greek, Hindu, and Persian Medicine.* New York.

Simonini, Laura. 1979. "Il fr. 282 P. di Ibico." *Acme* 32:285–98.

Sirna, Francesco G. 1973. "Alcmane *heuretes ton erotikon melon.*" *Aegyptus* 53:28–70.

Sjöqvist, Erik. 1973. *Sicily and the Greeks.* Ann Arbor, Mich.

Skafte Jensen, Minna. 1980. *The Homeric Question and the Oral-Formulaic Theory.* Copenhagen.

Slater, Philip E. 1968. *The Glory of Hera.* Boston.

Slater, W. J. 1978. "Artemon and Anacreon. No Text without Context." *Phoenix* 32:185–94.

Snell, Bruno. 1953. *The Discovery of the Mind in Greek Philosophy and Literature.* Trans. T. G. Rosenmeyer. New York.

Snodgrass, Anthony M. 1964. *Early Greek Armour and Weapons from the End of the Bronze Age to 600 B.C.* Edinburgh.

———. 1967. *Arms and Armour of the Greeks.* Ithaca, N.Y.

———. 1971. *The Dark Age of Greece: An Archaeological Survey of the Eleventh to the Eighth Centuries B.C.* Edinburgh.

———. 1980. *Archaic Greece: The Age of Experiment.* Berkeley.

———. 1983. "Heavy Freight in Archaic Greece." In *Trade in the Ancient Economy,* ed. Peter Garnsey et al. London.

————. 1987. *An Archaeology of Greece.* Berkeley.

Snyder, Jane McIntosh. 1989. *The Woman and the Lyre: Women Writers in Classical Greece and Rome.* Carbondale, Ill.

Sokal, Robert R., Neal L. Oden, and Chester Wilson. 1991. "Genetic Evidence for the Spread of Agriculture by Demic Diffusion." *Nature* 351:143–45.

Sommer, Volker. 1990. *Wider die Natur? Homosexualität und Evolution.* Munich.

"Spuren von Konträrsexualität bei den alten Skandinaviern: Mitteilungen eines norwegischen Gelehrten." 1902. *Jahrbuch für sexuelle Zwischenstufen* 4:244–63.

Stefanovich, Mark R. 1989. "Can Archaeology and Historical Linguistics Coexist? A Critical Review of Colin Renfrew's *Archaeology and Language*—The Puzzle of Indo-European Origins." *Mankind Quarterly* 30, nos. 1–2:129–58.

Stéphanopoulos, Stéphane-Théodore. 1988. "L'affaire Harmodios et Aristogiton." In *Éros et droit en Grèce classique,* ed. Panayotis Dimakis. Paris. 67–74.

Stiebing, William H. 1980. "The End of the Mycenean Age." *Biblical Archeologist* (Winter):7–21.

————. 1989. *Out of the Desert? Archaeology and the Exodus/Conquest Narratives.* Buffalo.

Strom, Folke. 1974. *Nid, Ergi and Old Norse Moral Attitudes.* London.

Stroud, Ronald. 1979. *The Axones and Kyrbeis of Drakon and Solon.* Berkeley.

Suys, E. 1932. "Les chants d'amour du Papyrus Chester Beatty I." *Biblica* 13:209–27.

Svenbro, Jesper. 1984. "La stratégie de l'amour. Modèle de la guerre et théorie de l'amour dans la poésie de Sappho." *Quaderni di Storia* 19:57–79.

Swaddling, Judith. 1980. *The Ancient Olympic Games.* Austin.

Sweeney, Jane, Tam Curry, and Yannis Tzedakis, eds. 1988. *The Human Figure in Early Greek Art.* Washington, D.C.

Symonds, John Addington. 1873–76. *Studies of the Greek Poets.* 2 vols. London.

————. 1883. *A Problem in Greek Ethics.* London.

————. 1896. *A Problem in Modern Ethics.* London.

————. 1983. *Male Love.* Ed. John Lauritsen. New York.

Szarmach, Marian. 1982. "*Erotikoì lógoi* von Maximos Tyrios." *Eos* 70:61–69.

Szegedy-Maszak, Andrew. 1978. "Legends of the Greek Lawgivers." *Greek, Roman and Byzantine Studies* 19:199–209.

Tarán, Sonya Lida. 1985. "*Eisì tríches:* An Erotic Motif in the *Greek Anthology.*" *Journal of Hellenic Studies* 105:90–107.

Tarbell, F. B. 1910. "Architecture on Attic Vases." *American Journal of Archaeology* 14:428–33.

Tarn, W. W., and G. T. Griffith. 1952. *Hellenistic Civilisation.* London.

Taylor, G. Rattray. 1954. *Sex in History.* New York.

Taylor, Michael W. 1981. *The Tyrant Slayers: The Heroic Image in Fifth Century* B.C., *Athenian Art and Politics.* New York.

Tecusan, Manuela. 1990. "*Logos Sympotikos:* Patterns of the Irrational in Philosophical Drinking: Plato outside the *Symposium.*" In *Sympotica: A Symposium on the Symposion,* ed. Oswyn Murray. Oxford. 238–60.

Thomas, Rosalind. 1989. *Oral Tradition and Written Record in Classical Athens.* London.

Thompson, Wesley E. 1972. "Athenian Marriage Patterns: Remarriage." *California Studies in Classical Antiquity* 5:211–25.

Thorp, John. 1992. "The Social Construction of Homosexuality." *Phoenix* 46:54–61.

Tibiletti Bruno, Maria Grazia. 1969. "Un confronto greco-anatolico." *Athenaeum* n.s. 47:303–12.

Tiger, Lionel. 1969. *Men in Groups.* New York.

Tomlinson, R. A. 1972. *Argos and the Argolid.* London.

Trendall, Arthur D. 1990. "Two South Italian Red-Figure Vases in a Private Collection in Sorengo." *Numismatica e Antichità classiche* 19:117–34.

Tristram, Henry. 1935. "The Burning of Sappho." *Dublin Review* 197:137–49.

Trumpf, Jürgen. 1973. "Über das Trinken in der Poesie des Alkaios." *Zeitschrift für Papyrologie und Epigraphik* 12:139–60.

Tsagarakis, Odysseus. 1979. "Some Neglected Aspects of Love in Sappho's Fr. 31 L.P." *Rheinisches Museum für Philologie* n.s. 122:97–118.

Turcan, Robert. 1961. "Encore le sarcophage de Cadenet." *Revue archéologique* 1:159–63.

Tyrrell, William Blake. 1984. *Amazons: A Study in Athenian Mythmaking.* Baltimore.

Ulf, Christoph, and Ingomar Weiler. 1980. "Der Ursprung der antiken Olympischen Spiele in der Forschung." *Stadion* 6:1–38.

Ulrichs, Karl Heinrich. [1864–80] 1975. *Forschungen über das Rätsel der mannmännlichen Liebe.* New York.

Ungaretti, John. 1978. "Pederasty, Heroism, and the Family in Classical Greece." *Journal of Homosexuality* 3:291–300.

———. 1983. "De-moralizing Morality: Where Dover's *Greek Homosexuality* Leaves Us." *Journal of Homosexuality* 8:1–17.

Valckenaer, Lodewijk Caspar. 1739. *Animadversionum ad Ammonium grammaticum libri tres.* Leiden.

Van Baal, Jan. 1966. *Dema: Description and Analysis of Merindanim Culture (New Guinea).* The Hague.

Vanggaard, Thorkil. 1973. *Phallos: A Symbol and Its History in the Male World.* New York.

Vanhouette, M. 1954. *La Philosophie politique de Platon dans les 'Lois.'* Louvain.

Veneri, Alina. 1990. "La questione omerica oggi: sviluppi e tendenze." *Eirene* 27:15–26.

Vermeule, Emily. 1964. *Greece in the Bronze Age.* Chicago.

———. 1969. "Some Erotica in Boston." *Antike Kunst* 12:9–15.

Verstraete, Beert C. 1977–78. "Homosexuality in Ancient Greek and Roman Civilization: A Critical Bibliography." *Journal of Homosexuality* 3:79–89.

Vetta, Massimo. 1979. "La 'giovinezza giusta' di Trasibulo: Pind. *Pyth.* VI 48." *Quaderni Urbinati di cultura classica* 31 (n.s. 2):87–90.

———. 1981. "Poesia e Simposio (a proposito di un libro recente sui carmi di Alceo)." *Rivista di filologia e di istruzione classica* 109:483–95.

———. 1982a. "Il *P. Oxy.* 2506 fr. 77 e la poesia pederotica di Alceo." *Quaderni Urbinati di cultura classica* 39 (n.s. 10):7–20.

—. 1982b. "Recenti studi sul primo *Partenio* di Alcmane." *Quaderni Urbinati di cultura classica* 39 (n.s. 10):127–36.

Vickers, Michael. 1983. "Les vases peints: image ou mirage?" In *Image et céramique grecque: Actes du Colloque de Rouen 1982,* ed. F. Lissarrague and F. Thelamon. Rouen. 29–42.

—. 1987. "Value and Simplicity: Eighteenth-Century Taste and the Study of Greek Vases." *Past & Present* 116:98–137.

—. 1990. "The Impoverishment of the Past: The Case of Classical Greece." *Antiquity* 64:455–63.

Vickers, Michael, and E. D. Francis. 1983. "*Signa priscae artis:* Eretria and Siphnos." *Journal of Hellenic Studies* 103:49–67.

Vickers, Michael, and D. W. J. Gill. 1990. "Reflected Glory: Pottery and Precious Metal in Classical Greece." *Jahrbuch des deutschen archäologischen Instituts* 105:1–30.

—. 1994. *Artful Crafts: Ancient Greek Silverware and Pottery.* Oxford.

Vidal-Naquet, P. 1986. *The Black Hunter.* Baltimore.

—. 1974. "Les jeunes. Le cru, l'enfant grec et le cuit." In *Faire de l'histoire,* ed. Jacques Le Goff and Pierre Nora. 3 vols. Paris. 3:137–68.

Villers, Robert. 1959. *La Femme.* Brussels.

Villoison, Jean Baptiste Gaspard d'Ansse de. 1788. *Homeri Ilias ad veteris codicis Veneti fidem recensita.* Venice.

Vogt, Joseph. 1960. "Von der Gleichwertigkeit der Geschlechter in der bürgerlichen Gesellschaft der Griechen." *Akademie der Wissenschaften und der Literatur in Mainz. Abhandlungen der geistes- und sozialwissenschaftlichen Klasse* 2:209–55.

Vorberg, Gaston. 1932. *Glossarium eroticum.* Stuttgart.

Vox, Onofrio. 1977. "Un pederasta dell'Agorà." *Zeitschrift für Papyrologie und Epigraphik* 26:118.

Wade-Gery, H. T. 1944. "The Spartan Rhetra in Plutarch Lycurgus VI." *Classical Quarterly* 38:1–9.

Walbank, F. W. 1981. *The Hellenistic World.* Cambridge, Mass.

Warren, Edward Perry (see Raile, Arthur Lyon).

Watkins, Calvert. 1986. "The Language of the Trojans." In *Troy and the Trojan War: A Symposium Held at Bryn Mawr College, October 1984,* ed. Machteld J. Mellink. Bryn Mawr, Penn. 45–62.

Watrous, Livingston V. 1984. "Ayia Triada: A New Perspective on the Minoan Villa." *American Journal of Archaeology* 88:123–34.

Watzinger, Carl. 1924. *Griechische Vasen in Tübingen, beschrieben von Carl Watzinger.* Reutlingen.

Webster, T. B. L. 1964. *From Mycenae to Homer.* 2d ed. London.

Weinrich, James D. 1987. "A New Sociobiological Theory of Homosexuality Applicable to Societies with Universal Marriage." *Ethology and Sociobiology* 8:37–47.

Welcker, Friedrich Gottlieb. 1816. *Sappho von einem herrschenden Vorurtheil befreit.* Göttingen.

—. 1824–26. *Die Aeschylische Trilogie.* Darmstadt.

————. 1856. "Ueber die beiden Oden der Sappho." *Rheinisches Museum für Philologie* n.s. 11:226–59.

Werner, Dennis. 1979. "A Cross-Cultural Perspective on Theory and Research on Male Homosexuality." *Journal of Homosexuality* 4:345–62.

West, M. L. 1965. "Alcmanica." *Classical Quarterly* n.s. 15:188–202.

————. 1966. *Hesiod, Theogony.* Oxford.

————. 1970a. "Burning Sappho." *Maia* n.s. 22:307–30.

————. 1970b. "Melica." *Classical Quarterly* n.s. 20:205–15.

————. 1978a. *Hesiod, Works and Days.* Oxford.

————. 1978b. "Phocylides." *Journal of Hellenic Studies* 98:164–67.

————. 1984. "New Fragments of Ibycus' Love Songs." *Zeitschrift für Papyrologie und Epigraphik* 57:23–32.

————. 1985. *The Hesiodic Catalogue of Women: Its Nature, Structure, and Origins.* Oxford.

————. 1988. "The Rise of the Greek Epic." *Journal of Hellenic Studies* 108:151–72.

————. 1990. "The *Anacreontea.*" In *Sympotica: A Symposium on the Symposion,* ed. Oswyn Murray. Oxford. 272–76.

Westermarck, Edward. 1906–8. *The Origin and Development of the Moral Ideas.* London.

Wiedemann, Thomas. 1981. *Greek and Roman Slavery.* Baltimore.

Wilamowitz-Moellendorff, Ulrich von. 1891. *Euripides Hippolytos griechisch und deutsch.* Berlin.

————. 1913. *Sappho und Simonides.* Berlin.

————. 1922. *Pindaros.* Berlin.

————. 1982. *History of Classical Scholarship.* London.

Wilamowitz-Moellendorff, Ulrich von, and Benedikt Niese. 1910. *Staat und Gesellschaft der Griechen und Romer.* Berlin.

Wilhelm, Friedrich. 1902. "Zu Achilles Tatius." *Rheinisches Museum für Philologie* n.s. 57:55–75.

Wilkenson, L. P. 1978. "Classical Approaches. IV: Homosexuality." *Encounter* 51, n. 3: 20–31.

Willetts, R. F. 1955. *Aristocratic Society in Ancient Crete.* London.

————. 1965. *Ancient Crete: A Social History from Early Times until the Roman Occupation.* London.

————. 1967. *The Law Code of Gortyn.* Berlin.

Williams, Craig Arthur. 1992. "Homosexuality and the Roman Man: A Study in the Cultural Construction of Sexuality." Ph.D. dissertation, Yale University.

Williams, F. E. 1936. *Papuans of the Trans-Fly.* Oxford.

Williams, G. W. 1951. "The Curse of the Alkmaionidai. I. The Origin and Early History." *Hermathena* 78:32–49.

Wills, Garry. 1992. "Athena's Magic." *New York Review of Books* Dec. 17:47–51.

Winckelmann, J. J. 1849. *The History of Ancient Art.* 3 vols. Boston.

————. 1887–1912. *Werke.* Weimar.

Windekens, A. J. van. 1986. *Dictionnaire étymologique complémentaire de la langue grecque: Nouvelles contributions à l'interprétation historique et comparée du vocabulaire.* Louvain.

Winkler, John J. 1990. *The Constraints of Desire: The Anthropology of Sex and Gender in Ancient Greece.* New York.

Wolf, F. A. [1795] 1985. *Prolegomena to Homer.* Princeton.

Wolff, Hans Julius. 1944. "Marriage Law and Family Organization in Ancient Athens." *Traditio* 2:43–95.

Wright, F. A. 1932. *A History of Later Greek Literature from the Death of Alexander in 323 B.C. to the Death of Justinian in 565 A.D.* London.

Wright, H. E., Jr. 1968. "Climatic Change in Mycenaean Greece." *Antiquity* 42:123–27.

Wright, Wilmer Cave. 1907. *A Short History of Greek Literature.* New York.

Wrigley, E. A. 1969. *Population and History.* New York.

Wyneken, Gustav Adolph. 1921. *Eros.* Lauenberg/Saal.

Young, Norman H. 1990. "The Figure of the *Paidagogos* in Art and Literature." *Biblical Archaeologist* 53:80–86.

Young, Rodney S. 1939. *Late Geometric Graves and a Seventh Century Well in the Agora. Hesperia: Supplement 2.* Athens.

Index

Drama, classical, 181, 185–86
Drerup, E., 213n17
Drews, Robert, 20
Dromeus, 66–67
Dromos, 67, 114
Dryopis, 139
Dumézil, Georges, 23
Dunbabin, T. J., 165

Easterling, P. E., 91
Effenterre, Henri van, 60
Eglinton, J. Z., 9
Egyptians: plastic art of, 115; possible influence on kouroi, 115; mentioned, 84, 149, 195n10
Eispnelas, 88
Ekdysia, 201n13
Elea, 153
Eleans. See Elis
Eleutheria, 112
Elis: reputation for pederasty, 6; anal intercourse at, 7; lovers fighting together in battle, 45, 126; fame for athletes, 125–26; male beauty contests in, 126, 127; ancient comments on mores of, 126; Cicero on pederastic lust among Elean men, 126; Josephus on pederasty at, 126; mentioned, 29, 122, 123, 124, 134, 190
Empedocles, 124, 164
Epaminondas, 10
Ephorus: on origin of Dorians, 28; account of Dorian pederasty on Crete, 61, 64–67; mentioned, 5, 23, 24, 28, 61, 63, 69, 70, 71, 75, 97, 144, 203n29
Epicharmus of Syracuse, 124
Epimenides: purported influence on Athenian laws, 174–76; mentioned, 60, 63, 79
Epirus, 123, 139
Erastes: age of lovers, 8; role as described by Ephorus, 64–67; bonds with eromenoi in Archaic Athens and Sparta, 64–65; depicted on vases, 119–20; role defined by Theognis, 130; mentioned, 1, 34, 96, 123, 194n17

Eretria, 67, 140
Eromenos: role as described by Ephorus, 64–67; bonds with erastes in Archaic Athens and Sparta, 64–65; role when bearded and adult, 88; praised in scolia, 117; depicted on vases, 119–20; mentioned, 1, 21, 34, 96, 116, 123
Eros: factor in Spartan agoge, 89; honored by pederasts, 98, 112; in Alcaeus's verse, 146; mentioned, 81, 91, 132–33, 136, 138, 147, 157, 182, 206n9
Etruscans, 81, 163, 166
Euboea: geography and accomplishments, 140, 141; institutionalized pederasty in, 140–41; mentioned, 56, 71, 123, 150, 211n32
Eubulus, 45, 54
Eumulus of Corinth, 124
Eunapius, 97
Eunomia: need for, 77; ascribed to Lycurgus, 78; laws and practices prescribed by, 80–84; prescribed exposure of infants, 86; mentioned, 73, 79, 85, 90, 91
Eunus, 132
Eupalinus, 154
Eupolis, 212n5
Euripides: play on Laius and Chrysippus, 57, 186; lover of, 186; mentioned, 6, 66, 83, 136, 190
Eurypyle, 158, 212n5
Eusebius, 79, 80
Eusebius-Jerome, 155
Eustathius of Thessalonica, 5, 62, 66, 97, 202n19, 202n22
Euxunthetus, 61
Everson, Michael, 20–21
Exposure of infants, 86, 176

Farces, Megaran, 130
Fellatio, 7, 121
Firmicus Maternus, Mathesis, 9
Flacelière, Robert, 112
Fluck, Edward J., 120
Forrest, W. G., 75, 76–77
Foucault, Michel, 9

Overpopulation (*continued*)
seventh-century Crete, 62; in Late
Archaic Sparta, 77, 86; Solon's response
to in Athens, 176–77
Ovid: *Ars Amatoria,* 216*n7;* mentioned, 55,
157, 211*n12*

Paestum, 164, 167
Page, Denys, 211*n12*
Palaephatus, 169
Palaestra: of Taureas, 114; specific mean-
ing, 206*n12;* mentioned, 82, 84, 112,
178, 179. *See also* Gymnasia
Pampaides, 67
Panathenaia, 181, 182
Pantarkes, 126
Panteus, 88
Parastates, 24, 45, 98
Parry, Milman, 37
Patroclus: relationship with Achilles, 38–
40, 188; portrayed in Aeschylus, 186;
mentioned, 37
Patzer, Harald: theory of lustless pederasty,
34–35; mentioned, 23
Pausanias (author): on Spartan human
sacrifice, 83; on origin of nude sports,
84; on Anacreon, 157; mentioned, 28,
29, 44, 75, 79, 80, 97, 124, 125, 134, 168
Pausanias (victor at Plataea), 10, 88, 184
Pedagogy, pederastic: appreciation of by
Wilamowitz-Moellendorf and Jaeger,
33–34; at Corinth, 130; at Megara, 132;
Spartan, 149; advances in at Samos,
154; at Croton, 166; views of classical
era on, 185–88; reflected in Theocritus, 189; defense of in Plutarch and
pseudo-Lucian, 189–91
Pederasty: "pure" (chaste), 7, 29–35, 196*n3;*
anal intercourse, 7, 8, 31, 61, 85, 88,
89, 119, 173; intercrural intercourse, 7,
86, 119, 173; distinct from androphilia,
8–10; Celtic, 18, 33, 195*n3,* 195*n4;*
Germanic, 18–19, 33; in pre-Christian
Scandinavian laws and literature, 19;
depicted in vase paintings, 118–20

—initiatory: among Indo-Europeans, 15–
16; among Eurasians, 16, 17; Melanesian,
16, 17, 32; views on Dorian, 32–35
—institutionalized: Marquis de Sade on,
1; defined, 1–2; as understood by Patzer,
34–35; absent from Homer and Hesiod,
37–41; effect of situational homosexuality on, 43; purported Levantine
influence on, 47–48; Cretan origins of,
59–72; Dorian forms of, 64–67, 123–24;
projected effect on population, 68–69;
diffusion from Crete to other areas of
Greece, 69–72, 205*n2;* Spartan form
of, 73–74, 80–92; sources on spread of,
96–98; tyrants' criticism of, 120–21;
Euboean form of, 141; as portrayed by
Alcaeus, 146; in Ionia, 150; introduction
into Magna Graecia and Sicily, 162–64;
in Athens, 176–79
Peisander, 41, 56, 57
Pelopidas, 124
Pelops, 37, 53, 55, 56, 57
Periander of Ambracia, 129, 139
Periander of Corinth, 129–30, 145, 166
Pericles, 177
Perioikoi, 77, 81, 82, 88
Persians: closing gymnasia, 113; fear
of pederastic tyrannicides, 121, 129;
conquest of Ionia, 160–61; defeat at
Marathon, 183, 185; defeat at Salamis,
184; defeat at Plataea, 184; mentioned,
48, 72, 124, 144, 148, 149, 150, 153, 154,
157, 170, 180, 182
Petronius, 3, 8
Phaedo, 125–26, 127
Phaistus, 22
Phalanx, Spartan: origin of, 76–78;
mentioned, 71, 82, 87, 149, 204*n3*
Phalaris, tyrant of Agrigentum, 121, 167
Pheidon, 127–28
Phidias, 10, 126, 128
Philetor, 24, 30, 66, 72, 98
Philip of Macedonia, 10, 135, 185
Philistius of Syracuse, 165
Philolaus, 30, 134

WILLIAM ARMSTRONG PERCY III is the senior professor of history at the University of Massachusetts at Boston. He is the co-author with Jerah Johnson of *The Age of Recovery: The Fifteenth Century* in *The Development of Western Civilization* and with Warren Johansson of *Outing: Shattering the Conspiracy of Silence*, "Homosexuals in Nazi Germany" in the *Simon Wiesenthal Center Annual* (1990), and "Homosexuality" in the forthcoming *Handbook of Medieval Sexuality*, edited by James Brundage and Vern L. Bullough. Also with Warren Johansson he is an associate editor of the *Encyclopedia of Homosexuality*, edited by Wayne R. Dynes.